Southern Theories

This book critically explores Global South perspectives, examining marginalised voices and issues whilst challenging the supremacy of Global North perspectives in literature. The unique value of this book lies in its extensive coverage of various Southern challenges, including disaster management, climate change, communication, resilience, gender, education, and disability. It also underscores the relevance of indigenous philosophies such as animism, *Buen Vivir*, Buddhism, Confucianism, Daoism, Neozapatism, *Qi* vitality, Taoism, and *Ubuntu*. Stemming from regions as diverse as Sub-Saharan Africa, Asia, and Latin America, these philosophies are brought into public discourse. By demonstrating their practicality in designing intervention programs and influencing policy-making, the book fills a critical gap in global Southern literature while promoting context-specific knowledge for improving well-being in the Global South contexts. This book's content resonates with a diverse audience, encompassing students, academics, researchers, NGOs, and policymakers from postcolonial states in the Global South and those from Global North countries.

Furthermore, it is highly relevant to communities within the Global North that mirror the Global South – those grappling with equity issues for indigenous populations. It has a versatile appeal that transcends disciplinary boundaries, encompassing cultural studies, sociology, international development, philosophy, and postcolonial studies, thus making it accessible to all educational levels. It holds particular interest for those in development studies, indigenous studies, government departments globally, international organisations, and universities worldwide.

Oliver Mutanga is a disability scholar with a PhD in development studies from the University of the Free State in South Africa. He is an assistant professor at the Graduate School of Education at Nazarbayev University, Kazakhstan, and a research associate at the University of South Africa's College of Education. Oliver has been honoured with prestigious awards such as the Marie Sklodowska Curie Postdoctoral Fellowship at the University of Oslo, Norway and the Global Challenges Research Fellowship at University College London's Institute of Education.

Tendayi Marovah is a research fellow at the Open Distance Learning Research Unit, College of Education, University of South Africa (UNISA). He is also a lecturer at Midlands State University in Zimbabwe. His research interests include curriculum and pedagogy, higher education, social justice, human development, and theorising using the capability approach and Ubuntu philosophy. Tendayi holds a PhD in Africa studies (history) from the Centre for Africa Studies at the University of the Free State in South Africa. Tendayi's current practice is grounded in transformative pedagogies informed by Ubuntu philosophy, which aims to develop the knowledge, skills, values, and attitudes needed to create a more just, peaceful, and sustainable world.

Routledge Advances in Sociology

6 **Exoskeletal Devices and the Body**
   Deviant Bodies, Extended Bodies
   Denisa Butnaru

7 **Social Protection Programmes**
   Narratives of Nigerian Women and Anti-Trafficking Practitioners in Italy
   Michela Semprebon

8 **Universities and Academic Labour in Times of Digitalisation and Precarisation**
   Thomas Allmer

9 **Economic Sociology in Europe**
   Recent Trends and Developments
   Andrea Maurer, Sebastian Nessel and Alberto Veira-Ramos

10 **The Politics of the Elite**
   Ideological Orientations, Mothering, and Social Mobilities in Neoliberal Chile
   Modesto Gayo and María Luisa Méndez

11 **A Sociological Genealogy of Culture Wars**
   Maya Aguiluz-Ibargüen and Josetxo Beriain

12 **Southern Theories**
   Contemporary and Future Challenges
   Edited by Oliver Mutanga and Tendayi Marovah

For more information about this series, please visit: www.routledge.com/Routledge-4Advances-in-Sociology/book-series/SE0511

'This well-curated and superb collection of essays – wide in scope, deep in analysis, and refreshing in its breadth – showcase the intellectual beauty, power and necessity of inter-epistemic dialogue as a leitmotif of decolonisation and democratisation of knowledge. Southern thought, theories and concepts are artisanally unearthed, meticulously articulated, and confidently displayed across the contributions. Oliver Mutanga and Tendayi Marovah have done a superb academic job in conceiving this project and assembling a stellar group of scholars to participate in its execution. The South is a majority world, and the voices, thoughts, concepts, and theories from this epistemic site enrich comprehension of the world and offer alternative visions of the future. This book is a compelling and timely scholarship.'

Sabelo J. Ndlovu-Gatsheni, *Professor/Chair of Epistemologies of the Global South and Vice-Dean of Research in the Africa Multiple Cluster of Excellence, University of Bayreuth, Germany*

'This is a courageous and exciting collection of essays that seeks to accomplish multiple goals. The common description of the world split between the North and South gives the wrong impression of two equal and balanced forces. The North is the few richest nation-states of the modern world that were built on imperialism and settler colonialism. The South is made up of all the other countries. This volume seeks to pierce through the centuries of epistemic domination of Northern countries, their institutions, their narratives, and their academic paradigms. The diverse topics of the chapters bring forward voices and perspectives that have been ignored and marginalised in global conversations. The chapters also describe internal disagreements, perspectives on priority challenges for non-rich countries, and agenda for collective action against epistemic, structural, and social injustices. This collection harkens a new kind of voice – not "third-world voices" or "southern perspectives" but global perspectives from voices based in the South.'

Sridhar Venkatapuram, *Associate Professor in Global Health and Philosophy, King's College London, UK*

'What challenges are Global South communities themselves concerned with? What innovative philosophies and knowledge-making practices do these communities utilise in the face of these challenges? What philosophies and knowledge-making norms impede community-led solutions? This book answers these questions by weaving together diverse Global South philosophies, practices, and on-the-ground solutions. Documenting personal reflections and local contexts alongside global concerns that traverse the environment, communication, resilience, education, disability, gender, and development, the authors bring rich perspectives for

rethinking the role of local communities in global change. By positioning Global South communities' challenges, innovations, and experiences as central, this book provides a platform to decolonise and transform the way knowledge and solutions are produced and consumed.'
Krushil Watene, *Peter Kraus Associate Professor in Philosophy, University of Auckland Waipapa Taumata Rau, New Zealand*

Southern Theories
Contemporary and Future Challenges

Edited by Oliver Mutanga and
Tendayi Marovah

LONDON AND NEW YORK

First published 2024
by Routledge
4 Park Square, Milton Park, Abingdon, Oxon OX14 4RN

and by Routledge
605 Third Avenue, New York, NY 10158

Routledge is an imprint of the Taylor & Francis Group, an informa business

© 2024 selection and editorial matter, Oliver Mutanga and Tendayi Marovah; individual chapters, the contributors

The right of Oliver Mutanga and Tendayi Marovah to be identified as the authors of the editorial material, and of the authors for their individual chapters, has been asserted in accordance with sections 77 and 78 of the Copyright, Designs and Patents Act 1988.

All rights reserved. No part of this book may be reprinted or reproduced or utilised in any form or by any electronic, mechanical, or other means, now known or hereafter invented, including photocopying and recording, or in any information storage or retrieval system, without permission in writing from the publishers.

Trademark notice: Product or corporate names may be trademarks or registered trademarks, and are used only for identification and explanation without intent to infringe.

British Library Cataloguing-in-Publication Data
A catalogue record for this book is available from the British Library

Library of Congress Cataloging-in-Publication Data
Names: Mutanga, Oliver, 1979– editor. | Marovah, Tendayi, editor.
Title: Southern theories : contemporary and future challenges / edited by Oliver Mutanga and Tendayi Marovah.
Description: Abingdon, Oxon ; New York, NY : Routledge, 2024. | Series: Routledge advances in sociology | Includes bibliographical references and index.
Identifiers: LCCN 2023036165 (print) | LCCN 2023036166 (ebook) | ISBN 9781032415970 (hardback) | ISBN 9781032415987 (paperback) | ISBN 9781003358879 (ebook)
Subjects: LCSH: Developing countries—Social policy—Citizen participation. | Developing countries—Economic policy—Citizen participation. | Indigenous peoples—Developing countries. | Ethnophilosophy—Developing countries.
Classification: LCC HN980 .S639 2024 (print) | LCC HN980 (ebook) | DDC 306.09172/4—dc23/eng/20231003
LC record available at https://lccn.loc.gov/2023036165
LC ebook record available at https://lccn.loc.gov/2023036166

ISBN: 978-1-032-41597-0 (hbk)
ISBN: 978-1-032-41598-7 (pbk)
ISBN: 978-1-003-35887-9 (ebk)

DOI: 10.4324/9781003358879

Typeset in Sabon
by Apex CoVantage, LLC

Contents

List of figures and tables   ix
List of contributors   x
Preface   xiv
Acknowledgements   xv

1 Embracing Southern theories for an inclusive future   1
 OLIVER MUTANGA

2 Chinese philosophy's contributions to the homoverse   16
 GEIR SIGURÐSSON AND PAUL J. D'AMBROSIO

3 *Qi* vitality and virtue cultivation: embodying and educating for eco-cosmic citizenry   33
 JING LIN, TOM CULHAM, AND YISHIN KHOO

4 De-Westernising communication thought from a Global South perspective: the contributions of indigenous approaches from Latin America   53
 ALEJANDRO BARRANQUERO CARRETERO AND EVA GONZÁLEZ TANCO

5 The role of indigenous religion in building community resilience: the case of the Karen, an ethnic minority group in the Myanmar-Thailand border region   68
 HEE-CHAN SONG

6 Disability, inclusion, and Gross National Happiness: the complex case of Bhutan   87
 SEYDA SUBASI SINGH AND MATTHEW J. SCHUELKA

7 Philosophical and practical challenges of *Ubuntu*: application to decolonial activism and conceptions of personhood and disability 104
MARIA BERGHS

8 Decolonising gender and development: the influence of *Ubuntu* philosophy on the articulation of African feminism 117
NYAMWAYA MUNTHALI AND THOMAS KITINYA KIRINA

9 Neozapatista decolonial pedagogy: an approach to the disruptive conceptualisation of the learner 133
JON IGELMO ZALDÍVAR, GONZALO JOVER, AND PATRICIA QUIROGA UCEDA

10 Southern theories: implications for epistemic justice and sustainable development 152
TENDAYI MAROVAH

Index 160

Figures and tables

Figures

Figure 3.1	Yin-yang symbol	39
Figure 7.1	*Ubuntu* as a practice	112
Figure 8.1	*Ubuntu*'s philosophical positions	126

Tables

Table 5.1	External political turmoil that directly or indirectly threatened the Karen community and their response to threats	75
Table 5.2	Role of animism in promoting community resilience among the Karen people	80
Table 8.1	Subcultures/various forms of African feminism	122

Contributors

Alejandro Barranquero Carretero is an associate professor in the Communication & Media Studies Department at Universidad Carlos III de Madrid in Spain. His research interests include the relations between communication and social change, such as community and citizen media, journalism and human rights, media literacy, critical and decolonial communication theories, and the techno-politics of social movements. Currently, he holds chair positions on the boards of the IAMCR Section on 'Community Communication and Alternative Media' and the Spanish AE-IC Group on 'Communication and Citizenship.' Additionally, he is the founder and director of the Community, Alternative and Participatory Communication Research Network-RICCAP (www.riccap.org).

Maria Berghs is an associate professor at De Montfort University in the United Kingdom. She is an anthropologist with a PhD in sociology and social policy. She works in medical anthropology and sociology, specialising in disability studies and chronic illness. Her research interests include disability, chronic illness, global health (sickle cell), and the application of Southern theories like *Ubuntu* philosophy.

Tom Culham had a PhD in education from Simon Fraser University later in his career. He is a lecturer and researcher in ethics education at Simon Fraser University's Beedie School of Business. Tom has authored or co-edited five books that propose incorporating neuroscience, psychology, virtue ethics, Daoist contemplative practices, and emotional intelligence into education. Tom co-authored the book *Daoist Cultivation of Qi and Virtue for Life, Wisdom, and Learning,* which examines how Daoism can inform contemporary education published in 2020. He also co-edited *Honing Self-Awareness of Faculty and Future Business Leaders: Emotions Connected with Teaching and Learning.*

Paul J. D'Ambrosio is a fellow of the Institute of Modern Chinese Thought and Culture, professor of Chinese philosophy, and dean of the Center for Intercultural Research at East China Normal University in Shanghai,

China. He is also the founder of the 四海为学 'Collaborative Learning' lecture and seminar series. D'Ambrosio received his PhD in philosophy from the National University of Ireland in 2013. He specialises in Chinese philosophy and technology-human relations, including artificial intelligence and social media. His publications include works such as 真假之间; *You and Your Profile*; *Genuine Pretending*, co-authored with Hans-Georg Moeller; and *Encountering China*, co-authored with Michael Sandel. He has authored almost 100 articles, chapters, and reviews and translated over a dozen books on Chinese philosophy.

Eva González Tanco is an associate professor of social communication at the University of Valle in Colombia, a visiting lecturer at the Intercultural Indigenous Autonomous University (UAIIN) in Colombia, and a member of the Community, Alternative, and Participatory Communication Research Network (RICCAP). Her research focuses on the contribution of indigenous communication and other social movements to the perspective of Good Living (*Buen Vivir*) as an alternative to developmentalism. With over 20 years of experience as a journalist in Spain and other countries, she has managed or collaborated on international cooperation and research projects funded by social and indigenous organisations.

Jon Igelmo Zaldívar is an associate professor in the faculty of education at the Complutense University (UCM) in Spain. He was a postdoctoral fellow at Queen's University in Canada from 2013 to 2014, supported by the Basque Country Government Postdoctoral Program in Spain. He defended his PhD thesis in 2011 at UCM and is a Cultura Cívica y Politicas Educativas research group member. His research focuses on unschooling theories, the theoretical foundations of alternative pedagogies, and the historiography of education. He has published books with prestigious publishers.

Gonzalo Jover earned his PhD degree in education in 1987. He is currently the dean at the Faculty of Education of the Complutense University (UCM) in Spain, where he has also held several notable positions. In addition to his academic roles, Jover has been an adviser for the Ministry of Education during the 9th Parliamentary Term. Furthermore, Jover has been elected as president of the Spanish Pedagogical Association (SEP) and serves as a member of the councils of the European Educational Research Association (EERA) and the World Educational Research Association (WERA). Jover's research interests encompass educational theory, history, and politics of education.

Yishin Khoo is a research associate and instructor at the University of Windsor, Canada. Her research is bifocal. She earned her PhD in curriculum studies and teacher education from the Ontario Institute for Studies in Education at the University of Toronto, Canada. Firstly, she investigates intercultural reciprocal learning within K–12 global citizenship and sustainability education. Secondly, she examines the role of mindfulness in climate justice education. In addressing contemporary socio-ecological challenges, Yishin applies Eastern wisdom traditions.

Thomas Kitinya Kirina is an agriculturist and expert in natural resource management. He is a PhD candidate in water systems and global change at the Wageningen Institute of Environment and Climate Research, Netherlands. His research and drive are on understanding the food-water nexus dynamics under climate change and developing better adaptation responses for sustainable agriculture. He is currently looking at the impact of scaling climate-smart agriculture interventions on agriculture and ecosystem services. Previously, Kirina was a junior professional with the Netherlands Development Organisation (SNV) based in Cambodia. As a private practitioner, he had extensive consultancy experience in climate-smart agriculture and climate risk assessment in East Africa, Southern Africa, and Southeast Asia.

Jing Lin, the Harold R. W. Benjamin Professor of International Education at the University of Maryland, specialises in Chinese culture, African gender issues, peace, and environmental education. She holds a doctorate from the University of Michigan and has contributed significantly to contemplative inquiry, holistic education, and the revival of wisdom traditions for educational reform. Lin has published extensively on these topics and has developed and taught several courses, including Ecological Ethics and Education and Global Climate Change and Education.

Nyamwaya Munthali is a senior lecturer at Cavendish University in Zambia. She received her PhD in communication for development at Wageningen University and Research Centre, Netherlands, in 2021. Her research interests include the influence of social context on information and communication technology (ICTs) application, strategic (digital) communication mechanisms to foster development, and decolonising development studies. She has over 8 years of experience in the Zambian agriculture sector on mobile innovation, livelihood enhancement, and business and social enterprise development projects, working as a project manager and contributing to developing and implementing monitoring, evaluation, and communication systems.

Matthew J. Schuelka is Lecturer of Organizational Leadership, Policy, and Development at the University of Minnesota. He holds a PhD in Educational Administration and Policy Analysis, with an emphasis in comparative and international education, from the University of Minnesota. Previously, he has held faculty positions at the University of Birmingham (UK and UAE), University of Nottingham Malaysia, and Royal Thimphu College in Bhutan. He is also an international development consultant, and Founder and CEO of Fora Education, having worked on projects with organizations such as UNICEF, UNESCO, World Bank, and USAID.

Primarily his academic and development focus is on South and Southeast Asia and on issues related to disability-inclusion, quality education, educational values, and transition to employment.ka.

Geir Sigurðsson is a Chinese studies and philosophy professor at the University of Iceland and holds a PhD from the University of Hawaii. Having studied in multiple countries, Geir's work emphasises the dialogue between Western and Chinese philosophy, advocating for more inclusivity. He examines methodologies, epistemological approaches, and differing views of education and life values. Notable works include an interpretation of Confucian propriety, an Icelandic translation of Sunzi's *Art of War,* and numerous articles. Currently, he is focusing on Chinese philosophical perspectives on ageing.

Seyda Subasi Singh, PhD, works at the Center for Teacher Education of the University of Vienna in Austria as a senior lecturer. She conducts research and teaches at the Inclusive Education Research Unit. Her teaching concentrates on diversity and educational equity with an intersectional focus on disability, migrant background, gender, sexual orientation and poverty. Her research areas are justice and equity in education, inclusive education, multicultural teacher education, intersectionality, flight and education, education under challenging conditions, and emergency education. She is involved in several research projects at the national and international level, including projects with Uganda, Nepal, Bhutan, Thailand, Indonesia, North Macedonia, and several other European Union countries.

Hee-Chan Song is an assistant professor of management at Sasin Graduate Institute of Business Administration, Chulalongkorn University in Thailand. He received his PhD in 2019 from the Ivey Business School, University of Western Ontario in Canada. His research draws on ethnographic fieldwork in unconventional contexts, such as Buddhist temples and minority villages, and explores how business can contribute to sustainable development. He has conducted long-term fieldwork in Buddhist temples across Asia, particularly interested in applying Buddhism to corporate sustainability and organisation studies.

Patricia Quiroga Uceda, an assistant professor in the faculty of education at the Complutense University (UCM) in Spain, has previously held postdoctoral roles at UNED and Universitat Autònoma de Barcelona. She obtained her PhD in pedagogy from the Universidad Complutense de Madrid in 2015 with a focus on Waldorf Education in Spain. As part of the Cultura Cívica y Políticas Educativas research group and the Theory and History of Education International Research Group in Canada, her research explores the history of education, highlighting alternative educational movements like Waldorf, Montessori, Pikler approaches, homeschooling, and slow education.

Preface

Sankofa yenkyi – embracing past lessons for a brighter future.

(Akan proverb)

Acknowledgements

We express our deepest gratitude to the scholars whose diligent review of this manuscript has significantly enhanced its quality, notably Oliver Gore, whose insightful suggestions have been invaluable. Our recognition extends to several institutions, including the Faculty of Health and Life Sciences at De Montfort University in the United Kingdom, the Graduate School of Education at Nazarbayev University in Kazakhstan, and the Department of Humanities, Business Development, and Arts Education at Midlands State University in Zimbabwe. The generous time allocation and supportive research environment provided a solid foundation for this extensive project. Moreover, we hold the British Academy (British Academy/Leverhulme Small Research Grants) and the Arts and Humanities Research Council (AH/T005459/1) in high regard for their generous financial support that has been instrumental in the successful execution of this book project. We are greatly indebted to those who have shown unwavering faith in our research pursuits and invested in them.

1 Embracing Southern theories for an inclusive future

Oliver Mutanga

Introduction

In the social fabric of most Global South communities, self-determination and self-worth are fundamental components. These communities serve as steadfast stewards of their ancestral lands and repositories of diverse cultural and traditional heritages. However, this fabric faces strain from the encroachment of Western capitalist paradigms. An array of factors, such as the imposition of national and international legal frameworks and governance systems, insidiously undermines the autonomy and stability of these communities. This systematic erosion, often executed covertly, renders the communities of the Global South increasingly precarious.

Nevertheless, amidst these challenges, specific communities are engaged in the reinvigoration and practical application of indigenous knowledge systems to counterbalance external pressures. These traditional systems, revered for their historical significance, are summoned and adapted with ingenuity to address contemporary challenges.

This book emphasises the significance of integrating Southern[1] perspectives or theories into global development discussions. Scholars, policymakers, and practitioners must acknowledge the significance of these philosophies and concepts in tackling present and future challenges. Embracing pluralism and inclusivity in knowledge production can lead to a more equitable and sustainable world. It is essential to acknowledge that the Global South is not uniform, and the impact of global challenges varies across countries and regions. The Global South has significant innovation potential, and many countries actively address challenges through policy, collaboration, and community-based initiatives.

This section provides the book's background, aims, objectives, structure, and organisation.

DOI: 10.4324/9781003358879-1

This book aims to address the marginalisation of Southern theories and promote their contributions across various fields by

- Showcasing Southern theories and concepts overlooked or dismissed
- Providing a platform for scholars from the Global South to share their insights and experiences, promoting a more diverse and inclusive academic discourse
- Critically analysing the impact of Western theories on the Global South, highlighting their limitations and biases
- Exploring Southern theories to address contemporary challenges in the Global South, emphasising context-specific and sustainable solutions.

The Western world's intellectual dominance has historical roots in colonialism, imperialism, and the spread of Western education systems (Amin, 1968; wa Thiong'o, 1986; Shizha, 2013). It is a unified brutal ongoing project with different programmes with one main goal – dominance. This dominance has achieved one of its objectives of marginalising Southern theories and concepts, leading to injustices in the global academic discourse.

Where does the recent surge in interest surrounding artificial intelligence (AI) tools such as ChatGPT fit into the conversations raised in this book? The functioning of these tools hinges on the data and language they have been trained on, and consequently, their responses rely on the substance of that data. Predominantly, this data originates from Western societies, specifically from Western intellectuals. This creates a significant epistemic imbalance as intellectuals and languages from the Global South need to be adequately represented. As such, the ongoing development of AI tools necessitates a greater demand for Southern-based tools and platforms that are context specific.

There are pressing global challenges, such as pandemics, environmental degradation, migration and refugees, and social inequalities. Culturally relevant and context-specific solutions are required for these complex issues, highlighting the need for Southern theories in academic discourse and policy-making. This quest can be achieved by decolonisation – defined here as 'shutting ourselves up in our cultural past' (Hountondji, 2002, p. 190) and reflecting and acting without being trapped in Western academic and scientific dependence; Hountondji (2002, p. 255) calls this 'intellectual extraversion,' where we need Western validation for our Southern concepts and theories to be deemed valid or relevant.

This collection of work presents various perspectives and approaches that highlight the significance of Southern theories in addressing present and future challenges. It is organised thematically, each section addressing a specific field or challenge in the Global South. Southern theories and concepts discussed include animism, Buddhism, *Buen Vivir*, Dao, *Qi*, *Ubuntu*, and Zapatista pedagogy. These theories and concepts can address social inequalities, environmental degradation, and cultural erosion across different fields. This edited collection primarily features personal reflections, experiences, and case studies, which aligns with the fact that most studies in this field are still in the conceptual phase due to the nascent stage of the discourse. To challenge the limitations of Western methodologies, which often prioritise objectivity in research, and bearing in mind our inescapable subjectivity as researchers inherently affected by the issues we examine, we purposefully encouraged personal reflections in this book. This book is practical in its approach to elevating Southern perspectives. As you will notice in Chapter 6, some references and citations include two names. This is unusual from a Western academic writing perspective, but in Bhutan, this practice is common because they don't have family names.

The book's contributors have diverse backgrounds and hold various academic and professional positions. They are located on various continents: North America, Europe, Africa, and Asia. Their research interests include education, disability studies, philosophy, communication, and the social sciences.

Reflection

This book originated from personal reflections and discussions with Tendayi Marovah, who explored *Ubuntu* philosophy during our doctoral studies in South Africa. The main objective of this book is to challenge misconceptions in the literature that misrepresent the cultures and traditions of Global South communities.

Two instances highlight the problem of Global South misrepresentations in literature. Some literature portrays Global South cultures, such as African cultures, inherently discriminatory against females and promote gender inequity. My personal experience growing up in an African village contradicts this perception. I witnessed gender equity mechanisms and African women holding essential roles in decision-making within our villages. Village women made important agricultural decisions, such as the type of crops to plant, the time to plant, and how the produce was used. This may appear trivial to those unfamiliar with the crucial roles of agriculture and land in Global South economies. I grew up witnessing the autonomy and influence of women.

Additionally, I saw women, including widows who inherited the land after their husbands' deaths, frequently making independent decisions due to the high number of men working in urban areas. Colonial administrations imposed taxes on Africans, forcing men to work in towns and live in cramped accommodations while women and children remained in villages. It is this historical fact that helps us to recognise the role of colonialism in the creation of gender inequalities in Africa, something that is solely attributed to culture. It is inaccurate to attribute gender inequalities in Africa solely to African culture and traditions. This realisation led me to explore oral history and traditional concepts as alternative ways to comprehend current challenges in the Global South.

I went beyond Western concepts and philosophies to understand issues in the Global South. I discovered Nzegwu Ngwcru's work (1994), which questions the Western gender binary and reconsiders women's roles in Africa examining pre-colonial Yoruba society. She emphasises women's agency and power in politics, religion, and economics. She challenges the Western feminist assumption that all women in African societies were oppressed and subordinated. Ngweru is not alone in her thesis; Oyewumi (1997, p. ix) states, 'As the work and my thinking progressed, I came to realise that the fundamental category "woman" – which is the foundation of gender discourses – simply did not exist in Yorubaland prior to its sustained contact with the West.' This is also true in other African societies. For example, in traditional societies in Zimbabwe, an aunt (the father's sister) who plays a significant role in the family decision-making assumes the female father role (*baba vechikadzi*) and is referred *to as ubabakazi* in Ndebele. This has no equivalence in Western gender discourses.

Lastly, another example which highlights the importance of Global South theories and concepts is being shown in the field of social research. Despite its long-standing presence in Global South societies, storytelling is often presented as a ground-breaking discovery in the growing body of research. The resurgence of storytelling is not a discovery but a revival of an ancient communication tradition. This book explores underappreciated perspectives as we seek to understand our lost identities.

Chapter overview

The chapters build upon each other, demonstrating the connection between these Southern theories and their relevance in addressing global challenges.

In Chapter 2, Geir Sigurðsson and Paul J. D'Ambrosio establish the book's foundation by discussing disharmony and environmental degradation worldwide. They explore five classical Chinese philosophical perspectives that provide alternative perspectives for human coexistence, environmental protection, and cultural appreciation – promoting a more harmonious world or 'homoverse.' These perspectives promote respect and responsibility towards the environment, including sustainable resource management, biodiversity preservation, and climate change mitigation. The emphasis of *Qi*'s (氣) notion on harmony and community's care underscores the importance of prioritising the well-being of every individual in society. This approach promotes mutual understanding, reduces tension, and resolves peaceful conflict. By embracing a fluid self-identity and acknowledging the impermanence of roles, individuals can build resilience against mental health issues caused by rigid self-identification or external validation pressures. This chapter introduces classical Chinese philosophy as an alternative approach to global challenges, setting the stage for subsequent chapters.

Building on the theme of human-environment interconnectedness in Chapter 2, Chapter 3, by Jing Lin, Tom Culham, and Yishin Khoo, explores the challenge of disconnection from nature and the cosmos. Using their experiences, they continue discussing *Qi* and introduce the *Qi* vitality theory, which emphasises the importance of nurturing and amplifying life energy through contemplative practices, fostering a more interconnected and harmonious existence with all living beings. The alternative perspectives *Qi* vitality theory offers counter-dominant Western worldviews that often prioritise rationality, linear analysis, and detachment from nature. By promoting *Qi* vitality, virtue cultivation, and eco-cosmic citizenship, they argue for a shift towards a more balanced and compassionate worldview. By incorporating these principles into educational curricula and policy directions, the authors aim to foster personal and spiritual growth, ultimately leading to more harmonious societies that can collectively address complex global challenges in a sustainable and regenerative manner. The authors present a compelling argument by drawing from diverse cultural and philosophical perspectives, including Daoism, emphasising the need for a more balanced and interconnected worldview.

Expanding the scope of communication, in Chapter 4, Alejandro Barranquero Carretero and Eva González Tanco tackle the global challenge of communication inequalities and the dominance of Western perspectives in the field. They present Latin American indigenous approaches that emphasise participatory, educative, and biocentric values, connecting with previous chapters' themes of interconnectedness and alternative worldviews. The authors argue that *Buen Vivir* and *Sumak Kawsay* can offer a framework for addressing the global challenges of climate change and unsustainable development by emphasising holistic and relational ways of living and promoting eco-social justice and an intersectional understanding of exclusions. They challenge the Western-centric theories of development and progress and advocate for a universal approach incorporating diverse worldviews and knowledge systems. Communication plays a significant role in this approach, enabling a dialogue of knowledge that fosters more democratic and equitable practices. *Buen Vivir*'s emphasis on community and solidarity over individualism and competitiveness, as well as a process over immediacy, aligns with the principles of sustainable development and offers an alternative to the extractive and exploitative practices of the dominant global economic model. This philosophy has similar views to *Ubuntu*, a Sub-Saharan African philosophy (discussed by Maria Berghs in Chapter 7, see also Mutanga, (2023)).

In Chapter 5, Hee-Chan Song continues the discussion on alternative Southern approaches by focusing on the challenge of community resilience in the face of external shocks, particularly among ethnic minority groups. The chapter emphasises the importance of indigenous religions, specifically animism, as a resilience factor. It shows how these belief systems can help communities adapt and thrive in adverse circumstances, echoing the themes of interconnectedness and harmony found in earlier chapters. Hee-Chan Song's key argument is that understanding the balance between system persistence and flexibility is crucial for unpacking the adaptive aspects of a resilient system. He examines how the Karen communities in Southeast Asia have integrated external ideas from foreign religions through unique hybridisation with animism, which plays a crucial role as a resilience factor that strengthens ethnic identity in response to external political turmoil. He also argues that cultural resilience is essential for ensuring the survival of a community and protecting its unique cultural identity.

Furthermore, he challenges theories conceptualising resilience as recovery capacity and operationalising it based on return time or survival. Instead, he draws upon an ecological perspective that emphasises a system's dual capacity: system persistence and flexibility. He challenges the idea that formal rules, practices, and institutions are the only factors that can improve a system's resilience. He argues that a community's ethnocultural, informal element can also be a resilience factor. Again, he highlights the urgent need to explore community resilience in ethnic minority groups facing diverse external risks.

In Chapter 6, Seyda Subasi Singh and Matthew J. Schuelka explore the challenges of inclusive education for students with disabilities in Bhutan. They explore the tension between Bhutanese Buddhism's view of disability and the country's commitment to social justice and equity in education, showcasing how Bhutan's efforts align with the broader goal of achieving inclusive education systems globally. This chapter emphasises the importance of cultural understanding. The chapter discusses the concept of Gross National Happiness (GNH) in Bhutan, which measures progress towards sustainable development based on a holistic approach to well-being. They argue that inclusive education is necessary for achieving an inclusive society and GNH and that Bhutan can teach the rest of the world how inclusive education can extend Buddhist and GNH philosophy. The authors challenge Western theories of disability and argue that the interconnected dialectic of dis/ability espoused in Buddhist philosophy is only being rediscovered in Western disability theory. However, they also acknowledge the challenges and contradictions in Bhutan's implementation of inclusive education. However, they suggest that GNH offers a unique opportunity to reconceptualise disability in terms of a continuum of ability interconnected with the collective suffering of communities.

In Chapter 7, Maria Berghs examines the global challenge of understanding diverse conceptions of rights, personhood, and disability. By exploring *Ubuntu*'s philosophical and practical challenges, Maria highlights how this African humanist and ethical worldview can contribute to decolonial activism, which is public activities and campaigns to confront and fight injustices related to colonialism and neo-colonialism. *Ubuntu*'s philosophy addresses global challenges by emphasising the interdependence of individuals and collectives and the importance of social relationships. By prioritising the community's well-being, *Ubuntu*'s philosophy encourages practices that promote social harmony and cooperation, such as hospitality, generosity, and compassion. One example of *Ubuntu* in action cited is the work of African environmental activists, such as Ken Saro-Wiwa and Wangari Maathai, who fought against the environmental destruction of their homelands by Western multinational corporations. Through their activism, they sought to protect the environment and the rights of their communities, illustrating how *Ubuntu* can inform environmental justice.

In Chapter 8, Nyamwaya Munthali and Thomas Kitinya Kirina build on decolonising knowledge by addressing the global challenge of gender inequality. They emphasise the importance of understanding cultural differences and context when developing and implementing feminist interventions. They focus on marginalised epistemologies and articulate alternative, culturally sensitive interpretations of feminism. These authors analyse Chimamanda Ngozi Adichie's book, *We should all be feminists*, through the *Ubuntu* philosophical lens to offer a new perspective on the influence of African culture on African feminism. Furthermore, they argue that universally applying Western feminist theories and practices may not be practical or appropriate in non-Western contexts, particularly African societies. The authors challenge Western feminism by highlighting its individualistic nature, focus on self-interest, and promotion of retributive justice. Munthali and Kirina also explain how African feminism prefers a Gandhian feminist approach, reflecting aspects of restorative justice over retributive justice. They show how African feminism's approach to identity formation aligns with the relational nature of *Ubuntu* philosophy and how rational choice in African societies is based on community well-being rather than self-interest. This chapter ties together the themes of alternative Southern perspectives, interconnectedness, and cultural understanding presented throughout the book.

Jon Igelmo Zaldívar, Gonzalo Jover, and Patricia Quiroga Uceda, in Chapter 9, tackle the challenge of reimagining education in the context of decoloniality and alternative approaches. They examine the Zapatista pedagogical proposal and its conceptualisation of the learner/student, focusing on the Sistema Educativo Rebelde Autónomo Zapatista de Liberación Nacional (SERAZ-LN), the Universidad de la Tierra (University of the Earth), and the Universidad Intercultural (Intercultural University) projects that inspire Neozapatista ideology. The chapter provides a roadmap for articulating decolonial pedagogy in the 21st century, which promotes emancipation and interconnectedness. The key argument of the authors is that the Zapatista decolonial pedagogy in Chiapas, Mexico, offers a disruptive conceptualisation of the learner on four dimensions: breaking from the individual/society dichotomy, prioritising a care ethic over an individualist rational model, seeing education as a path to emancipation, and defending incidental learning – which has the potential to create more just and equitable societies. The authors draw on the Zapatista movement's resistance to marginalisation, oppression, and destruction of the environment to demonstrate how their pedagogy challenges traditional Western concepts of education and identity. They challenge Western theories and concepts, including individualism, rationality, and institutionalised education.

In Chapter 10, Tendayi Marovah integrates the book's focus on Southern theories and their invaluable contributions to sustainable development. Examining the implications and offering pragmatic, sustainable development recommendations, Marovah's analysis showcases the unique insights that Southern perspectives can provide in confronting epistemic injustices. The chapter emphasises the importance of adopting a collaborative and multidisciplinary approach that focuses on the voices and experiences of the Global South, as well as learning from their innovative strategies and solutions. By reflecting on the richness of Southern theories and expertise shared in the previous chapters, this conclusion offers an empowering roadmap for policymakers, academics, and professionals to navigate and address global challenges' dynamic and complex landscape, ultimately fostering a more equitable and socially-just world.

Global challenges and the Global South

Building on the overview of the earlier chapters, this section discusses the critical global challenges that disproportionately affect the Global South and their implications for the region's development. The Global South's susceptibility to environmental changes, exacerbated by economic factors and infrastructural limitations, is compounded by interrelated global challenges such as poverty, unemployment, and limited essential services. Conflicts, environmental disasters, and displacement coincide with ecological degradation, inadequate healthcare infrastructure, and susceptibility to pandemics. Political instability also perpetuates displacement and socio-economic disruption.

Recognising that the Global South has predominantly relied on Western concepts and theories to address these challenges is crucial. While some Western-informed interventions have succeeded, most have failed to effectively address the unique contexts and complexities in the Global South. In the next section, I will explore the dominance of Western theories and their impact on the Global South's ability to confront and overcome these challenges, emphasising the need to consider alternative approaches.

The dominance of Western theories and their impact

Western theories dominate in various fields, including economics, development studies, education, gender studies, and environment management. This section will explore some of the specific theories that have dominated some of these fields and discuss the consequences of this domination, such as marginalisation and distortion of reality:

- In development studies, modernisation theory and neoliberalism have controlled the field. It assumes that the Global South (developing countries/third world) must follow the path of the West (developed countries/first world) to achieve progress. The dominance of these theories has distorted the reality of Global South contexts by imposing one-size-fits-all models, ignoring the unique historical, cultural, and socio-economic contexts of each society. These theories have marginalised and overlooked local knowledge, experiences, and strategies for development. These theories

encourage reliance on Western aid and technology, which perpetuates cycles of underdevelopment in the Global South.
- Anthropological theory classified societies into hierarchical stages of development, often placing Western societies at the top (first world). Though its classification is still being used, this Western perspective has been critiqued for reinforcing stereotypes and justifying colonial and neo-colonial domination by portraying Global South societies as underdeveloped.
- Some Western educational theories and practices neglect indigenous knowledge systems and epistemologies, critical for meaningful learning experiences in Global South contexts (de Sousa Santos, 2015).
- Gender theories, such as liberal feminism, radical feminism, and socialist feminism, have shaped gender studies and policies in the Global South (Nzegwu, 1994). These theories often ignore the intersectionality of gender with other social factors like race, class, and culture, which is particularly relevant in the Global South (Chiumbu, 2022). By prioritising these theories, the experiences and knowledge of Global South citizens have been marginalised, resulting in a distorted understanding of gender issues in the Global South. I have examined Nkiru Nzegwu's (2004, 1994) work on gender and feminism in Africa, and I am astonished by the limited citations her insightful and forthright scholarship has received. Perhaps this can be attributed to her deviation from mainstream Western-informed feminist perspectives.

The importance of Southern theories in addressing global challenges

In contrast to the dominance and impact of Western theories discussed in the previous section, this section explores the importance of Southern theories in addressing global challenges. By incorporating diverse perspectives and frameworks from different geographical and cultural backgrounds, Southern theories offer alternative ways to understand and respond to pressing global issues often overlooked in dominant Western perspectives.

Southern theories play a crucial role in several areas, such as providing unique insights into the lived experiences of marginalised populations, challenging dominant paradigms, offering alternative models of development and governance, and fostering inclusive global dialogue. For example, *Buen Vivir* (Good Living), which originates from indigenous Andean communities in Latin America, emphasises the importance of harmonious living with the environment, community, and oneself (see Chapter 4 in this book). By offering a valuable perspective on sustainable development, *Buen Vivir* addresses the challenge of environmental degradation, a pressing global concern.

Moreover, Southern theories challenge dominant paradigms and encourage critical examination of issues under consideration. Decolonial theories, rooted in the Global South, critique the power dynamics and colonial legacies shaping contemporary global relationships (Adams & Estrada-Villalta,

2017). By challenging Western assumptions and biases, decolonial theories address the challenge of unequal power relations and neo-colonialism in the international system, contributing to a more equitable global order.

Southern theories offer alternative models of development. For instance, the Gandhian model of development, derived from the ideas of Indian leader Mahatma Gandhi, prioritises self-sufficiency, non-violence, and local decision-making. This Southern theory addresses the challenge of top-down, exploitative development practices by promoting a grassroots approach that empowers local communities and emphasises sustainable, inclusive growth.

Southern theories foster inclusive global dialogue. The *Ubuntu* philosophy highlights the interconnectedness of all human beings and the importance of human relations, empathy, and community (see Chapter 7 and Chapter 8 in this book, Metz, 2022 and Mutanga, 2023). By promoting dialogue and understanding among diverse stakeholders, *Ubuntu* addresses the challenge of social fragmentation and conflict, fostering a more inclusive and collaborative global community based on communal relationships.

In conclusion, engaging with and learning from Southern theories can help scholars, policymakers, and practitioners work towards more comprehensive, contextually relevant, and inclusive solutions to complex global challenges. The following section will briefly examine some Southern theorists and their contributions to global discourses.

Southern theorists

In the previous section, I discussed the importance of Southern theories in addressing global challenges. Building on that premise, this section explores the contributions of several Southern theorists from various regions. By presenting the works of these selected scholars, I highlight the appreciation and recognition of Southern theories across different regions. The following regional overview of selected Southern scholars showcases their commitment to challenging Western hegemony and advocating for recognising and appreciating non-Western cultures, values, and knowledge systems.

In Latin America, Rodolfo Kusch critiqued Western philosophy's dominance and marginalisation of other forms of knowledge (Escobar, 2007). His work sought to bridge the gap between Western and indigenous thought by demonstrating the richness and depth of indigenous knowledge systems, challenging Western assumptions that often dismiss these traditions as less valuable (Rozzi, 2015). One example of Kusch's influence can be seen in developing intercultural education policies in several Latin American countries, which aim to promote mutual respect and understanding between different cultural groups (see Chapter 9). Similarly, Boaventura de Sousa Santos (2015) argues for recognising and validating diverse knowledge systems from the Global South, which Western epistemologies have silenced. He calls for decolonisation[2] of knowledge production and promotes 'cognitive justice,' which refers to the equitable treatment and recognition of all knowledge systems to achieve a more equitable global order (de Sousa Santos, 2015, p. 237). Arturo Escobar (1992) critiques the dominant development discourse, which he argues has perpetuated Western narratives and contributed to the marginalisation of knowledge systems and practices from the Global South. He calls for alternative, locally grounded development approaches that respect the diversity and complexity of societies in the Global South. An example of the impact of Escobar's work can be seen in the emergence of alternative development paradigms, such as *Buen Vivir* or *Sumak Kawsay*, which prioritise holistic well-being and harmony with nature over conventional economic indicators (see Chapter 4 in this book). Moving to Africa, we find similar efforts to challenge Western hegemony and promote Southern theories.

With specific reference to Africa, Marimba Ani (1994) emphasises the importance of understanding the distinct ways of knowing and interpreting the world rooted in African culture. She argues that African cultures have a solid spiritual and moral foundation integral to their worldview, and this foundation often needs Western thought, which tends to prioritise materialism and dominance. Sabelo J. Ndlovu-Gatsheni's work (2018, 2021) focuses on decolonising knowledge production and challenging the dominant Eurocentric narratives that often misrepresent African history, politics, and development. By advocating for the recognition of African epistemologies and promoting a more inclusive and decolonial understanding of Africa and its diverse societies, Ndlovu-Gatsheni's work contributes to the broader discourse on epistemic freedom as it 'would be naive for peoples of the Global South. . . . to continue looking to Europe and North America for usable knowledge, relevant ideas, critical theories and solutions to modern problems.' (Ndlovu-Gatsheni, 2018, p. 38). Next, we turn our attention to contributions from Asia.

In India, Rabindranath Tagore criticised the Western model of education and its influence on Indian society (Sabareesh & Reeta Sony, 2022). He believed Western education promoted materialism and alienated Indians from their cultural roots (Mukherjee, 2022). Tagore advocated for an educational system that fostered creativity, critical thinking, a connection to the natural world, and a deeper understanding of India's cultural and intellectual heritage (Porselvi, 2022). The Visva-Bharati University, founded by Tagore, is an example of his educational vision, offering an alternative approach to learning that emphasises holistic and culturally rooted education. In China, Tu Weiming advocated for the revival of Confucianism to counter Western cultural hegemony. He emphasised the importance of embracing traditional Chinese values, such as humaneness, righteousness, and wisdom, and fostering a more harmonious and moral society (see Chapters 2 and 3 in this book for Chinese traditions). The recent resurgence of Confucianism in China and the establishment of Confucius Institutes worldwide can be seen as a manifestation of Tu Weiming's ideas (Huang, 2022). As we will see, the Middle East also has its share of influential Southern theorists.

From the Middle East, Ali Shariati sought to revive Islamic and Iranian cultural identity as a means of resisting Western imperialism (Tortolini, 2020). He emphasised the need to return to the core principles of Islam and reinterpret them in a contemporary context, advocating for a more socially engaged and politically active form of Islamic thought. Shariati's ideas have significantly impacted contemporary Iranian society, particularly in the context of the Iranian Revolution and its emphasis on Islamic values as a source of national identity and resistance against external influence (Ghazizadeh & Mollanazar, 2022).

Even in the West, some Indigenous scholars have contributed to Southern theories. Vine Deloria Jr. (1988) criticised the United States government's treatment of Native Americans and the assimilation policies that sought to erase Indigenous cultures. He emphasised the importance of Indigenous sovereignty and the revitalisation of Native American traditions and knowledge. Deloria's work has influenced the development of Native American studies as an academic discipline and contributed to the growing awareness of Indigenous rights and perspectives (Perley, 2021).

In New Zealand, Linda Tuhiwai Smith (2012) critiques how Western research methods have marginalised indigenous perspectives and knowledge. Tuhiwai Smith advocates for developing research practices focusing on indigenous voices, values, and worldviews. Her book, *Decolonizing Methodologies: Research and indigenous peoples*, has become an influential resource for researchers working with indigenous communities to incorporate more respectful and inclusive methodologies.

Leanne Betasamosake Simpson (2017) focuses on the resurgence, decolonisation, and renaissance of Nishnaabeg intellectual traditions. She emphasises the importance of reconnecting with indigenous knowledge systems, languages, and cultural practices to resist colonialism and build sustainable, self-determining communities. Bruce Pascoe (2018) uses historical records and archaeological evidence to argue that Indigenous Australians engaged in sophisticated agricultural practices and land management systems. He debunks colonial myths about Aboriginal societies and challenges the widely held belief that pre-colonial Aboriginal societies were exclusively hunter-gatherers. Pascoe's book, *Dark Emu*, has sparked renewed interest in pre-colonial Indigenous Australian societies. It has influenced efforts to incorporate indigenous land management practices in contemporary environmental conservation and land use strategies (Konish, 2019).

These scholars commit to challenging Western hegemony and advocating for recognising and appreciating Southern cultural identities and values. Their work has significantly contributed to the critique of Western dominance and promoted a more inclusive and balanced understanding of the world.

This book follows the footsteps of these and other pioneering and current Southern scholars. By examining the works of these selected scholars, I emphasise that Southern theories are appreciated in different regions and have the potential to reshape the way we address global challenges.

Conclusion

This book highlights the value of Southern theories and philosophies and their application to various fields and contexts. These theories provide nuanced and context-specific perspectives on the worldwide complex and interconnected challenges and offer valuable insights into the root causes and potential solutions. By leveraging the perspectives and approaches of Southern theories, we can work towards creating a more inclusive and equitable world that recognises and addresses the needs and perspectives of all people, regardless of their geographic location. We hope readers will be inspired to engage with these theories and philosophies, promote their significance, and continue discussing how indigenous knowledge can be applied to addressing contemporary and future global challenges.

Notes

1 Southern theories, philosophies, and traditions encompass diverse approaches originating from the Global South. These approaches aim to critique and challenge Western hegemony and narratives, and advocate for the recognition and appreciation of perspectives, knowledge systems, and values from the Global South. In this book, the terms 'Global South' and 'Southern' will be used interchangeably. It is important to note that whilst the term 'Global South' primarily refers to geographical location (countries in the southern and eastern parts of the globe), in this book, it also serves as a metaphor for native and indigenous communities within Western regions which experience subjugation and injustices. While some scholars such as Ghai (2012) and Nguyen (2018) use the term 'Southern theory' in the singular form, this book will use 'Southern theories,' 'Southern philosophies,' and 'Southern traditions' in the plural form to acknowledge the vast array of philosophical concepts across Global South.
2 In this book, decolonisation refers to elevation, acknowledging and application of Southern theories, concepts and philosophies when evaluating, conceptualising, theorising and designing policies aimed at addressing challenges in the Global South.

References

Adams, G., & Estrada-Villalta, S. (2017). Theory from the South: A decolonial approach to the psychology of global inequality. *Current Opinion in Psychology*, *18*, 37–42. https://doi.org/10.1016/j.copsyc.2017.07.031

Amin, S. (1968). *Le development du capitalisme en Cote d'Ivoire*. Minuit.

Ani, M. (1994). *Yurugu: An African-centered critique of European cultural thought and behavior*. Africa World Press.

Chiumbu, S. (2022). Reporting sexual and gender-based violence: A decolonial gaze on women journalists in South Africa. In G. Daniels & K. Skinner (Eds.), *Women journalists in South Africa: Democracy in the age of social media* (pp. 31–47). Springer International Publishing.

Deloria, V. (1988). *Custer died for your sins: An Indian manifesto*. University of Oklahoma Press.

de Sousa Santos, B. (2015). *Epistemologies of the South: Justice against epistemicide*. Routledge.

Escobar, A. (1992). Imagining a post-development era? Critical thought, development and social movements. *Social Text*, 31–32, 20–56. https://doi.org/10.2307/466217

Escobar, A. (2007). Worlds and knowledges otherwise: The Latin American modernity/coloniality research program. *Cultural Studies*, 21(2–3), 179–210. https://doi.org/10.1080/09502380601162506

Ghai, A. (2012). Engaging with disability with postcolonial theory. In D. Goodley, B. Hughes, & L. Davis (Eds.), *Disability and social theory* (pp. 270–286). Palgrave Macmillan.

Ghazizadeh, A., & Mollanazar, H. (2022). The activist role of translation in promoting cultural anti-imperialism: A historical analysis of translations rendered by Ali Shariati. *Journal of Language and Translation*, 12(3), 115–127. https://dorl.net/dor/20.1001.1.17350212.1401.20.3.9.2

Hountondji, P. (2002). *The struggle for meaning: Reflections on philosophy, culture and democracy in Africa*. Ohio University Press.

Huang, Y. (2022). Tu Wei-ming's Tizhi and the confucian contribution to contemporary epistemology. *Philosophy East and West*, 72(3), 739–757. https://doi.org/10.1353/pew.2022.0056

Konishi, S. (2019). First nations scholars, settler colonial studies, and indigenous history. *Australian Historical Studies*, 50(3), 285–304. https://doi.org/10.1080/1031461X.2019.1620300

Metz, T. (2022). *A relational Moral Theory: African Ethics in and beyond the Continent*. Oxford University Press.

Mukherjee, M. (2022). Decolonising education: Critical reflections from India. *Aula de Encuentro*, 215–237.

Mutanga, O. (ed). (2023). *Ubuntu Philosophy and Disabilities in Sub-Saharan Africa*. Routledge.

Ndlovu-Gatsheni, S. J. (2018). *Epistemic freedom in Africa: Deprovincialization and decolonisation*. Routledge.

Ndlovu-Gatsheni, S. J. (2021). The cognitive empire, politics of knowledge and African intellectual productions: Reflections on struggles for epistemic freedom and resurgence of decolonisation in the twenty-first century. *Third World Quarterly*, 42(5), 882–901. https://doi.org/10.1080/01436597.2020.1775487

Nguyen, X. T. (2018). Critical disability studies at the edge of global development: Why do we need to engage with Southern theory? *Canadian Journal of Disability Studies*, 7(1), 1–25. https://doi.org/10.15353/cjds.v7i1.400

Nzegwu, N. (1994). Gender equality in a dual sex system: The case of Onitsha. *Canadian Journal of Law and Jurisprudence*, 7, 73–95. https://doi.org/10.1017/S0841820900002575

Nzegwu, N. (2004). Feminism and Africa: Impact and limits of the metaphysics of gender. In K. Wiredu (Ed.), *A companion to African philosophy* (pp. 560–569). Blackwell Publishing.

Oyewumi, O. (1997). *The invention of women: Making an African sense of western gender discourses*. University of Minnesota Press.

Pascoe, B. (2018). *Dark Emu: Aboriginal Australia and the birth of agriculture* (new ed.). Magabala Books.

Perley, B. (2021). Indigenous anthropology. In *Oxford research encyclopedia of anthropology*. Oxford University Press. https://doi.org/10.1093/acrefore/9780190854584.013.98

Porselvi, P. M. V. (2022). The Cambridge companion to Rabindranath Tagore (book review). *Journal of Comparative Literature and Aesthetics*, *45*(2), 137–140.

Rozzi, R. (2015). Earth Stewardship and the biocultural ethic: Latin American perspectives. In R. Rozzi, F. S. Chapin III, S. T. A. Pickett, M. E. Power, J. J. Armesto, & R. H. May Jr. (Eds.), *Earth stewardship: Ecology and ethics* (pp. 87–112). Springer.

Sabareesh, P. A., & Reeta Sony, A. L. (2022). Ecocentric approach of science from the perspective of Mahatma Gandhi and Rabindranath Tagore: Exploring sustainability and ethics amidst British colonialism. *Journal of Scientific Temper*, *10*(1–2). https://doi.org/10.56042/jst.v10i1-2.66005

Shizha, E. (2013). Reclaiming our indigenous voices: The problem with postcolonial Sub-Saharan African school curriculum. *Journal of Indigenous Social Development*, *2*(1), 1–18.

Simpson, L. B. (2017). *This accident of being lost: Songs and stories*. House of Anansi.

Smith, L. T. (2012). *Decolonising methodologies: Research and indigenous peoples* (2nd ed.). Zed Books.

Tortolini, A. (2020). The defence of national identity as a revolutionary concept: *Gharbzadigī*, Islamic modernisation, and anticolonialism. *International Journal of Islam in Asia*, *1*(1), 91–115. https://doi.org/10.1163/25899996-01010006

wa Thiong'o, N. (1986). *Decolonising the mind: The politics of language in African literature*. James Currey.

2 Chinese philosophy's contributions to the homoverse

Geir Sigurðsson and Paul J. D'Ambrosio

Introduction

The term 'homoverse,' coined by the late comparative Chinese-Western philosopher Henry Rosemont, Jr., refers to the specific world of humans with all their daily physiological and mental needs, as distinct from a 'universe,' which suggests a metaphysically objectified and single-ordered world arrangement (cf. Rosemont & Smith, 2008). This chapter outlines five interrelated perspectives of Chinese philosophy that could make accurate and meaningful contributions to our contemporary homoverse if they were more widely adopted. The first perspective is a stance of *nondualism* that acknowledges the equal importance of both physical and mental aspects of reality and persons, manifesting itself, for instance, in the notion of *Qi* 氣 that emphasises the unity of both aspects of reality. The second is the relational notion of *person*, where interactions, roles, and relationships constitute the person. Here, the agency is ideally relatively dispersed within the environment. The third is the predominantly Confucian idea of *cultivation* that understands persons (human becomings) and culture as primarily developmental. The fourth is the notion of *harmony* that celebrates differences between interacting components (whether of society or nature) and opposes a tendency to impose sameness upon them. The fifth, finally, is a post-comparative notion developed out of Daoist origins coined by one of the authors, namely *genuine pretending*. This suggests confronting contemporary societies without either submitting to their demands or turning their back on them entirely. It is a mode of coping psychologically in reality largely gone amok while at the same time contributing towards reducing its madness and maintaining ease.

In the following sections, we shall often discuss the Chinese philosophical perspectives mentioned earlier by juxtaposing them with corresponding, often contrasting, Western views. In the concluding section, we will summarise and draw further inferences from our discussion.

A note on methodology

This chapter is based on our interpretation of early Chinese philosophy. Having both worked extensively with early Chinese philosophical sources in their

DOI: 10.4324/9781003358879-2

original classical Chinese language, we offer, for the most part, our interpretations of the perspectives and notions discussed in this chapter, but we also claim that our interpretations would generally be considered neutral. Still, we often reference other scholars of early Chinese philosophy to substantiate our views and understanding. While we would like to avoid being too technical, it will also be necessary to refer to some early Chinese philosophical writings and Western ones to support our arguments.

Our methodological approach is most appropriately characterised as aligning with philosophical hermeneutics in the spirit of Hans-Georg Gadamer and Paul Ricoeur. While we rely on our sinological training, i.e. our command of both the classical and modern Chinese languages and our acquired insights into the Chinese historical tradition and culture, we approach the issues in question primarily from a philosophical point of view. It entails two stages; firstly, we endeavour to interpret the Chinese philosophical insights from a holistic view that contextualises them within their original philosophical tradition. In other words, they are interpreted as belonging to a configuration of elements that can only be made meaningful insofar as they are related internally to each other and thus contribute to the complex whole. Secondly, we then decontextualise them so that we can subsequently recontextualise them in a more global philosophical dialogue, whereby they are juxtaposed with, in particular, Western philosophical treatment of comparative spheres of human living. The second stage entails a certain 'distancing' from the original Chinese context, but such a divergence is necessary for the ability to construct commensurable global philosophical concepts (cf. Gadamer, 1990; Ricoeur, 2016).

First perspective: nondualism, interrelationality, one-world theory

Let us begin with an issue related to metaphysics or reality's fundamental structure and makeup. Early Chinese philosophy is undoubtedly non-dualistic (Wang, 2012). Suggesting a negative category as an integral aspect of Chinese philosophy may seem peculiar. However, because philosophical discourse primarily takes its cue from mainstream Euro-American philosophy, non-Western philosophies sometimes have no choice but to define themselves relationally and negatively. Since the days of its ancient Greek predecessors, mainstream Western philosophy has been radically dualist in its outlook (Hall & Ames, 1995). There are many manifestations of dualism – and thus also of its contrast. Some of the most consequential and potentially pernicious ones are matter-spirit dualism, gender dichotomy, and the two-world theory.

Matter-spirit dualism has a long history in Western thought. It is at least present in the earliest stages of philosophical development and is undeniably a fundamental aspect of Christianity. Descartes established its corollary, mind-body dualism, quite explicitly as a necessary condition for human freedom because the scientific view of reality suggested that a mechanistic and thus deterministic chain of causes and effects applied to all material things, including the human body. By arguing that the two substances are entirely 'distinct' and thus independent, Descartes believed that he had liberated the human mind from mechanistic determinism. However, by disjoining them, he had trouble accounting for their mutual interaction (Störig, 1990). Interestingly, this issue is far from being an outdated problem belonging to the 17th or 18th centuries; the very same difficulty is still being discussed among contemporary Western philosophers (Scheffel, 2020).

In early Chinese philosophy, there is certainly an acknowledgement of the difference between the material and the spiritual sides of reality. However, these are seen as sides or aspects of the same entity, not as two distinct substances. Instead of substance dualism at the metaphysical level, there are 'provisional distinctions' on the linguistic level, while the emphasis is on the underlying unity (Wang, 2012).

In this case, another way of speaking of nondualism is 'interdependence.' Reality is understood as a vast network in which everything is interconnected. Thus, seemingly contrasting elements are, in fact, necessary features of the whole, indispensable for each other. Such a vision produces the inescapable penchant to 'envisage' a contrast whenever an aspect of reality is expressed. Thus, we may speak of spirit, but spirit always suggests something material. The two cannot be realistically envisaged in isolation from each other. In early Chinese philosophy, this is a fundamental dialectic view of reality. Ames (1998) has referred to this view as 'holographic,' whereby everything entails all other things 'as conditions for its continued existence,' including its contrasts.

This logic of interconnection between all components of reality is expressed through the categories of yin 陰 and yang 陽 (Wang, 2012; Linck, 2000; Rošker, 2021). While yin and yang symbolise distinct characteristics, features, and aspects of things, yin always entails yang, and yang entails yin. Neither can ever be absolute nor make sense individually except through their interrelations. We may illustrate this by considering the meaning of the terms 'in' and 'up,' neither of which make sense unless we simultaneously keep in mind 'out' and 'down,' respectively. In Chinese philosophy, the same applies to all other characteristics of reality, including matter and spirit.

An early Chinese notion going beyond dualist categories is *Qi* 氣, which means, at the same time, matter, energy, and life (Wang, 2012; Rošker, 2021). In early Chinese cosmology, *Qi* is presented as the fundamental 'stuff' or 'raw material' of existence, containing spiritual and mental aspects. All existing things have material, spiritual, and vital aspects, though their proportions differ.

Gender relations are also an illustrative example of the yin-yang interrelational scheme. The tendency in Western thought has been to construe the genders as entirely distinct and therefore draw an absolute line between them in terms of two opposite sexes and, as Derrida (1967) and others have shown, place them in a hierarchical logocentric relationship that ultimately justifies the domination of one through the other. In the more sophisticated

Chinese philosophical accounts, gender relations are envisaged much more nuanced and complexly. The labels 'feminine' and 'masculine' signify a variety of characteristics belonging to everyone, irrespective of sex (cf. Lai, 2017, pp. 250–251). These characteristics are then made meaningful through their correlations with their opposites. This means that, first, no absolute distinction can be made between them, and second, there is no philosophical justification for domination. However, it must be readily admitted that this philosophical understanding did not prevent male dominance in the actual history of Chinese society.

Lastly, a two-world theory was probably an inevitable outcome of Plato's demand for absolute and unconditional truth. His intentions were undoubtedly good, but it has had many fateful consequences. The most obvious one is the emergence of the Christian value-laden distinction between the human and the divine worlds, according to which Christians disregard their life here and now to focus on an unlikely afterlife in some other transcendental realm (Störig, 1990). The two-world theory may, admittedly, also have enabled a particular abstract conceptualisation of reality, possibly facilitating the mental construction of natural laws. However, these have also generated absolutist categories with many pernicious consequences, including the firm belief in obtaining the unconditional truth about life and the world, leading to intolerance against differences, racial prejudice, and violence against other cultures.

Early Chinese thought has no space – or need – for a two-world theory. Our empirically experienced and constantly changing reality is the only available reality. This generates a reluctance to accept truths as unconditional and a continuous effort to adapt to reality. This underlying tendency comes through quite clearly in the following sections on person and cultivation.

Second perspective: person, agency and morality

Early Chinese philosophy's conception of the person is most clearly articulated through contrasts with general approaches in some mainstream discourses found within Western thought. Here again, a foundation in a one-world theory is crucial. When there is no split between mind and body, the person is conceived of as wholly within this world and thus not an 'individual' in the modern sense of the term. No soul, indivisible self, or abstract sense can be isolated from the world's contingencies. Everything that makes a person who they are, from their characteristics to personality, predilections to volitions, are inextricable in this world. Nothing higher or beyond commands them. There are no strings from another world pulling actions, thoughts, or emotions in this one. The individual or self-divorced from the concrete particulars of this world does not exist (Li, 1999; Hall & Ames, 1995).

While not necessarily entirely based on 'materialism,' some fundamental congruence between this thinking and early Chinese philosophy is evident. A person is an incredibly complex cluster of characteristics and predispositions which are given. One's height is thereby not categorically distinct, in some sense, from their capacity for any particular moral virtue or ethical understanding (Behuniak, 2005). However, this does not mean that persons are wholly predetermined. While some attributes may have specific limitations, such as physical ones, many aspects of one's personality, and most importantly those associated with the moral and ethical, can be cultivated. Everyone starts with some essential 'sprouts' for being moral, ethical, and living well in society, but the starting points are different. Further, our motivation and desire to cultivate differs from person to person. Early Chinese philosophy thus presents a relatively unique view of agency or autonomy, of morality, as well as the motivation to develop oneself accordingly.

According to individualist views, there is always some element of the person that exists outside of worldly contingencies. The will, intention, self, soul, or something of the sort, is anchored somewhere beyond this world – a second pure, absolute world. Morality, too, echoes that which is beyond contingencies, which allows it to have the bearing it does on this world. Suppose either the will (or something like it) or morality is seen to be contingent or include too high of a degree of contingency. In that case, it is no longer considered moral or truly wilful. A moral code that allows, for example, for 'moral luck' is subject to criticism. Likewise, a person who acts according to contingencies is not considered thoroughly (morally) responsible. Early Chinese thought does not consider either the person or morality to reside, in any degree, in a world outside of this one. There is nothing that transcends the world of contingencies.

We can begin by noting the irreducibly social nature of persons. Their social environments largely determine who a person becomes and how they transform. The dispositions one is born with transform through interactions. Those changes are dependent upon what the person already is, the way others are, and how the relationships between them bear out. In a simplified sense, people are more or less constituted by their social roles and relationships. Outside of these, little, if anything, makes the person who they are (Rošker, 2021). What qualities, if any, have meaning in and to one's life without being products of exchanges with others? Early Chinese thinkers do not find much in the way of an answer. Mostly, they took the more obvious explanation: those we relate with make us who we are, and we make them who they are. Each person is a conglomerate of their environment, especially their social environment (Ames, 2011).

Again, this can be readily contrasted with an individualistic approach. If we take the person to have something outside of social interactions, environmental factors, and given dispositions, then one is not simply reducible to roles and relationships. There must be something more that can reflect on these contingencies and is categorically distinct from them. Whatever this separate thing is, it is the house of autonomy – understood here simply as the ability to critically reflect on one's condition independently (Rosemont,

2015). However, early Chinese thinkers did not require autonomy in this sense. Many discovered resources to explain our ability to reflect on our circumstances without the need to posit anything abstracted from them (Ames, 2011; Rošker, 2021; Fingarette, 1972).

In Confucianism, agency develops from the multifarious and incongruent dispositions that constitute a person (Lao & Ames, 1998). Socially, other sets of multifarious and incongruent expectations, such as various roles and relationships, guides and models, pull the person in all directions. For example, one desires two different foods, or to eat ice cream but also to stay in good shape, or to be a good son but also a good friend – and the demands conflict. Life is full of conflicting contingencies, both internal and external to the person. These various feelings, thoughts, and influences generate a sense of agency. This allows the person to reflect on their own dispositions and external factors critically. Confucians argue that strengthening our ability to reflect critically is paramount to being a (good) person (Ames, 2011). Far from being a determinist view based on materialism, early Chinese thought embraces contingencies and finds them to be a well-spring of meaningful critical reflection.

The attitude towards developing a robust sense of personhood, agency, and living morally might be summarised as 'no excuse.' Indeed, everyone is born with and experiences vastly different contingencies. As a result, some find it easier to excel in these areas. However, even when someone is exceptionally unlucky in all areas of life, their striving, committing to positively influence others, reflecting on their situations, and cultivating themselves morally is enough. Not viewing people as individuals, early Chinese thought only held one bar or standard for everyone to follow. As long as one sincerely works hard, that is all that matters. Achievement in any area is based on the particular person and their circumstances. Thus, everyone can be accomplished in some sense, and there is no excuse not to work hard.

Morality is, in this sense, a moving target. The basic vocabulary underlying what is considered good in each context is based on a *jing* 經-*quan* 權 dynamic, in other words, weighing doctrines, codes, and models with the particulars of a situation, the persons involved, and their relationships (which is just another way to say 'persons'). As many modern scholars have noted, in some sense, using the word 'morality' is misleading when discussing early Chinese thought. Instead, we might say that the concern revolves mainly around 'appropriateness.' This term gives us a better sense of the constant variation based on ever-transforming particulars and the lack of abstractness, objectivity, and absoluteness in this realm. We are chiefly concerned with how people feel as well as their reasons. Moreover, everyone involved, their relationships, and all the contingencies constituting and surrounding them must be considered.

A generalised contrast serves us well here. While in Plato's work, we find vigorous attempts to clear away concrete particulars to get at the 'essence' of the matter and are supposed to judge from there, we have precisely the opposite orientation in early Chinese texts. In the *Analects of Confucius*, we gather as many concrete particulars as possible to feel all the details. Moral considerations are as authentic as the person and agency conceptions.

Third perspective: cultivation, virtue, ritual

The Confucian philosophy envisages human life holistically as, ideally, a continuous cultivation process, implying growth or improvement through time. For Confucians, such growth or learning constitutes the very meaning of human existence. The ancient Confucian philosopher Xunzi begins his voluminous work by stating that learning can never be regarded as being concluded (*Xunzi*, 2006–2022).[1] As long as we are living, we should also be learning.

We have our abilities, roles, and responsibilities in each phase of life. Naturally, as newcomers in life, or infants, our abilities are remarkably undeveloped. Thus we depend almost entirely on the benevolence of our caretakers, who must attend to all our needs. Through interaction with the persons around us during the first phase of our existence, we gradually learn to behave as humans and develop characteristics seen explicitly as human. Education is, therefore, also a process of humanisation.

This does not entail, however, that we are a blank slate by birth. Our abilities grow out of an inborn source, a sort of potentiality that the ancient Confucian philosopher Mengzi called 'sprouts' (*duan* 端; *Mengzi*, 2006–2022, 2A6). Being inborn, the sprouts are a part of our constitution by birth, given to us by nature, and thus the development of human characteristics, which we could also refer to as the process of civilisation, is considered an entirely natural process: Confucians, then, consider their cultural tradition, or civilisation, to be an outgrowth of nature. To cultivate oneself along these moral lines is what it means to be human. ('Human' is a moral rather than a biological designation in early Confucian texts. Daoist considerations of the same issue will be outlined later.)

Civilisation is supervenient on excellent human abilities or virtues. The more we have of these virtues, the more advanced and thus 'humane' the civilisation. Among the virtues or excellences, we can mention reason or understanding, moral judgement, the capacity for meaningful communication through language and physical gestures, affection or love, and emotional capacities such as empathy, trustworthiness, and loyalty. Mengzi identified four kinds of sprouts that could be said to match the first four virtues: *zhi* 智, *yi* 義, *li* 禮 and *ren* 仁. In later developments of Confucianism, *shu* 恕, *xin* 信, and *zhong* 忠, corresponding to the final three, were emphasised as cardinal virtues.

At first sight, it may seem unusual to see emotions among these virtues. Are emotions not spontaneous and natural, opposite to reason, acquired to control and dominate emotions? Such a view would constitute a typical assumption resting upon the Western dualistic categories of emotion and reason. Early Chinese philosophers accepted emotion but instead regarded the human being as an emotio-rational creature (Li, 2016). Furthermore, they emphasise that while emotions are indeed based on the naturally inborn 'sprouts,' they still need to be trained. Affection for others is, therefore, an entirely natural emotion. However, it needs to be nurtured in the person, for otherwise, it will likely fail to develop and bloom as a fundamental ability. As Xunzi (2006–2022) points out metaphorically at the beginning of his work, the colour blue is made from the indigo plant but is bluer than indigo; ice is made from water but colder than water. Our natural sources must be worked on and improved. Another significant correction to be learned from early Chinese philosophy is that emotion is not something to be repressed or rejected but instead nurtured and integrated into the social lives of human beings – or rather 'human becomings,' because as the complex creatures that we humans are, we are continually developing through changing circumstances and experiences (Ames, 2011).

Among the emotions, the interrelational ones of affection and empathy particularly require interpersonal communication. These abilities can only be learned through interacting with and emulating others in our surroundings. Thus, it is of utmost importance what sort of experience we have as children, what we are taught, and what sort of people will be our role models.

Confucians place a particular emphasis on education and learning. It is no coincidence that the *Analects of Confucius*, the first and most fundamental Confucian text, begins by accentuating the importance of learning as a crucial human activity. In this context, 'learning' indicates studying, learning from texts or reflecting on specific ideas, norms, principles, modelling, and emulation. Sometimes, to grasp something, especially at a young age, one is encouraged to follow in the footsteps of others until they come to have the appropriate sentiments, thoughts, and emotions. For example, a child is told to say thank you. Even if they only begrudgingly follow along, parents encourage them to do so until they eventually actually think and feel gratitude.

Furthermore, learning is a joyful activity that constitutes a happy life. This can be understood from two points of view. On the one hand, a meaningful process of learning and growth can only occur given that certain preconditions for material and spiritual well-being are met: we must have both access to material subsistence and enjoy sufficient freedom to attend to and practice learning. Therefore, it makes an implicit but apparent socio-political demand for everyone's bare subsistence. The ability to cultivate oneself is an indicator of justice and existential well-being. On the other hand, we should adopt a view of learning first and foremost as an enjoyable activity, both in our approach to and pursuit of it and in the way we design formal educational activities.

Additionally, the Confucian understanding of learning is foundational in that it signifies the continuous endeavour of human beings to figure out and adapt to their natural and social environments. Learning is, therefore, a continuous process of life, not restricted to formal institutions of education, although these constitute an essential part of the overall scheme. This also entails that learning occurs here and now: we learn – or should learn – from any mundane activity or interaction with other people. 'Whenever in a company of three,' Confucius said, 'I have teachers present.' (*Analects of Confucius*, 2006–2022, 7.22)

A crucial tool in Confucian cultivation is the notion of *li* 禮, often translated as 'ritual' or 'propriety.' *Li* initially designated religious sacred rituals but later referred to an extensive range of social or communal behaviour trained and structured according to established tradition or convention. It can therefore refer to the simplest of 'rituals', such as social greetings, and the most elaborate ceremonies, such as weddings or coronations. Its original sacredness gradually became attached to tradition and, more immediately, to the society within it. The primary function of *li* is to make social interactions efficacious and ease awkwardness (Fingarette, 1972). *Li* functions as an educational tool, not unlike the forms used in the practice of martial arts to cultivate a keen sense of one's physical surroundings. They are mainly physical actions and gestures and embody, in this sense, the cultural tradition and its values. Their repetition and eventual mastery as interactive and social habits train an entirely parallel sense of one's social environment. They make one aware of its norms, how to adapt to them but also how to change them – critique them, so to speak, through their modification.

In this sense, education is a fundamental requirement for a well-functioning and civilised society. It is through self-cultivation that one improves communication within the family, and it is through such improvement that society is more civilised, happier, and harmonious. Through such learning, we both realise our identity as necessary members of a community and the importance of serving that community – which, in many cases, may require critique and new meaningful creation.

Fourth perspective: harmony, happiness, community

Given everything thus far, harmony as a goal in early Chinese thought should be no surprise. Specifically, early Chinese thinkers were interested in promoting harmony between people in society. On the personal level, a particular type of harmony, i.e. maintaining a good balance of various emotions, thoughts, intentions, and the like, can definitively be attributed to early Chinese concerns. However, as already partly demonstrated earlier, behind the impetus to cultivate oneself into a better person, to be moral, and to pass down rituals and traditions is the ever-present concern for interpersonal relationships (Rošker, 2021). This is frequently misinterpreted as an emphasis on the value of community. A more nuanced appreciation recognises that while there is some truth to this, the focus should be on relationships and the intersubjective nature of the person as constituted by roles and relationships. In this way, the 'individual' is not subordinate to the community; instead, the entire dynamic between a person and those they live with is treated with far more detail. Accordingly, harmonious interactions become, naturally enough, a significant goal.

Harmony has occasionally been misinterpreted as 'identity,' 'conformity,' and other oversimplified characterisations that reject creativity and idiosyncrasies. Borrowing from the *Analects of Confucius*, harmony in the Chinese tradition has often been summarised as 'harmonised but not the same' (*he er bu tong* 和而不同) (*Analects of Confucius*, 2006–2022, 13.23). Indeed, the early Chinese thought, contrary to popularised caricatures, is replete with not only the recognition that persons are unique and must always reestablish, recreate, and reinvent patterns of being and interaction, it further demands this. Looking again at the *Analects of Confucius*, we find the phrase 'people broaden the way; the way does not broaden people' (*Analects of Confucius*, 2006–2022, 15.29). The 'way' here is *dao* 道, which can also be translated as path, road, method, or understood with more cosmological, metaphysical, or even ontological connotations. It functions almost like 'Truth' in some strains of Western philosophy. The *Zhuangzi*, too, a classic of Daoism – which gets its label from *Dao* – similarly rejects any 'conformity.' In it, we find that 'the dao is made by walking.' Today some scholars use phrases such as 'making the most of' one's 'ingredients' or 'experience' (see Ames, 2011) to highlight the uniqueness and nuance required for this robust notion of harmony.

To explain again through contrast, early Chinese thought was less interested in 'justice' than many other traditions.[2] In its stead, we have 'harmony' and can learn much through a generalised comparison. Justice usually attempts (though often unsuccessfully) to treat people equally. Ideally, nothing about the person, such as age, race, sex, and the like, should be considered. Relations are also typically minimised, and the situation's essence should be dealt with coldly and strictly. Reason dominates, and emotions should be highly minimised. Otherwise, we risk violating the principle of justice. The individual is theorised as an abstract and atomic agent; theories of justice are likewise abstract and isolated from the particulars and concreteness of this world (Rosemont, 2015).

While broadly contested, justice is often defined with a fair degree of precision in fixed contexts. This is due primarily to the abstractness accompanying these understandings. Discussions of justice often begin with hypotheticals, which seek to minimise the importance of contingencies. With these types of models, the application can be complex. The actual practice may be messy and include all sorts of particulars, though the definition and principles it is based on are abstract. Ideally, everything should be dealt with on the essence level; unfortunately, this is not always true.

Finally, something strange about theories of justice has often been noticed; namely, justice does not necessarily claim to promote the happiness of the parties involved or do much besides enforce fairness. While happiness has not been central in many Western theories of justice, 'well-being' is sometimes considered important, though it should be noted that this is most often connected with the idea of people being fundamentally rational. Thus 'justice as fairness,' or other driving mantras where justice is based strictly on reason, dominate.

Classical Chinese conceptions of harmony can be understood as almost opposed to these characteristics of justice. It thereby does not subvert the need for justice, or even developments of theories of justice, but calls for a different way of thinking about how people should relate and what types of communities should be promoted (Ames, 2011). Harmony and justice can be complementary, or we can think of one being built upon the other.

Harmony itself is difficult to define. Unlike many theories of justice, Chinese thought has almost no overarching 'theories' of harmony. Indeed, many major Chinese concepts are famously resistant to definitions. The virtues mentioned earlier, *dao* and harmony, should all be understood within their particular contexts (Wang, 2012). Only a general guide can demarcate some of their respective boundaries. Harmony does not establish a model for order or boast necessary prescriptions or foundational ideals. It does rely on shared expectations, but these vary in different contexts. The order harmony proffers is necessarily contextually determined.

To 'make the most of one's ingredients,' we must know what we are making – the same ingredients can be used to make various concoctions. So smaller social groups, where expectations are widely shared, and participants generally interact accordingly, are fertile grounds for establishing harmony. Precisely what that harmony may look like is determined by those involved. Outsiders may not understand how a harmonious situation has come about, why it is, or even what it is. Nevertheless, none of this is essential. Harmony does not require abstract explanations, theory, or any claim to objectivity. It thrives on concreteness, actual practice, and subjectivity. This extends beyond the understanding of 'what harmony is' – which is not particularly important in Chinese thought – and dominates the more pertinent question of 'how can harmony be established and maintained?'

People involved in harmony-based projects are not treated as atomic; they are not 'individuals' but relationally defined persons. Accordingly, treating people as equals is neither desirable nor possible. Thinking about harmony requires thinking about people as distinctive and particular. All the nitty-gritty concreteness that makes them who they are is central to establishing harmonious relations. The more abstract people are treated, the more 'equal' they become in an atomic sense and the less material we have for figuring out how harmonious interactions can occur. Relatedly, harmony is not based on reason alone. Chinese thinking understands that reason and emotions are intertwined. When separated, we can think of the cultivation of one bolstering the cultivation of the other.

Most importantly, distinguishing them is highly abstract and should be deemphasised when considering practical applications. Harmony thus considers not just what is 'right,' 'fair,' or other rational perspectives; it takes very seriously emotional elements. How particular persons feel in situations, interactions, and various contexts is central to harmony. Reason can be used to balance and ensure that emotions do not become overly subjective, just as emotions are used to counter overly rational, abstract, and objective thinking.

Harmony further considers two aspects of social order that justice often downplays: community and happiness. Understanding persons as constituted by their environment and social relations means determining how interactions should proceed is inextricably connected to broader communities. It is neither possible nor desirable to isolate interactions between persons from more enormous webs of connections. Further contextualisation is essential for establishing harmony and ensuring positive reflections by those involved. Indeed, harmony strives to make people happy. Whereas justice can sometimes be a zero-sum game, harmony almost always wants to avoid losses on either side – sometimes to a fault. To continue with game-theory terminology, we can say that harmony hopes for positive-sum or win-win situations. However, we argue that harmony is better understood outside such calculative thinking.

Fifth perspective: Daoism, wandering, genuine pretending

While Confucian views have arguably been dominant in this discussion, we want to include a perspective inspired by Daoist sources because Daoism may have been equal to Confucianism regarding historical influence and relevance to contemporary philosophy and comparisons.

A saying, which comes from the Daoist classic *Zhuangzi* (2006–2022), perfectly illustrates the relationship between Daoism and Confucianism in China's history: inner sage and outer king *neisheng waiwang* 內聖外王 (*Zhuangzi*, 2006–2022, ch. 33). 'Outer king' refers to complying with external social, moral, and political expectations. Indeed, one may even excel in these areas. 'Inner sage' speaks to not being overly attached to these standards and in other words, not allowing them to become oppressive or even definitive for how one thinks about themselves or others. Guo Xiang 郭象 (d. 312), who famously understood Confucianism and Daoism as quite similar and certainly complementary, notes that while one's body might be in the palace, working as a minister of the state, their heart-mind could be in a mountain temple, free from over-commitment to social, moral, and political entanglements. A person may be completely integrated and involved with ordinary worldly affairs without being too disturbed by their failures or successes – thereby maintaining a relatively even-keeled mentality. Vacillating between involvement and non-attachment, with a perspective not lost in its adherences and bond, is often referred to as *you* 游, which means 'wandering' or 'playing' and can be 'swimming' in other contexts.

The most famous philosophical reflections on *you* 游 or 'wandering' come from the *Zhuangzi*. Throughout Chinese history, this text has been lauded for providing an outlet for any who feel stifled by social, moral, and political pressures. The text is a mixture of poetry, literature, and philosophical reflection. Important as it has been philosophically, it has also been exceedingly influential in art, fashion, poetry, literature, and basically every part of life. The text has fantastical stories, humorous encounters, and deafeningly penetrating insights. At any moment, just when it seems to say something definitive, it immediately undermines itself, leaving readers with unstable though somehow not unsettling footing. For example, Confucius is sometimes a mouthpiece of the text's ideas, saying things that seem 'unConfucian.' At other points, Confucius is a fool, the butt of a joke. Moreover, in still other places, Confucius expresses another point of view, one which the *Zhuangzi* does not necessarily endorse.

In terms of philosophical content, a great example of the 'unstable yet not unsettling' place the *Zhuangzi* loves to play in is expressed in the phrase '*dao yi you dao* 盗亦有道' (*Zhuangzi*, 2006–2022, ch. 10). It has become an idiom used regularly in China today and for the past 2,000 years. The phrase simply means 'Robbers also have a way.' However, the point is quite striking. Firstly, the way or *dao* is somewhat sacred, so attributing it to robbers seems scandalous. Secondly, this phrase is used to express that while Confucian virtues are usually thought of as noble, they can equally be found in the deeds of people doing 'bad' things. In other words, morality and doing good in any context, socially or politically – including the most mundane everyday interactions – is ineffable. Whatever we grasp hold of and say 'that is it' can be turned on its head in the next moment or a different context. This is true of moral ideas just as any claiming 'that is it,' 'that is right,' or 'that is the way it should be.' Moreover, the reverse, 'that is not it,' 'that is wrong,' or 'that is not the way things should be,' is subject to the same contextualisation that makes any of them only a temporary lodging at best.

The cultivation and firm adherence to social, moral, and political expectations can be a heavy burden, particularly for those who do not do well – for whatever reason. Daoism provides resources, then, not only to view one's successes as not indicative of who one is and the actual values one should live by but also for those who fail. Both those who do well, who cultivate themselves, gain social praise and a good reputation, and those who do not can, through reliance on Daoist sources, understand themselves as not being limited therein.

A type of ethos based on role-based understandings of one's self and others and interlocked with social values, communal commitments, and mutually binding expectations is often taken, to some degree or another, as a marker of pre-modern societies. Abstaining from the pre-modern/modern/post-modern discourse, we can note the generality of this ethos. Western civilisations functioned according to different models, including a two-world theory with God, absolutes, objectivity and highly abstract notions. It was nevertheless no less important than in China. Overcoming the role-based ethos required a strong notion of the individual harbouring some content,

Chinese philosophy's contributions to the homoverse 29

value, or meaning that could be self-sustaining. Instead of constantly turning outward to understand oneself, relations with others, and values in general, the individual could look within. The person could be a source for (nearly) everything previously supposed to exist only externally. Another way to think about this trajectory is found in 'authenticity,' which is described by Charles Taylor as:

> Involv[ing] (i) creation and construction as well as discovery, (ii) originality, and frequently (iii) opposition to the rules of society and even potentially to what we recognise as morality.
> (Taylor, 1992, pp. 67–68)

The person is thus wedged free from the power of society and all the pressures and potential oppression of social conventions.

Readers of Daoism have often noticed a particular affinity between this way of thinking in China and the discourse surrounding individualism and authenticity. Both reject the ethos of externally determining powers. However, classifying Daoism as individualism or authenticity completely misconstrues some of the most fundamental tenets of this tradition.

In Confucianism, individuals are encouraged to pursue 'cultivation' by broadening their connections, learning, and increasing their influence. On the other hand, Daoism offers a contrasting path. Rather than focusing on 'learning,' which signifies growth and development, Daoism teaches that practising the Dao leads to a reduction (Laozi, 2006–2022). This way of thinking emphasises the minimisation of the individual in various aspects. There are discussions of 'losing one's self' or 'having no self' and generally 'acting through non-action' and being 'self-so.' These counterweights to Confucian projects do not fit at all with the individualism or authenticity described in Western philosophy. In other words, Daoism provides unique reflections on a role-based ethos not popular in Western thought. Rather than turning the trajectory from the outside to the inside, as individualism and authenticity advance, Daoist thought suggests temporarily lodging in external expectations but not losing one's hold on what is prior – that is to say, the self before cultivation, behaviours before virtues, relations before categories, and generally a pre-value state. This position is unique when compared with mainstream Western thought. Upon closer inspection, it has contributions to make regarding content and its relation to the ethos of roles and external expectations.

As mentioned previously, the Chinese tradition has endorsed Confucian thought for establishing norms that allow society to function, people to cultivate themselves, and harmony to be realised. In doing so, however, it has also celebrated Daoist reflections wherein these practices are called into question. Students who were unable to pass the state exams, officials who fell out of favour, and ordinary people who – for whatever reason – did not fit well in society could all find in Daoism a rich resource for reimagining identity and meaning outside of norms. In less extreme cases, people could think of themselves as constantly vacillating between Confucian and Daoist modes of thought or, in other words, embodying the 'inner sage outer king' ideal.

We thus find a resource for rethinking the relationship between society and the individual, which does not rest on a solid sense of self (e.g. individualism or authenticity) but also one that completely rethinks how a person can live according to the role-based ethos.

The Daoist position has been described as 'genuine pretending' (Moeller & D'Ambrosio, 2017). It speaks to the 'wandering' or 'playful' aspects, the total commitment, which is also allowed, and the movement between them. The 'genuine' is found in that one can completely fulfil role-based expectations. One's thoughts, feelings, desires, and intentions can align with their roles and identify themselves and others accordingly. This is, however, only a temporary state and not the way one *should always be*. That does not mean this is 'pretending.' The significant difference between 'pretending' and genuine pretending is, obviously, the 'genuine' aspect. There is no substantial notion of self or individual in Daoism. Instead, people are 'empty' and are viewed as being able fully, or genuinely, to take on roles without becoming attached to them or constructing a corresponding understanding of themselves, others, or the world. We are, to borrow an image from the *Daodejing* and the *Zhuangzi*, like vessels that are constantly filled with social expectations, only to be emptied, filled again, emptied again, and so on – none of them belongs to us; they are all only temporarily held.

Genuine pretending does involve adapting to external transformations, but goals, intentions, or ideas do not back it. The genuine pretender is internally empty – and does not cultivate a full consciousness of being 'upright' or having an authentic self. Pretending here can be understood in how children play, that is, without attachment to whatever is temporarily adopted, recognising both the contingency and transience of transformations. The 'genuineness' of genuine pretending is also reflected in child play. Children take on their roles and 'become' them, but again only while affirming the contingency and transience of their roles. They do not essentially identify themselves as *really being* a doctor, cop, or robber. Unlike doctors, cops, and robbers, who sometimes get carried away with their roles, a child only identifies as such in a particular situation and for a fixed amount of time. Genuine pretending suggests that this attitude might help alleviate some of the stress and anxiety associated with overzealous over-commitment to social roles. Perhaps more significantly, this approach also offers resistance against the 'bad faith' associated with falsely over-identifying oneself with social roles. Paradoxically, genuine pretending also implies the absence of inauthenticity and cultivates a certain resilience against vanity induced by social pressures.

Conclusion

The world today is facing an unprecedented array of challenges spanning political, social, and environmental spheres. We do not claim that adopting the five perspectives outlined in this chapter will resolve all these issues; however, we believe they can potentially create significant positive change. We can foster more respectful and responsible engagement with nature and our fellow humans by embracing an interrelational understanding of the world and human development. As the cornerstone of a flourishing life, a comprehensive, integrated approach to cultivation or education can enhance collaboration across borders and between cultures. Emphasising harmony and community care can cultivate a 'global' consciousness, while adopting a mindset of 'wandering' or 'genuine pretending' can help alleviate societal oppression, allowing for a healthy degree of individual freedom.

It is essential to acknowledge that much of our discussion, particularly perspectives 2, 3, and 4, is based on Confucian thought, which may be criticised. Although the Chinese tradition is undeniably rich and diverse, many influential ideas stem from early Confucian sources and their subsequent developments. Legalism, Mohism, and Buddhism have also substantially developed Chinese philosophical discourse. While we have not explored these 'schools' in depth within this chapter, we recognise their significance and encourage further exploration. Our goal in presenting these perspectives from early Chinese philosophy is not to promote any ideology but to showcase viable alternatives to dominant worldviews that may constrain human development. We hope readers will be inspired to explore these ideas further through the readings listed in the references. These resources offer comprehensive and nuanced treatments of the Chinese philosophical tradition, providing readers with a deeper understanding of various texts and thinkers contributing to this rich intellectual heritage.

In conclusion, the adoption of these perspectives has the potential to contribute to a more respectful, collaborative, and sustainable world. By embracing an interrelational perspective, fostering a comprehensive and integrated approach to cultivation or education, emphasising harmony and community care, and adopting a mindset of 'wandering' or 'genuine pretending,' we can build a healthier and more equitable society for all.

Notes

1 All the early Chinese classics are accessible on the Chinese Text Project webpage: www.ctext.org (see also Bibliography for individual references). While English translations are often included, we prefer using our translations or paraphrases throughout the chapter.
2 This perspective, of course, depends on one's understanding of justice. Although the equivalent term for justice was not found in Chinese when interactions with Western thought were established, it is essential to note that some similar ideas did

exist. Compared to other models in Global South philosophies and thought, there are substantial similarities regarding theories of justice. For instance, in the Global South, we find traditions where justice is not based on autonomous individuals but is constructed within a communal context.

References

Ames, R. T. (1998). East Asian philosophy. In *Routledge encyclopedia of philosophy*. www.rep.routledge.com/articles/overview/east-asian-philosophy/v-1
Ames, R. T. (2011). *Confucian role ethics: A vocabulary*. The Chinese University Press.
Analects of Confucius. (2006–2022). https://ctext.org/analects
Behuniak, J. (2005). *Mencius on becoming human*. State University of New York Press.
Derrida, J. (1967). *De la grammatologie*. Les Éditions de Minuit.
Fingarette, H. (1972). *Confucius – the secular as sacred*. Harper & Row.
Gadamer, H. G. (1990). *Wahrheit und Methode: Grundzüge einer philosophischen Hermeneutik* (6th ed.). J.C.B. Mohr.
Hall, D. L., & Ames, R. T. (1995). *Anticipating China: Thinking through the narratives of Chinese and Western cultures*. State University of New York Press.
Lai, K. L. (2017). *An introduction to Chinese philosophy*. Cambridge University Press.
Lao, D. C., & Ames, R. T. (1998). *Yuan Dao: Tracing Dao to its source*. Ballantine Books.
Laozi. (2006–2022). https://ctext.org/dao-de-jing
Li, Z. (1999). Subjectivity and "subjectivity": A response. *Philosophy East and West*, 49(2), 174–183. https://doi.org/10.2307/1400201
Li, Z. (2016). A response to Michael Sandel and other matters. Translated by Paul D'Ambrosio and Robert A. Carleo. *Philosophy East and West*, 66(4), 1068–1147. https://doi.org/10.1353/pew.2016.0084
Linck, G. (2000). *Yin und Yang: Die Suche nach Ganzheit im chinesischen Denken*. C.H. Beck.
Mengzi. (2006–2022). https://ctext.org/mengzi
Moeller, H. - G., & D'Ambrosio, P. J. (2017). *Genuine pretending: On the philosophy of the Zhuangzi*. Columbia University Press.
Ricoeur, P. (2016). *Hermeneutics and the human sciences: Essays on language, action and interpretation* (J. B. Thompson, Ed. & Trans.). Cambridge University Press.
Rosemont, J. H. (2015). *Against individualism: A Confucian rethinking of the foundations of morality, politics, family, and religion*. Lexington Books.
Rosemont, J. H., & Smith, H. (2008). *Is there a universal grammar of religion?* Open Court.
Rošker, J. S. (2021). *Interpreting Chinese philosophy: A new methodology*. Bloomsbury Academic.
Scheffel, J. (2020). On the solvability of the mind-body problem. *Axiomathes: Quaderni del Centro Studi per la Filosofia Mitteleuropea*, 30(3), 289–312. https://doi.org/10.1007/s10516-019-09454-x
Störig, H. J. (1990). *Weltgeschichte der Philosophie*. W. Kohlhammer Verlag.
Taylor, C. (1992). *The ethics of authenticity*. Harvard University Press.
Wang, R. R. (2012). *Yinyang: The way of heaven and Earth in Chinese thought and culture*. Cambridge University Press.
Xunzi. (2006–2022). https://ctext.org/xunzi
Zhuangzi. (2006–2022). https://ctext.org/zhuangzi

3 *Qi* vitality and virtue cultivation
Embodying and educating for eco-cosmic citizenry

Jing Lin, Tom Culham, and Yishin Khoo

Introduction

This chapter promotes a theory about *Qi* vitality, which helps individuals deepen their experiences of interbeing (or interconnectedness of all things), practices of eco citizenship, as well as their cosmic wisdom and capacity to integrate wellness, wisdom, and love in the creation of new global development trajectories. The *Qi* vitality theory posits that we live in an interconnected web of energy, and all exist with others. This vital energy, called *Qi*, permeates the whole universe. It is the primordial energy and spirit in all existence, making all beings sacred and at one with the creative force. The material world is not isolated as this invisible, energetic *Qi* field infuses it. Universal equality is built into the foundation of our being because this creative, vital energy is present in everything, including humans, animals, trees, mountains, rivers, and stars. The chapter posits that we can cultivate and expand this energy through an integrated meditation process that uses virtues as technologies. In our view, virtues are not just values but are mechanisms that establish structures in the universe and human society. Culham and Lin (2020) put forward that love, service, cooperation, humility, gratitude, forgiveness, reconciliation, and gratitude are energy-guiding principles that sustain harmony and the exchange of life forces among all beings. The *Qi* vitality theory focuses on contemplative practices as pathways to expand our vital energy and connect with all humans and species on Earth and in the universe. As we all breathe and have *Qi* propelling the energy in our body reaching out to the universe, meditation has been explored to cultivate *Qi*; this practice is exemplified by spiritual teachers who engage in meditation to find their inner self and enlightenment (Culham & Lin, 2016, 2020; Lin, 2018, 2019; Lin et al., 2016; Lin & Khoo, 2022).

In this chapter, we will discuss the cultivation of vital life energy *Qi* and illustrate the aspirations of many generations of alchemists and countless people in human history for spiritual growth, health, longevity, wellness, and the remarkable ability to serve and help the world. The chapter draws from philosophies and contemplative practices embedded in Daoism, Confucianism, and Buddhism, as well as indigenous wisdom and world spiritual

DOI: 10.4324/9781003358879-3

traditions, both philosophical work and embodied personal practices. We also draw from classical Chinese medicinal thinking that emphasises the importance of connecting our energy, meridians, consciousness, and *Qi* – in other words, the microcosm of the human being – with the macrocosmic universe and the cosmic creative force *Qi*. We posit that the ideal of education is to cultivate this vital energy, foster wisdom and compassion, and take love as this cosmic, vital *Qi* energy that makes all life possible and meaningful. The *Qi* vitality theory focuses on exploring ourselves as incredibly complex and intelligent, with huge potential to be tapped into and developed. Peaceful and sustainable development in the world starts from cultivating a harmonious and sustainable flow of *Qi* within ourselves and being connected to the universe forming an eco-cosmic citizenry with all beings and existence connected in heart, spirit, and *Qi*.

Methodology

Starting from our personal experience

The three authors embarked on a unique journey to make the writing of this chapter an immersive and personal experience, reflecting our cultivation of the *Qi* life force. We held three extensive meetings, each lasting over two hours, delving into *Qi*'s philosophy, exchanging personal experiences related to *Qi* cultivation, and enriching our understanding. Moreover, we conducted comprehensive research on the topic before and after our discussions. Jing, who originally hails from China, has a background in practising Daoist, Confucian, and Buddhist meditation. Yishin, originally from Malaysia, has dedicated years to practising Buddhism and, more recently, Daoist *qigong*. These diverse experiences and cultural backgrounds have contributed significantly to our exploration and comprehension of *Qi* and its transformative power. Tom comes from Canada and has a background in Christianity and science but has engaged in *qigong*, or Daoist meditation, for two and a half decades. The three of us work in education and have engaged in development projects in the Global South at different times. We believe that through dialogues and reflection about our *Qi* energy practice, we will be able to sharpen our understanding of *Qi* vitality and its relevance to promoting a framework from the Global South that conceptualises an alternative way of thinking and being that transforms the overall purpose of education. *Qi* is to be experienced and cultivated; hence, we use the opportunity to write and cultivate the chapter. This means we incorporated some meditation practices into our dialogue sessions and found them very energising.

First-person research and Daoism

> A way to describe what we are doing is to call it first and second-person research. This provides the framework for emphasising observing personal experience

(first person), discussing our personal stories amongst ourselves, and theorising and reflecting on them (second-person research). Any references we include in the document are third-person research which we can minimise.

(Tom's comments, dialogue on June 8, 2022)

The first- and second-person research approach is consistent with Daoism and Zen Buddhism, which emphasise personal experience over intellectual thought as a path to enlightenment. This is the opposite of the Western view, which emphasises conceptual thought. Huang Po, a 9th-century Zen master, articulates the Zen view: 'give up all indulgence in conceptual thought and intellectual processes. When such things no longer trouble you, you will unfailingly reach Supreme Enlightenment' (Blofeld, 1958, p. 130).

Reason and logos rooted in the argument were the focus of ancient Greek philosophy following Plato's example. At the same time, the Chinese emphasised the living embodiment of wisdom in sages and the Dao. Before Plato, the Greeks saw philosophy as a way of life to be practised (Davidson & Hadot, 1995); later, they focused more on understanding the realities of life by arguing the logic of abstract ideas. Unlike the Greek focus on developing and defending logical propositions, Daoists paid attention to self-transformation through the cultivation of virtue to 'attain full integration with life's deepest realities' (Kirkland, 2004, p. 75). The practice of storing and building one's *Qi* (life energy), having embodied experience, taking sages as teachers and guides, and taking virtues as energy-guiding principles in their effort to live life well were considered vital to Daoists (Culham & Lin, 2020).

Daoists were interested in the practice of *Qi* vitality and the experience of living in harmony with the universe and, therefore, living well. Daoism was not the only spiritual tradition that emphasised personal experience as a guide to learning. According to the Buddha, his teachings should only be accepted if practitioners have experienced them and personally discovered them to be true (Palmo, 2002). Confucius also held that experience was critical to personal cultivation and understanding one's place in the universe (Culham & Lin, 2016; Lin, 2018).

Daoism seems particularly suited to guide first-person research as it involves inner work for 'discovering the mechanisms of cultural inculcation and shedding off cultural habits (so) that one approaches Dao. Dao does not exist in metaphysical abstraction but could be felt concretely' (Yen, 2008, p. 87). Dao cultivation is a process of returning to a state of oneness unconstrained by habit and culture. As mystical as this may seem, it is practical and physical and can be experienced incrementally in everyday life. An important outcome of Daoist *Qi* cultivation is an ultimate state of oneness and harmony where one has direct intuitive knowledge of the universe and where the self 'is seen as intimately connected with other people, creatures, and things in ways that conduce to their greater happiness, advantage, and well-being' (Ivanhoe et al., 2018, pp. 1–2). Some of the first-person research methods employed in Daoist training are meditation, tai chi, practising virtues, reflection, following the teaching of enlightened master teachers, receiving energy imparted by master teachers, calligraphy, music, dance, art, and poetry.

This chapter will consider why these approaches make sense given the current knowledge of the human brain, as articulated by McGilchrist (2009). In addition, the methods of first-person research informed by Daoist cultivation practices that might be applicable in a Western setting will be discussed, and the outcomes that may be beneficial to teachers and students will be articulated.

Questions for dialogue

As stated earlier, this chapter is grounded in our experiences, understandings, and cultivation of *Qi* using first-person research methods informed by Daoist cultivation practice. Through dialogues, we went deeper and reflected upon our own experiences. We dialogued on many topics. The following are some questions we discussed:

- What are your experiences with *Qi*? How do you work with *Qi*?
- What is *Qi* in Chinese philosophy, cosmology, traditional Chinese medicine, language, and daily life?
- How is the cultivation of *Qi* related to interbeing, eco citizenship, cosmic wisdom, integration of wellness, wisdom, and love?
- What is the Confucian and Daoist notion about *Qi* and cultivating *Qi* vitality and virtues? What are the goals they aspire to?
- What is yin and yang? Why do we meditate?
- How are *Qi* and virtues related to each other? What pathways do spiritual leaders take to embody love as foundational in our well-being, peace, and stewardship?
- How do ancient and contemporary people cultivate *Qi* vitality to connect with elements of earth, wood, metal, fire, water and everything in nature, and the human body? How do we understand consciousness is energy, and humans and nature/cosmos are one?
- What is development? What is the Anthropocene? What is our relationship with nature and with each other? Where are capitalism and technology leading us? What should be the roles of education? How do we revive lost wisdom from the South/China? How can we reprogramme our minds with new ideas and visions?

In the ensuing sections, we first share our experience of *Qi* and its cultivation. Then, we present our understanding of the cosmology that focuses on *Qi* and its virtues. Next, we discuss different methods of cultivating *Qi* and virtues. Finally, we contemplate the implications of *Qi* and its cultivation on our life and education.

What is *Qi*? Our personal experiences

What is *Qi*? We start from our personal experiences. Tom first experienced *Qi* in a seminar offered by a coordinator of a qigong community in Vancouver. He was introduced to the idea of *Qi*, and due to his education in Western science, he thought the idea was ridiculous. Nevertheless, the following day, when he was sitting in his office looking out at the ocean, he felt very calm and appeared floating in his chair. Because of this experience, he was motivated to investigate more profoundly. He attended a conference in the eastern United States on the science of qigong (literally meaning the power and application of *Qi*), where a qigong master was present. Following the conference, he felt a profound sense of tranquility and peace on his way home. Since then, he became interested in *Qi* and the qigong practice and dedicated himself to understanding the science of *Qi*. Seven years later, after he was laid off from his management job, he returned to university and completed a PhD in education to further his understanding of *Qi* and qigong in Western terms. Cultivation of virtue is a central tenet of qigong; consequently, Tom completed a thesis that considered the implications of this view on contemporary ethics education (Culham, 2013).

Jing experienced *Qi* when she started to do the Chinese qigong meditation method mentioned by Tom, and suddenly, everything started to come alive and become sacred. She started to feel the spirit and energy of everything, from trees, stones, and people, even from an electrical pole. She felt a fallen broom had a spirit begging her to pick it up. She used to love fishing, but suddenly, she started to feel the pain of the hook in the mouth of the fish, and she stopped fishing. Her awareness was greatly expanded, and she felt a connection to heaven and earth and all beings' emotions, sharing their joy and suffering. She started to feel a profound love for people and things on a new level, and her awareness stretched far beyond what she could imagine.

Yishin has just started learning classical Chinese medicine. One of the classes involved learning the science of nourishing life (*yang sheng* 养生) through a body shaking practice originated from the Jinjing Qigong (筋经气功) or the Tendon and Channel Qigong. The shaking exercise made her more aware of the life force *Qi* that flows in her body. In this exercise, one practised shaking off the physical and emotional tensions in her joints, muscles, internal organs, and bones, moving into a state of ease and flow that enables a person to connect with the universe's life force. Practising daily shaking with the mantra, 'ease, ease, ease, and flow, flow, flow,' she began to feel her whole body unblocking. She had more energy and better concentration to observe what was happening inside her and around her (including her own body, mind, and colleagues) to find more effective solutions at her workplace and in the community.

A cosmology of *Qi* vitality

In our journey of deepening our experience and cultivation of *Qi*, we found it helpful to understand the notation of *Qi* in Chinese worldview and cosmology. In Chinese philosophy, all existence comes from *Qi*, the primordial energy that creates all beings and existence. *Qi* is invisible, unnameable, and the unified force that is beyond the hearing range of our ears (Zhuangzi, 天籁之音; Laozi, 大音稀声) and beyond our vision (Laozi, 大象无形). As a great creative force, Dao is wrapped in everything. Dao is this vast energy field called Void that contains the mighty *Qi*, and from the Void appears the One, the spirit or consciousness, which becomes Two, the yin and yang forces, that interact and create humans, which forms Three. These Three become the fundamental forces that generate myriads of existence (Culham & Lin, 2020). In Chapter 25 of *Dao De Jing*, Laozi says

> There is something
> that contains everything.
> Before heaven and earth,
> it is.
> Oh, it is still unbodied,
> all on its own, unchanging,
> all-pervading, ever-moving.
> So it can act as the mother of all things.
> Not knowing its real name,
> we only call it the Way [Dao].
> If it must be named, let its name be Great.
> Greatness means going on,
> going on means going far,
> and going far means turning back.
> So they say: "The Way [Dao] is great,
> Heaven is great,
> Earth is great,
> and humankind is great;
> four greatnesses in the world,
> and humanity is one of them."
> People follow the earth,
> Earth follows heaven,
> Heaven follows the Way [Dao],
> the Way [Dao] follows what is.
>   (Le Guin, 1998, pp. 34–35)

Our life has a critical mission: to return to Dao by following the way of the Dao, which can be known by virtues, as illustrated in the book of *Dao De Jing*. Dao or enlightenment can be acquired through cultivating *Qi* energy and virtues simultaneously (Culham & Lin, 2020).

Dao and *Qi* cultivation

Dao unifies everything, which divides into the pulsating force of yin and yang that enables the creation of myriad of things in the whole universe. This process is best captured in the yin-yang symbol in Figure 3.1, which simultaneously represents the unending dynamism of apparent opposites, such as night and day, and the perfection and tranquility of the Dao in the form of the circle.

To align with the perfection of Dao, one must learn to be tranquil in the presence of the dynamic interplay of the apparent opposite. Meditation is the means to cultivate tranquility and align with the Dao; meditation enables us to reach our inner Dao-given wisdom, connecting us to the whole universe (Culham, 2013). *Qigong* is another name for meditation practice. It means the cultivation of the power of *Qi*. There are two types of qigong practices: Wai Dan (external cultivation) involves movement meditation (coordinating physical movement with breathing in concentration), and Nei Dan (internal cultivation) involves sitting meditation and guided imagery or visualisation (Her, 2016).

Qi and virtue cultivation need to go hand in hand. Through breathing, visualisation, and various meditation practices, including qigong, tai chi, martial arts, and yoga, we regulate our *Qi*. However, we must remember the importance of cultivating virtue as our *Qi* relates to others' *Qi* and all things and beings in our environment. Virtue is the energy-guiding principle of the universe that enables all to exist, sustain, and be interdependent. When we give, we receive; when we give without thinking about the fruits of our actions, we receive *Qi* in abundance. This practice of virtue is the foundational teaching of Daoism, which is likened to the collection of 'yin virtues' (Culham & Lin, 2020). Virtue creates a reciprocal loop of energy and expands the sense of self, so much so that it extends to the universe. Hence, *Qi* vitality practices always combine the inner and the outer, spirit and matter, emphasising cultivating virtuous deeds and our bio-magnetic,

Figure 3.1 Yin-yang symbol

bio-informational vital life *Qi* energy. We live in a vast boundless vital life energy field, and we are complexly wired with all spirits and energies of the universe.

Based on this ontological foundation, the whole universe is matter, energy, information, and spirit simultaneously, and the universe is moral and intelligent. As Jing reflected

> If we observe the workings of the universe, it is easy to derive such a perspective. Stars in the solar system revolve around the sun, and the Milky Way moves in an orderly manner without collapsing into each other. Human society will not survive without love and support built into our genes – babies cannot survive without the inherent love built into parents, which is also the case for animals. In all, there is a mechanism of cooperation and love built into the whole structure of the universe.

Virtue cultivation is *Qi* cultivation, and the Chinese philosophy of *Qi* focuses on *Qi* as the vital life energy in everything. *Qi* cannot be forced; rather, it flows spontaneously. When we are relaxing, *Qi* can be cultivated more easily. Further, virtues are essential to relax our mind and heart, including the body, as virtues such as loving-kindness, humility, compassion, letting go, service, yielding, and peace enable a tranquil mind and positive energy flow. Laozi's *Dao De Jing* says that instead of competition, grabbing, and hoarding, we know Dao (as the Creative Power) and reach Dao (as the unmeasurable energy *Qi*) through giving and serving, reconciliation, and balance.

Everything, including mountains, oceans, trees, rivers, and stars, has the vital life energy *Qi*, and all exchange vital energy *Qi*. As such, by working in harmony with the energy of nature, we can cultivate *Qi* and balance our body, mind, heart, and spirit too. Human interrelationships also involve *Qi* exchanges. Given that we live in an ever-changing world in constant interactions with others and nature, we need to find a middle way to avoid losing our harmony and balance within ourselves and with the world. In our experience, the most practical way to seek the middle way is to turn to ourselves and attend to our body (the microcosm of the universe) through the practice of meditation. During meditation, we calm our mind and stay in the present moment to better sense the movement of *Qi* and observe its working in our inner system. We become more aware of the dynamic changes in nature. Subsequently, we can fine-tune our *Qi* and become integral to our inner and outer selves, with others and nature.

For instance, Yishin shared about how through practising walking meditation, she was able to experience a feeling of oneness between the earth and her; the boundary between herself and her surroundings dissolved, and there was a moment of ease, freedom, and love experienced during the act of walking. Similarly, Bai (2015) discussed how in a meditative walk, she entered a state where everything became animated and alive, and in contemplation and oneness with nature, she got 'recharged.' Pokharel (2019) felt the life and will of a mosquito and even the joy of a gecko. This is *Qi*. Lin and Parikh (2019) felt their chakras opened, connecting them to the deeper realms of their energy through meditation. Jing highlighted the following in her experience of *Qi* cultivation:

> At a particular stage of our *Qi* cultivation, we let *Qi* teach us how to lead our lives. We follow the rhythm of nature and the rhythm of our body intuitively. We tap into the *Qi* in nature, cultivate and accumulate it. We start noticing that *Qi* can be refined to have extraordinary power for healing and many benefits, including enhanced cognition, more compassion, wisdom growth and better health. As we enhance our practice, we will also learn that groups have *Qi*, nature has *Qi*, everything has *Qi*, and the whole universe is involved in exchanging *Qi*. Then we realise that the whole universe is a cultivation site that involves more than humans. As our awareness expands, we know that we are working with everything else in the universe. The basic notion in Chinese philosophy is that heaven, earth, and humans are One. We resonate and correspond with each other. Human affairs affect the functions of the sun and moon and vice versa. These are embodied experiences of ancient Chinese philosophers, derived from the cultivation of their vital life energy *Qi* and lived experiences, as first-hand knowing and emergence from the inner heart.

The Chinese philosophy of *Qi* is similar to the philosophy of many other Global South traditions (see other chapters in this book; Metz 2023; Mutanga, 2023). Essentially, we are connected holistically to everything in our environment; internally and externally, we are interconnected. The crises we face, whether health, environmental, economic, or political, happen because such a connection is lost. Healing practices in ancient China aimed to restore the interconnection between our internal and external *Qi*, and this restoration requires the engagement of mind, heart, body and spirit, treating virtues as technologies in our lives (Culham & Lin, 2020). When people are treated, healing occurs at all levels – physically, emotionally, and spiritually – just like in some indigenous practices (Andrey, 2009).

Our body is built to work harmoniously, with every part contributing to the whole. This is simple: when one main organ fails, the body dies. We are also part of the holographic universe. In science, the theory of homeostasis says that all the cells in our body are working together to be in balance to enable the body to work and function; hence, the cells all align with the ruling principle of the body. Tranquility is a state we can cultivate to allow the body to maintain homeostasis. We need close understanding and inner knowledge about our body to notice the effects of the environment and maintain the balance of yin and yang. In Chinese philosophy, virtues are essential technologies to regulate our emotions. Our emotions affect the working of our organs, and our emotions arise from our relationship with others. When we are angry, we damage our liver. When we are kind to others, we receive positive feedback from others in a subtle energy exchange. Hence, we need to cultivate *Qi* and virtues simultaneously.

Daoist alchemists' cultivation of health, longevity, immortality, and sagehood

The practice of *Qi* cultivation has a long history in China and is primarily used in Daoism to cultivate physical and spiritual immortality. Many Daoist-informed approaches to *Qi* cultivation can still be found and learned today. The Daoist belief is that life is precious and that we can nurture our vital life energy *Qi* and live a healthy, long, fulfilling life. Further, Daoism believes it is pathetic that we can only live for a few dozen years and that we should aspire to control our destiny. We can extend our life and transform our life by following the way of Dao. Dao is immortal; Dao is the way or virtue, which is to be treated like technologies, meaning as mechanisms upholding the universe and human society and as principles governing our wellness and life course (Culham & Lin, 2020). Those who aspire to be like Dao, who are loving, giving, and yielding, helping bring peace to the world – are called Junzi (君子) or sages. They go through rigorous cultivation to achieve tranquility, self-control, wisdom, and inner peace, and afterward, they strive to work to bring peace to the world (Lin, 2018). Simultaneously, they use breathwork and visualisation to gather *Qi*, accumulate *Qi*, transform *Qi*, attain health and longevity, and become immortals and sages.

The Chinese medicinal classic *Huang Di Nei Jing* (the Inner Sutra of the Yellow Emperor) named the great masters in ancient times by their levels of *Qi* cultivation and virtues. They are called Zhenren (真人), Shenren (神人), Zhiren (至人), and Xianren (贤人), who all lived very long lives, knew the deep secrets of the universe, and were completely kind. With them, Zhenren and Shenren were immortals who had cultivated their *Qi* to such a high level that they coexisted with heaven and earth, and they had immense powers and supernatural abilities (*Huang Di Nei Jing*, Su Wen, Chapter 1: Shang Gu Tian Zhen[1] 黄帝内经素问:上古天真论; Lin, 2018).

Daoist practitioners use their bodies as vehicles to know Dao. They believe we have corresponding organs mimicking nature and the universe, and we are energetically wired with the stars, the earth, and the seasons. They undergo rigorous self-cultivation and endeavour to transform their whole life energy toward growing the immortal child, or the golden flower (Culham & Lin, 2020), and go through what alchemists call the process of distilling and refining energy – dissolution, calcination, conjunction, fermentation, and purification – and expand their bodies outward toward the universe (Andrey, 2009).

Thousands of methods have been discovered or invented to preserve our *Qi* and bolster our *Qi* energy in Daoism, and all aim to expand our awareness toward knowing the secret of life, nature, and the universe. It is to engage our energy, body, heart, mind, and spirit with the energy that creates and propels the universe.

Chinese philosophy, language, and embodied cultivation of *Qi* energy

Chinese philosophy, language, and embodied cultivation of *Qi* energy are inherently linked. In Confucianism, the emphasis has been on ren (仁), meaning embodying love for all people; zhong (忠), meaning centring on the cultivation of the heart (values, virtues, intentions, relationships); and cheng (诚), meaning we must be sincere in intentions. In the Chinese language, *Qi* is written as 炁, with the top part 无 meaning that it comes from a vast energy field called the Void, and the dots at the bottom mean they are boundless, flowing in everything like gas and water. *Qi* also manifests as various functional qi 气, which flows in our organs, in nature, among stars, and so on. Virtue is written as De, or 德, which shows on the left side as two people or the collective, meaning for the good of all; on the right, the top part 十 can mean complete kindness and light shining from the head, the middle part can mean the heaven eye, or one's views and inner vision, and the bottom part means 一心, or one heart or wholeheartedly. So, virtue means working wholeheartedly for the collective good, shining the wisdom from our sincere heart, and glowing the energy of light and love. Eventually and ultimately, Dao 道, which represents the creator of the universe, has the parts of a pathway toward the opening of one's inner eye (knowledge and wisdom) and glowing with the energy of light on the top of one's head.

In Buddhism, much emphasis is on cultivating our true nature. The word xing (性) has our emotions or heart on the left part and our life on the right-hand side our life 生. We are to understand our hearts and know our true selves (明心見性). Buddhahood results from the cultivation of compassion, written in Chinese as 慈悲. 悲 is a word that means sadness if we are not following our heart (the top part means negative or not following, and the bottom part means heart). 慈 means a heart (心) that is always thinking about (兹) and sending light of love (the top part signals light) to those who suffer. Hence, in Buddhism, enlightened people are sad when they see people have lost their way, take delusion as reality, and want to help people find their true self with their love and energy. Ultimately, they all have a goal of connecting heaven and humans, cultivating both their wisdom and life energy, reaching xing ming shuang xiu (性命雙修) (working on both our higher Self and *Qi* energy), to build up this energy that transforms into the immortal dan (丹) or the golden flower that enables them to become citizens of not only the earth but also of the solar system and the universe.

Chinese classical medicinal thoughts on spirit, *Qi*, and body

The theory of *Qi* vitality and its cultivation is not esoteric and has been widely discussed and applied in Chinese medicine. According to the Inner Sutra of the Yellow Emperor, the earliest and most important written work of classical Chinese medicine, Jing (essence), *Qi* (energy), Shen (spirit or mental), and Xing (body) (Li & Merer, 2013) are 'resources' in our body that produce *Zhen Qi* which has been refined through meditation and accumulation of virtues, and our eating habits, social interactions, and living environment can influence that. *Zhen Qi* (真气) allows our body to function normally and not be attacked by pathogenic factors (Li & Merer, 2013). When we have a deficiency of *Zhen Qi*, and when our body is disconnected from nature and experiences emotional turbulence, our body cannot perform its *Qi* transportation and transformation functions. When the yin-yang balance of our bodies is at stake, we experience poor health. Classical Chinese medicinal tradition believes that we have medicine within ourselves and we are our own healers. To ensure the typical performance of *Zhen Qi* for our body's optimal health, our Shen or mental state needs to be relaxed, soft, tender, and concentrated; we need to have enough Jing (essence) stored in the kidneys. Stomach *Qi* must be expected, and the channels and collaterals through which *Qi* and blood circulate must be open. We also need to ensure that there are no pathogenic factors inside our body, blockage, deficiency, or excess at any level (Li & Merer, 2013).

One may work with the spiritual template or the spiritual/energy body to treat illness caused by the disturbances to the Shen (the spirit). Daoism has explored the methods, but only some people know them. The method basically treats people who have lost some parts of their souls and heals them with energy to return them to the normal state of their spiritual template. Healing methods include mental visualisation deploying energy or using mantras or rituals to call in deities to help, much like the practices of indigenous shamans. Doctors exert their *Zhen Qi* to cure the leakage in the patient's energy body or clear images of emerging illnesses that show up as shadows or images. These methods are quick and effective. They treat the body as an energy entity, interconnected with others in an interpenetrating universe. Souls can inhabit each other. Hatred or sadness from another soul can affect a person's spiritual body. Those who can treat people like this need to have direct transmission of knowledge and energy from teachers and to have cultivated a pure heart. Many illnesses are believed to be caused by negative karma in previous lives or this life or can be inherited from past generations. Our spiritual template is perfect, but holes can be punched into it, or deformation can happen; hence, treatment means bringing the template back to its normal state.

The second level of treatment is based on *Qi*. The treatment of *Qi* is often conducted through herbal medicines, acupuncture, massages, and moxibustions, among other ways. Chinese medicinal sages practice meditation, visualising the internal meridian system by entering a tranquil state and seeing how *Qi* flows in the body. Herbal medicines and acupuncture are based on this knowledge. The masters also see *Qi* in everything in nature and know how their composition of various *Qi* qualities, such as some herbs or minerals, can strengthen the kidney or how ginseng can calm down the Shen and add a lot of *Qi* to the body. Some masters spent their whole life documenting the yin and yang dispositions and capacities of various herbs, including minerals and animal parts, for the treatment of various illnesses. The most well known classics are *Shen Nong Original Herbal Sutra* (神农本草经) and *Ben Cao Gang Mu* (本草纲目). In these books, the masters prescribed a combination of different herbal elements to tackle the yin and yang imbalance in the body, making *Qi* energy to flow normally among the meridians, which cures the patient.

Because Chinese medicine emphasises treating the invisible (e.g., Shen and *Qi*), Chinese medicine practitioners are advised to meditate and cultivate their intuition to tune their senses and know their patients' *Qi* energy state intuitively. Chinese doctors/healers must be familiar with different factors that disturb the energy balance of yin and yang in the body, including emotional factors, social environmental factors, and one's cultural history. They need to know the patient's family relationships and the composition of the patient's yin and yang energy (e.g., some people tend to have less yang energy than others). Those who treat others need to train themselves to become reliable instruments for the diagnosis and treatment of a patient, as a portal for the spirit. The medicines they prescribe form a force field, like a group of soldiers and nurturers tackling the blockages of energy in the body, making the energy flow, and strengthening the vital energy in the body.

Given that *Qi* is the foundation of Chinese medicine, one needs to cultivate one's vital life energy *to have good health and live a long li*fe. As mentioned earlier, an excellent way to cultivate *Qi* is to return to a tranquil state. Excessive use of our openings, such as speaking too much or having too many desires, can all deplete one's energy. As warned by Laozi

> The five colours blind the eye.
> The five tones deafen the ear.
> The five flavours dull the taste.
> Racing and hunting madden the mind.
> (Laozi, *Dao De Jing*, chapter 12)[2]

Tranquility enables one to preserve energy and follow the rhythm of life. Instead of overwhelming ourselves to force things to happen, we follow the spontaneous movement of the Dao by being present and well-attuned to changes. Chinese medicinal masters know this secret and put it into practice. They cultivate what is the more refined and powerful energy, *Zhen Qi*, through effortless meditative practices of tranquility that enable one to gather the primordial *Qi* from the universal into the body and experience unity between the microcosmic self and the macrocosmic universe. A well-known master, Sun Simao, was titled China's King of Medicine or *yaowang* (药王藥王). An accomplished master who lived up to 141 years, he wrote the famous classics *Beiji Qianjin Yaofang* (Essential Formulas for Emergencies [Worth] a Thousand Pieces of Gold) and *Qian Jin Yi Fang* (Supplement to the Formulas of a Thousand Gold

Worth), which are milestone books in the history of Chinese medicine. He also taught meditation methods that help one to gather the primordial *Qi* from the universe into the body. One method is stated as follows:

> Close your eyes, turn inward, and visualise the harmonious *Yuan Qi* in the universe, coming like big purple clouds with five different shining colours, slowly descending onto your hair, and getting into your head as if the rain has just stopped. The sun is shining, and like the clouds entering the mountains, the *Qi* enters your skin and flesh, into your bones and brain, flowing slowly into your abdomen. All your four limbs and five organs are receiving this nourishment, like water flowing into the earth. Feel the sound of the flowing water in your stomach. Focus your mind, be concentrated, and do not be distracted by any outside influence, soon you find the *Yuan Qi* reaching your *Qi* Ocean (*Qi Hai* or the part below the navel), then reaching the bottom of your feet, and you sense energetic vibration in your body, even your bed is moving and vibrating with it.[3]

In sum, Chinese classical medicine treats meditation as a major pathway to regulate energies and bolster our life energy. It views following the way of nature and maintaining positive relationships with others as directly influencing the flow of *Qi* and, subsequently, our health. Our *Qi* is connected with plants, animals, mountains, rivers, stars, and galaxies. Virtues are technologies that produce a positive *Qi* reciprocal exchange system that enables *Qi* from everyone and everything else to support each other. In Chinese philosophy, meditation and cultivating virtues go in tandem and are hence called Xiu Dao (修道) or cultivating Dao.

Cultivating Dao is to return to our true selves. The quality and length of our life are directly related to the amount of *Zhen Qi* (真气) or *Yuan Qi* (元气)[4] one possesses. In Confucian teaching, cultivating *Qi* and doing well extends one's life; virtue cultivation changes one's destiny and gives one essential societal roles (Lin, 2018). From a *Qi* perspective, educational and development projects need to be carefully designed to promote ways of living that encourage tranquility and awareness, cultivate virtues and *Qi*, and promote harmony between humans and nature to protect the well-being of all.

New perspectives on development and education

We further dialogued on these questions:

- What is development? What is the Anthropocene? What is our relationship with nature and with each other? Where are capitalism and technology leading us? What should be the roles of education? How do we revive lost wisdom from the South/China? How can we reprogramme our minds with new ideas and visions (instead of resources, use live language with souls and spirits)?

International development models separate our world into the Global North, Global South, East, and West. We established world hierarchies, reflecting the horrible results of colonisation and capitalist expansion. Although we talked about learning from the Global South, White saviours and neo-colonialism still dominate the development field. Education is the key to development to change people's mindset, but this cannot be taken for granted, as what matters the most are the values and pedagogies underlying education. If we fail to educate learners to understand the interconnection of all things, love nature, and love each other, our education will perpetuate inequality and destruction. Educators need to sustain and regenerate their vital life energy to have the capacity to educate for a sustainable and regenerative world. The solution to the world's crisis is not technological but spiritual. We are having a spiritual crisis, and we need a new vision of education to address this crisis.

McGilchrist (2009) talks about right-brain and left-brain consciousness. He said Western thinking is dominated by left-brain consciousness, which is very narrow in awareness, self-centred, and does not consider the big picture. In contrast, the holistic and interconnection emphasised in Global South philosophy align with the attributes of the right brain. The right brain is related to unity and experiences connected with life. Many cultures from the Global South align with right-brain consciousness. However, because of the global dominance of Western culture, left-brain thinking is prioritised.

Further, European colonists believed they needed to 'civilise' the native people or the Global South because, in their minds, those people who did not follow their way were barbaric. With its insatiable desires for wealth, capitalism has pursued the Gross Domestic Product (GDP) with the deception that there are infinite resources on Earth for GDP growth. The international development model has not helped countries in the Global South as development aid has gone primarily to the wealthy and powerful people there, and the poor get very little.

The Global South is rich in the wisdom on how to learn from nature and inter-be with nature. We need to learn from this wisdom as it will shift our emphasis from left-brain consciousness to proper consciousness (McGilchrist, 2009). In Daoism, this is called 'following Dao manifested in nature' (道法自然). During the last four decades toward universal education, educational development is often practised as building schools that have children learning in them, but modern schooling separates children from nature and real life; modern education emphasises achievement based mainly on left-brain cognition. Nature is the most incredible school. When we take nature as our school and experience nature deeply, we are in touch with life, we see everything as alive, we experience yin and yang, we see the vital life energy *Qi* that constitutes our bodies and brings fruits and flowers, and that goes into rest, and then another cycle begins. To bring the knowledge of *Qi* back to education is to bring life back to education, and education back to life, knowing that life is not outside of us – it is everywhere inside and around us, above and beneath us. Contemplation allows deep learning to happen with nature. We also need to enliven the language we use in education. When we talk about plants and animals, we should not use abstract terms; we should see them as alive, hug them, make friends with them, and use the language of animacy when addressing them; we should paint their images with their spirits shining through. Ultimately, education is to develop a new and expanded awareness with new insights, and this requires spiritual development.

We must bring humility, gratitude, and reciprocity back to the centre of education. In this context, we encourage students to discover their unique true selves (*xing*) and to be immersed in our eco citizenship and mutuality with each other. Everyone, especially policymakers, educators, parents, and others in power, must have an expanded view and a deepened experience of the interconnection of life and the universe. The universe works in harmony because the principle of cooperation and interdependence forms its axis. Individualism and capitalism are not sustainable for nature and for our human society.

We need to recognise the creative force of the feminine by respecting women and respecting all that gives us life. We want to explore the unknown. Scientists say that 95% of the world is made of dark matter. We speculate that the so-called dark matter is not dark; it is the *Qi* energy and spirit that produce all the life forms in the universe. Guanzi, an ancient sage, stated in his essay 'Inner Work' that contemplative practices can join us with the *Qi* energy of everything. While cultivating and transforming that energy, we grow virtue and compassion, becoming sages (Lin, 2018). The bottom line is that we need to have humility, sincerity, love, and awareness, allowing us to recognise that we are one with the universe.

We are not discussing new concepts or notions but trying to recover and reiterate what the ancient sages and many cultures have said. For example, *Buen Vivir* is based on the notion that all life forces are interdependent and interrelated with each other; Greek philosophers talk about 'air,' which corresponds with the idea of primordial *Qi* in Chinese philosophy (Guthrie, 1975). They also talk about the underlying structure of the universe that represents beauty and harmony.

Educating for the world we want to see

We posit that education that focuses on our *Qi* vitality gives tools for students to nurture their bodies, master the skills of accumulating virtues, embody what they learn, and enable wisdom to emerge. It organically elevates the learners' spirit, allowing them to know their inner calling and aspire to seek the true self that is connected to all beings and existence (Lin & Khoo, 2022).

This type of education pays attention to reality's visible and invisible aspects. The invisible, energy, and spiritual aspects are as important or even more important than acquiring knowledge and skills catering to the external world. Effective education must include self-cultivation, which is valid for educators, students, and the larger community. Knowledge acquisition should include knowing by *Qi*, embodying *Qi*, and recovering our inner child who is pure in heart and curious about the universe. Quantum physics points us to an interrelated universe; in this framework, changing ourselves will affect changes in the world. Like a big tree, education should let us know what comprises our roots, which is the vital energy we have for living a fulfilling, healthy, and wisdom-oriented life. We need to rigorously challenge the disembodiment of education.

Learning through cultivating our vital *Qi* is an open process; it focuses on life in the whole spectrum of our being, not just the mind or the left brain. All individual experiences are a valuable part of this learning. We should see learning as a journey to find our true selves and join the chorus of life in the universe. We learn to know plants and animals at their deep level of being, i.e., their spirits and energy; we see mountains and rivers as our home and mother, and earth and the whole universe as breathing intelligent beings, and we build meaningful relationships with them, seeing them as not separate from ourselves. Going inward is as vital as going outward to learn; from the outside, we appreciate patterns and forces; from the inside, we sense the flowing energy in all existence and the heart of all existence.

Decolonisation of education must take place to enable such a kind of learning and promote education grounded in an understanding of *Qi* vitality. Decolonisation enables us to return to knowledge marginalised in the Western academy. We return to our inner being for knowing (Khoo & Lin, 2023). The knowledge institutions upheld by the Global North have objectified knowledge as external to us. *Qi* vitality theory says we are integrated multi-dimensionally, and the different disciplines established in our educational institutions should be unified.

In our dialogue, we further contemplated how we can teach and learn through *Qi*:

Tom: Dao manifests in the world through virtues. All are perfect, as Dao does not differentiate between good and evil. All beautiful and ugly flowers are all perfect expressions of the Dao in the world.
Yishin: All students are perfect expressions of Dao, too.
Jing: Dao is invisible, but Dao can be experienced.
Tom: Ten thousand books can be summed up in one phrase: Virtue is the essence. The concept of virtue is much bigger than that. If you want to manifest Dao in the world, you align yourself with the human virtue of the Dao – not wanting things beyond one's needs, not accumulating things, being generous and humble. Many religions talk about this. To enter the kingdom of heaven, you follow the model of Jesus, who loved unconditionally. Through your actions, you can merge with the Dao. Nevertheless, sometimes you need a teacher to help you to merge with the Dao.
Yishin: A good teacher can bring out the inner teacher in every student so that we can see reality more deeply, embodying the '*Qi*-verse.'
Jing: Hidden virtues translate into *Qi* energy. We must know our vital energy and the relationship between our Jing or body essence, *Qi*, and *Shen* (spirit). We nurture our body and spirit, taking our body as

	the foundation to know the universe. Life is precious; energy is precious; to preserve life and energy, it is most important to know our position in the universe and live a meaningful and harmonious life. We must be in peace, tranquility, and love with all existence.
Tom:	Parker Palmer – we teach who we are. We cannot just teach about *Qi*; we must cultivate ourselves as educators.
Jing:	*Qi* resonates. We are educating for the *Qi*-verse (universe made of *Qi*). We have put massive stress on teachers to meet external goals and neglect other parts of the teachers – teachers' being and interior wellness. We do not allow learning through ambiguity. Palmer said you must always work with contradiction. Cultivation is vital to come back to the state of integration.
Tom:	Dao expresses and manifests itself in tranquility.
Yishin:	Carving out quiet time for contemplation and reflection is essential in teaching and learning.

Conclusion

In this chapter, we have explored an ontology centred around the concept of *Qi*. This vital life energy propels the universe and binds us within interconnected energies. This energy profoundly influences our well-being, world peace, and Earth stewardship. We have proposed meditation as a crucial means of working with *Qi*, expanding our awareness, and fostering a deep connection with all beings and existence. We have critically examined prevailing notions of development and underscored the importance of a comprehensive and integrative education system. By merging various fields of study and focusing on experiential learning and understanding life, we can better grasp our humanity and how we interact. This approach is rooted in the premise that virtues form the foundation of both the universe and human society. We advocate for embodying and promoting interconnected eco-cosmic citizenship, recognising our inherent interconnectedness, and emphasising our shared responsibility in fostering cosmic harmony. It is vital to incorporate indigenous knowledge and wisdom traditions from the Global South to shape the future of education and development. Throughout the chapter, we have introduced *Qi* vitality and virtue cultivation as a viable pathway to actualising eco-cosmic citizenship. The journey towards this realisation commences with everyone, and there is no better time to start than the present.

Notes

1 www.quanxue.cn/CT_ZhongYi/SuWen/SuWen02.html
2 www.quanxue.cn/CT_DaoJia/LaoZi/LaoZi12.html
3 In Chinese, the original text is:《备急千金要方》养性篇中记载这样一种调气法：
"闭目存思，想见空中太和元气，如紫云成盖，五色分明，下入毛际，渐渐入顶，如雨初晴，云入山，透皮入肉，至骨至脑，渐渐下入腹中，四肢五藏皆受其润，如水渗入地若彻，则觉腹中有声汩汩然。意专思存，不得外缘。斯须即觉元气达于气海，须臾则自达于涌泉，则觉身体振动，两脚卷曲，亦令床坐有声拉拉然。"

4 *Zhen Qi* and *Yuan Qi* are similar yet can be different. They are both the most essential vital life energy in our body. *Yuan Qi* can mean mainly the energy that we were born with that propels our life, such as maintaining the heartbeat, and the harmonious working of the organs and the body, while *Zhen Qi* is a compelling energy that is refined from our Jin, which becomes more subtle and powerful *Qi*, and then *Shen* energy that has much power. Masters can apply *Zhen Qi* to do 'miracles,' such as causing rains to fall, healing people, or changing courses of events.

References

Andrey, J. (2009). *Shamanism for beginners: Walking with the world's healers of Earth and Sky*. Llewellyn.

Bai, H. (2015). Peace with the Earth: Animism and contemplative ways. *Cultural Studies of Science Education, 10*, 135–147. https://doi.org/10.1007/s11422-013-9501-z

Blofeld, J. E. C. (1958). *The Zen teaching of Huang Po: On the transmission of the mind*. Grove Press.

Culham, T. (2013). *Ethics education of business leaders: Emotional intelligence, virtues and contemplative learning*. Information Age Publishing.

Culham, T., & Lin, J. (2016). Exploring the unity of science and spirit: A Daoist perspective. In J. Lin, R. Oxford, & T. Culham (Eds.), *Toward a spiritual research paradigm: Exploring new ways of knowing, researching and being* (pp. 171–198). Information Age Publishing.

Culham, T., & Lin, J. (2020). *Daoist cultivation of Qi and virtue for life, wisdom, and learning*. Palgrave Macmillan, Springer.

Davidson, A. I., & Hadot, P. (1995). *Philosophy as a way of life: Spiritual exercises from Socrates to Foucault*. Blackwell.

Guthrie, W. K. C. (1975). *The Greek philosophers: From Thales to Aristotle*. Routledge.

Her, P. (2016). *Qigong*. www.takingcharge.csh.umn.edu/qigong#:~:text=There%20are%20two%20types%20of,and%20guided%20imagery%20or%20visualization

Ivanhoe, P. J., Flanagan, O. J., Harrison, V. S., & Schwitzgebel, E. (2018). *The oneness hypothesis: Beyond the boundary of self*. Columbia University Press.

Khoo, Y., & Lin, J. (2023, forthcoming). "Asia as method" as a quest for the spirit and we-togetherness: A collaborative autoethnography. *Asia Pacific Education Review*, 1–13.

Kirkland, R. (2004). *Taoism: The enduring tradition*. Routledge.

Le Guin, U. K. (1998). *Lao Tzu: Tao Te Ching: A book about the way and the power of the way*. Shambhala Publications.

Li, X., & Merer, C. (2013). *Traditional Chinese medicine: Back to the sources for a modern approach*. Arbre D'or Editions.

Lin, J. (2018). From self-cultivation to social transformation: The Confucian embodied pathways and educational implications. In Y. Liu & W. Ma (Eds.), *Confucianism and education* (pp. 169–182). State University of New York Press.

Lin, J. (2019). Enlightenment from body-spirit integration: Dunhuang's Buddhist cultivation pathways and educational implications. In D. Xu (Ed.), *The Dunhuang

Grottos and global education: Philosophical, spiritual, scientific, and aesthetic insights (pp. 113–132). Palgrave Macmillan.

Lin, J., Culham, T., & Oxford, R. (2016). Developing a spiritual research paradigm: A Confucian perspective. In J. Lin, R. Oxford, & T. Culham (Eds.), *Toward a spiritual research paradigm: Exploring new ways of knowing, researching and being* (pp. 141–169). Information Age Publishing.

Lin, J., & Khoo, Y. (2022). Knowing our true self and transforming suffering toward peace and love: Embodying the wisdom of the Heart Sutra and the Diamond Sutra. *Religions, 13*(5). https://doi.org/10.3390/rel13050403

Lin, J., & Parikh, R. (2019). Connecting meditation, quantum physics, and consciousness: Implication for higher education. In J. Lin, S. Edwards, & T. Culham (Eds.), *Contemplative pedagogies for transformative teaching, learning and being* (pp. 3–25). Information Age Publishing.

McGilchrist, I. (2009). *The master and his emissary.* Yale University Press.

Metz, T. (2022). *A relational Moral Theory: African Ethics in and beyond the Continent.* Oxford University Press.

Mutanga, O. (ed). (2023). *Ubuntu Philosophy and Disabilities in Sub-Saharan Africa.* Routledge.

Palmo, T. A. (2002). *Reflections on a mountain lake: Teachings on practical Buddhism.* Shambala Publications.

Pokharel, A. (2019). Mindfulness, meditation, and the cultivation of empathy. In J. Lin, S. Edwards, & T. Culham (Eds.), *Contemplative pedagogies for transformative teaching, learning and being* (pp. 27–42). Information Age Publishing.

Yen, H. C. (2008). *Is Daoism cultural? A study of Daoist cultivation.* UBC Conference on Daoist Studies, University of British Columbia, Vancouver.

4 De-Westernising communication thought from a Global South perspective

The contributions of indigenous approaches from Latin America

Alejandro Barranquero Carretero and Eva González Tanco

A new ecology of knowledge emerging from the Global South

Fields across the discipline of communication studies are increasingly attending to how different exclusions – ethnicity, gender, class, colonialism – have historically affected knowledge production and dissemination in postcolonial states. In this line, this chapter explores how Latin American scholars and practitioners have been actively engaged in de-Westernising and decolonising the field of communication studies, paving the way for critical communication theories emerging from the Global South. The notion of the Global South has recently been popularised as a critical concept that helps to understand the new forms of marginality stemming from global capitalism. Through the study of the trinomial modernity-coloniality-capitalism, scholars such as de Sousa Santos (2006) and Shome (2019) use this term not to refer to a geographical or even symbolic South but to the dispossession of a wide range of population sectors: from refugees fleeing economic exclusion and environmental disasters to urban peasant farmers losing their lands to land grabs by multinational corporations. According to Shome (2019, p. 197), 'these conditions – which we will call (and discuss below as) the Global South – cannot necessarily be mapped through our available Northern based theories of culture and Cultural Studies. In fact, many of these conditions have not even entered, in any remarkable way, our intellectual imaginations in Cultural Studies'. Adopting the Global South notion to enlarge cultural and communication studies involves at least two epistemological breaks: (1) with the monocultural character of critical theories, which underrepresented important forms of exclusion such as racism, sexism, ageism or castes; (2) with traditional Science, labelled as 'knowledge-regulation' since it objectifies and exoticises the *Other* avoiding all dialogue and epistemological tensions (de Sousa, 2006, p. 44).

Within this background, this chapter aims at constructing a new 'ecology of knowledge' (*ecología de saberes*) within the communication studies field in order to help it adapt to the increasing complexity of a range of intercultural realities as well as to open a dialogue between positivist and Eurocentric knowledge, on the one side, and secular, widespread, indigenous, marginal and peasant knowledge emerging from Latin America and the Global South, on the other (de Sousa, 2006).

Dependency theories and decolonial challenges

When analysing Latin American history in the different fields of social sciences, we can echo the importance of two native theoretical frameworks pointing to the epistemic emancipation of Latin America and the Global South: the 'dependency theories' and the more recent 'decolonial turn'. Those two paradigms highlight a local-based and emancipatory understanding of communication for social change, one of Latin American communication thought's historical and leading areas.

To reconstruct their profound implications for communication and media theories, it is crucial to see how communication studies in the region have been traditionally connected to the idea of 'development', modernisation, progress and social change. Especially from the second half of the 20th century, the idea of development signified not just a concept for Latin Americans, but also a political and economic horizon to which moved inexcusably. The philosophical foundations of this notion date back to the 16th and 17th centuries, just after the Colon's campaign (Castro-Gómez & Grosfoguel, 2007; Habermas, 1988). Descartes, Bacon and other philosophers built the meanings of a universe in which nature was supposed to be progressively conquered and controlled by male/white/Judeo-Christian rationality (Lugones, 2008). Within this framework, natural resources were understood as commodities that must be accumulated to advance towards well-being (Acosta, 2015; Gudynas, 2013). Therefore, poverty, or the lack of (natural) resources, was synonymous with an unworthy condition to escape from:

> Those are some of the foundational elements of the still dominant ideas of progress and civilisation. Ideas that have nursed development, turning it into a neo-colonial tool. Thus, America, being incorporated as a source of natural resources, and Africa, especially as a source of cheap energy, underpinned the birth of capitalism as a civilisation with a global scope.
>
> (Acosta, 2015, p. 307)

Later on, Harry Truman made his famous speech in 1949, splitting the world into two regions: developed nations and developing countries (or *not yet* developed). In this new approach to the historical ideal of 'progress', he was following the racist logic installed four centuries back, based on the opposition between the rational and 'civilised' people as 'modern' subjects and the *Others*, who were 'laggards', 'barbarian' and primitive objects to be reformed (Castro-Gómez & Grosfoguel, 2007). The novelty of the development paradigm lay in the soft aspiration that the statement imposed: The 'developed' ones must help the 'developing' others to reach presumably the 'developed' standards. This was thus a very compelling justification of the intellectual and moral superiority of the Global North and its model of intervention based on capitalist and geostrategic interests (Escobar, 2011).

Within this framework, communication and media were used as a unilinear instrument to persuade underdeveloped nations to imitate the 'modern' capitalist values of the North (Waisbord, 2020). Also, from a technocentric perspective, U.S. forerunners of communication for development (for example, Daniel Lerner and Wilbur Schramm) conceived media as compelling tools and even as 'magic multipliers' of growth and innovations (Barranquero & Saez, 2015).

Without steady opposition, this development model extended from the end of the Second World War to the 1970s, when Latin America assimilated different critical trends to enunciate the so-called 'dependency theories' (Waisbord, 2020). This framework criticised the imposture of a monitored and mandatory development designed and disseminated by media and campaigns from the United States of America (U.S.) and other Global North countries while encouraging a revalue of local knowledge and proximity methods to construct an endogenous self-centred idea of development. Dependency theories were the early precursors of the posterior shift towards indigenous practices and legacy (González Tanco & Arcila, 2022).

Foucault said: 'A day came when the truth was displaced from the ritualised, efficacious and just act of enunciation, towards the utterance itself, its meaning, its form, its object, its relation to its reference' (1971, p. 12). At the end of the 1990s, a new epistemological challenge emerged from a group of Latin American thinkers who had developed their career in the United States, which started to be known as the Modernity/Coloniality Group (Escobar, 2007) according to their focus: Enrique Dussel, Walter Mignolo, Catherine Walsh, Aníbal Quijano, Arturo Escobar, María Lugones and others. Since then, the 'decolonial turn' in social sciences has explored who determines the truth – 'those who rose to power after the conquest and their inheritors', they answer – and how it is spread, based on the ritualisation of the annunciation, the colonised structure of the acts of knowledge and also the rituals of research (Castro-Gómez & Grosfoguel, 2007; Maldonado et al., 2015; Mignolo, 2008; Sierra & Maldonado, 2017; Walsh, 2013).

Decolonialism, as a Latin American theory, does not just focus on power relations and hierarchies but also explores the strong connection of power with communication strategies:

> The 'coloniality of power' is, above all, a structure of domination to which the population of Latin America was subjected after the conquest. In this sense, the coloniality of power alludes to the invasion of

the imaginary of the *Other*, in this case, its westernisation. It is named through a discourse that is inserted in the colonised world but also reproduced in the *locus* of the coloniser.

(Soto, 2008, p. 21)[1]

This is how the coloniser subordinates or even destroys the imagination of the other, 'while by denying it reaffirms his own' (Soto, 2008, p. 21). The colonised replaces his values, worldview, lore, symbolic world and images with those that are imposed. 'The "coloniality of being" kills the hope of living, kills utopia, corrodes desire, puts it on hold' (Soto, 2008, p. 33).

The two approaches, dependency theories and the new decolonial paradigm, trace a theoretical frame to embrace new perspectives and possibilities of thinking, feeling and doing, such as those raised by the pedagogue Freire (2005, 2011) with the pedagogy of the oppressed and the pedagogy of hope, and Dussel (2015), as one of the leading philosophers of decolonisation and trans modernity. Others have also continued this tradition: Walsh (2013) with her decolonial pedagogies; de Sousa Santos (2016) and his epistemology from the South; Ghiso (2000) and his writings on the need to recognise diversity through dialogue; and Mejía (2020) with a set of new approaches of popular education. Among other scholars, this generation of decolonial thinkers is currently offering new emancipatory perspectives emphasising the globally hegemonic power as a whole and the local ways of producing knowledge, 'another way of thinking, *un paradigma otro*, the very possibility of talking about worlds and knowledge otherwise' (Escobar, 2007, p. 1179).

Beyond its epistemological potential, the modernity/coloniality paradigm has undergone expropriations that corrupt its original formulation, particularly when it is classified under or along with the former postcolonial studies (Bhabha, Said, Spivak) and when its vocabulary is used as an academic capital to build careers and prestige (Segato, 2013). Furthermore, decolonial thinking has tended to consider indigenous knowledge, media or education forms as an ethnic variant (Arcila et al., 2018) or an abstract source of inspiration. Therefore, these Latin American scholars still act as 'ventriloquists' of indigenous epistemologies, which became popular in the same period in the subcontinent. In other words, the Latin American academy accepted the challenge of incorporating some previously excluded topics, such as demands for specific communication rights and indigenous communication practices, but still needs to improve in accepting indigenous thinkers as peers.

The challenge of indigenous communication

In recent years, indigenous communication has become popular to refer to an extensive diversity of communicational practices and processes undertaken by the more than 800 indigenous peoples living in Latin America and the Caribbean (CEPAL & FILAC, 2020). This label has been widely accepted in various sectors, from academia and policymakers to Aboriginal collectives

(González Tanco, 2015; Orobitg et al., 2021). It is also shaping a promising and certainly autonomous research inquiry regarding older epistemological regional concerns such as development communication, liberation philosophies and dependency theories (González Tanco & Arcila, 2022; Herrera et al., 2016; Magallanes & Ramos, 2016; Sierra et al., 2020). Nonetheless, the notion of indigenous communication demands to be problematised with due caution since it is often used to describe and interpret a too diverse and heterogeneous compendium of indigenous wisdom and practices emerging from various regions such as the Amazon Basin, the Southern Cone, and the Andes.

New theorisations about indigenous communication encompass such diverse research topics as the new indigenous communication policies, planned from an ideal of 'restitution' and 'reinforcement' of the local and ethnic identities silenced for centuries (policies with identity); the digital divide and, specifically, the creative appropriations made by indigenous collectives of technologies 'imported' from the West – such as apps, mobile phones and social networks – until they become 'own' or 'appropriated' technologies; the allegations against external representations and narratives about indigenous peoples that dominate non-indigenous-mass media; and the use of media and information and communication technologies (I.C.T.s) as weapons of resistance, vindication and preservation of memory, among others (Arcila et al., 2018).

As mentioned earlier, indigenous communication implies new interdisciplinary dialogues between the communication field and complementary frameworks derived from anthropology, sociology, linguistics, humanities and environmental sciences. At the same time, this issue invites Latin American and Western academic communities to move away from the universal and universalist positions that were the hallmark of modern positivist science. In this sense, the US-based Colombian anthropologist Escobar (2011, 2020) reclaims the idea of the 'pluriverse', which indicates that it is impossible to construct a universal theory, valid and applicable to all cases, just as it is impossible to advance towards a single development model for all nations and human collectives.

From different fronts (academia, social movements) and thanks to a fruitful dialogue between historical (dependency theories, liberation theology and philosophies) and emerging theories (decoloniality, Good Living), Latin America has become a new epistemological locus from which to challenge modern/colonial thinking and build post-development and transition alternatives based on respect for human dignity and natural rights. Escobar (2011, p. 29) states that building transition models involves 'moving from the modern understanding of the world as a universe to the world as a pluriverse (without pre-existing universals)'. According to Escobar (2011), the modern world privileged 'globalisation' and 'universalisation'; that is, economic and cultural integration and homogenisation under a series of Eurocentric universal principles. Instead of globalised societies, building pluriverse and 'planetary' systems implies opening bridges, communication routes and dialogues between different epistemologies on the basis that both the Northern and Southern worlds must face a climate emergency that affects us all.

Universal thinking also means promoting and giving state and expert support to communities and territories so that they become more self-sufficient and resilient in the face of the current climate crisis, which involves exploiting food and energy sovereignty in a scenario of both resource austerity ('peak oil'), erosion and the constant threat of extraction and destruction of traditional ecosystems and wisdom. Incorporating universal conceptions in communication involves adopting a more critical perspective when facing the capitalist techno-mythification processes that persuade communities and populations worldwide to adopt technological innovations as if they were synonymous with economic progress, intellectual development and social well-being. In this line, Pedro-Carañana et al. (2022, p. 22) claim to adopt the pluriverse in terms of 'communicative justice', whose 'focus is not the media itself but the practices, relations, and mediations of communication'. In contrast to technocentric perspectives, communicative justice in the perspective of the pluriverse allows us to look beyond specific technologies.

From this perspective, the new political project emerging from indigenous thinking calls to articulate a new 'relational ontology' based on the principle that 'one cannot live well if others live badly' (Giraldo, 2020, p. 65). This means building new governance models from the critique and the dismantling of the older developmental model of overproduction and overconsumption. From indigenous perspectives, this path would involve a redefinition of what we understand as well-being or wealth since many indigenous communities connect these ideas to reclaiming harmony and commonality and advocating, through communication and education, for a new understanding of humans as living beings are materially and spiritually connected to the chain of natural life, which is also a source for food and survival. As such, indigenous communication revitalises the older ideals of the 1970s critical communication thinking based on incorporating the informative and expressive demands of marginalised populations and groups (Quiroz et al., 2021). However, this revitalisation of popular, alternative and community communication thinking and practices is now connected with new debates regarding collective identity vindication; a return to territory and a re-sacralisation of nature; and, finally, the blocking and deconstruction of modern and colonial thinking and its emphasis on individualism, competitiveness, consumption and exploitation of nature.

The vindication of indigenous Good Living/*Buen Vivir* epistemologies

In the 1990s, Latin America went through another breaking point to turn its gaze inward, commanded by new marginal actors. On the one hand, 1992 marked the commemorations of the 500th anniversary of what Spain, the Metropolis (and most of the Global North) called the 'discovery' of America

(Wynter, 1995). On the other hand, the prominent international economic institutions were arranging the full entry into market capitalism in the expansion phase of globalisation, when different social movements converged in a dynamic of rejection and affirmation 'from trade unions to peasant federations, from N.G.O.s to neighbourhood groups' (Gudynas, 2016, p. 6).

Indigenous participation started to be essential in different Latin American states. In Bolivia, as early as 1992, natives rejected the Spanish celebration and instead underlined their self-discovery in celebrating the former 'Día de la Hispanidad' (Columbus Day) (Deneulin, 2012; Ziegler, 2008). In 1994, the Zapatistas gained the world's attention in Mexico thanks to their innovative communication strategies and the leading hooded men emerging from the forest of Chiapas (Wolfson, 2012). In Ecuador, indigenous organisations gathered social discontent and opposition against corruption and discrimination (de la Torre, 2015).

These phases of actions and following reflections by marginal social movements and indigenous organisations founded a new and radical questioning attitude against developmentalism. During that same period, many groups also retrieved the holistic philosophy of Good Living (*Buen Vivir*) as a possible alternative to the older development ideal. For most Latin American indigenous groups, the concepts of wealth and poverty are not determined by the accumulation and lack of material goods but rather by a holistic vision to create the material and spiritual conditions to achieve harmonious lives (Acosta, 2015; Viteri Gualinga, 2002), or 'Good Livings', as it is today better expressed in plural.

These terms emanated from a pre-colonial Andean concept with many definitions, e.g. *Pacha kawsay*, *suma qamaña* (in *Aymara*), *ñande reko (guaraní)* or *their wares* (in Amazonic *Achuar*), and many others (Cubillo-Guevara & Hidalgo-Capitán, 2015a). Despite nuances and the plurality of applications of these terms, all of them are similar constructions that express a wish and a set of guidelines to find inspiration rules in ancient societal behaviour. This aspiration 'refers to humans living in harmony in communities, with nature (*Pachamama*) of which they form part, and of all nature with the structures of existence' (González Tanco & Arcila, 2022, p. 328). Viteri Gualinga (2002, p. 1) wrote a manifesto of what that expression means,

> In the indigenous worldviews/cosmovisions, in that understanding of the meaning that people's lives have and should have, the concept of development does not exist. In other words, there is no idea of a linear path in life which sets up an earlier or later state, namely underdevelopment and development, a dichotomy through which people must pass to achieve well-being, as occurs in the Western world.

He warns against the temptation of applying development solutions to indigenous societies because '*Alli Káusai* is highly transcendent beyond the mere satisfaction of needs' (Viteri Gualinga, 2002, p. 1). *Alli Káusai* or '*allín kawsay*' is a variant prior to the systematisation of *Sumak Kawsay*, which Viteri himself carries out. *Alli Káusai* is a more ambiguous term used by many Peruvian rural communities, which would mean 'the sweet life' as a state but not as an aspiration (Cubillo-Guevara & Hidalgo-Capitán, 2015b).

Those holistic interpretations have been questioned since the inclusion of Good Living into the Ecuadorian and Bolivian Constitutions in 2008 and 2009 (Gudynas, 2011). These normative texts disclosed diverse contradictions, revealing the difficulties of integrating something that is not developed and which tries to be a paradigm of living away from the capitalistic frame into nations still ruled by international mechanisms and their financial indicators (Unceta, 2014). Even so, it is undeniable that Good Living has been a primary influence on social movements and scholars seeking the decolonisation of knowledge (Forno & Weiner, 2020; Monni & Pallottino, 2015). Today we can find 'adaptations for daily life' among indigenous and non-indigenous communities that use the ancient *Sumak Kawsay* concept to make it fit other contemporary positions. Paradoxically, the construction of public policies adapted to its principles has created tensions within governments given its call for a higher state of autonomy for indigenous groups; the defence of the right of nature, degrowth, ecofeminism; and its dialogue with other anti-colonial struggles master frames. Good Living is part of the intersectional perspective for other communities that pays attention to every oppression that crosses human lives (Butler et al., 2019). Oppressions such as gender, race and social class are considered colonial categories of exclusion, as they are social constructs used to justify the domination and exploitation of certain groups by others. These categories were imposed on indigenous and other marginalised communities by colonial powers to maintain their power and control (Fanon, 2008; Mohanty, 1984). The intersectional critique can add developmentalism to the list of strategies 'of intervention in the name of progress, modernity, civilisation, and salvation' used by Western colonial history (Prashad, 2007, p. 2). Decolonialists agree that, in the name of progress, development has been used as a tool of domination, employed to perpetuate inequalities and maintain colonial relationships (Dussel, 2015; Escobar, 2011; Grosfoguel, 2011; Rivera Cusicanqui, 1987).

Many social movements today, including those advocating for eco-social justice, are challenging these colonial exclusion categories and working towards a more inclusive and equitable society. They see Good Living as a critical concept in this struggle, as it offers an alternative vision of development that prioritises social and environmental well-being over economic growth and individualism (Escobar, 2018; Soubbotina & Al-Shawarby, 2004).

Beyond (post)feminist studies, social movements are exploring intersectionality as a core concept to connect practices and reflections either emerging in the Global North, such as degrowth, austerity, slow living, the commons and responsible consumerism, or from the Global South, such as *Buen Vivir*, decoloniality and the rights of nature, all converging paths towards a way out of the crisis provoked by the unlimited progress model.

Southern theories for alternative living

Good Living/*Buen Vivir* is a powerful source of inspiration for social movements in Latin America through its gathering of philosophical and empirical frames from indigenous thinking, global activism and other Latin American critical traditions (González Tanco & Arcila, 2022). These are also applicable to the Global South and beyond: as a universal philosophy whose proposers claim that Good Living philosophies should be adapted and comprehended in every local context, according to specific needs, so it can also be helpful both for global peripheries and for the Global North (Thomson, 2011; Unceta, 2014).

Furthermore, this concept seems so transversal and inclusive to encompass different but universal needs because diverse cultures have achieved similar results in their attempt to build their living ontologies. In other words, digging into its epistemic conception, one finds the same holistic aspiration to a harmonious, relational and reciprocal life (Cruz et al., 2018) both in *Buen Vivir* and in other worldviews of the planet (i.e. in other communities and populations in Africa, Asia and other continents). Therefore, many communities that have yet to attend to the homogenisation patterns of the modern/colonial paradigm share conceptions of a desirable life that obviate or explicitly avoid the teleology of development and might be associated with a familiar concept, the so-called Good Living.

As previously mentioned for *Buen Vivir* in Bolivia and Ecuador, these holistic philosophies of existence and resistance have been recently included in other constitutional acts. This is the case of *Ubuntu*, a sub-Sahara African philosophy that emphasises compassion and relatedness. This worldview proposes that all persons are interconnected, as the aphorism summarises: 'I am because we are' (Gade, 2012; van Norren, 2020; see Metz, 2022). In 1994, the new South African Constitution was premised on the principles of *Ubuntu* for 'understanding' and 'reparation' after the apartheid (Derrida, 2004, p. 116).

With no unanimity about the meaning, some Afro-Latin American communities are bringing *Ubuntu* closer to the Good Living conceptions (Sánchez, 2021; Oñate, 2016). This might be an attempt to value the hybrid sources of critical and decolonial thinking in Latin America, both indigenous and Afro-descendant, and to increase the moral principles for social living through spiritual and environmental interactions (Terblanché, 2019). These exchanges are also shaping reviews of practices such as Colombian '*escuetería*', a way of life based on thrift and frugality, under theoretical features that remind one of *Ubuntu*, Good Living, and the idea of '*sentipensamiento*', the art of living based on thinking both with heart and mind proposed by Orlando Fals Borda (Escobar, 2016). Those conceptions overpass the older dominant meanings of progress and development and suggest new implications for these discourses, even challenging the nomenclature itself:

> There is a need for 'development as service' to one another and the Earth. Including these perspectives may lead to abolishing the word 'development' within the S.D.G.s, replacing it with inter-relationship; replacing end-result-oriented 'goals' with process thinking; and thinking in cyclical nature and earth governance, instead of static 'sustainability'.
> (van Norren, 2020, p. 431)

We can find implementations of those choices in Asia, such as the Gross National Happiness, applied in the Bhutan Constitution. This is defined as a 'calling for material and spiritual development that mutually reinforce one another, which aims at harmony between "inner skills" and "outer circumstances", respect for nature, compassion, and balance and moderation and interdependence of all things' (van Norren, 2020). This ontology serves as a basis for the so-called 'alter-development' index, laying its foundations in relations among culture, socio-economy, nature and governance.

Also, in Latin America, there are populations with very similar proposals that shift 'development' in their rules and laws. This is the case of Andean's Nasa indigenous people 'planes de vida', which are community life plans based on culture, unity, territory and autonomy. This living path entails considering the principles of 'reciprocity, redistribution, collectivity, caring, respect, dialogue, complementarity, duality' (Montoya et al., 2015, p. 28), which serve as a measure of good ways of living.

Regarding communication, Good Living principles are closely connected to popular and local experiences that emphasise community over individuality, solidarity over competitiveness and process over immediacy. We refer, for example, to such projects as the so-called 'time banks' in Paris or Madrid; media resistance collectives in Times Square in New York; Union movements advocating for the mental well-being of high school teachers in Spain; or urban gardens and cooperative markets in Berlin. Furthermore, experiences such as the 'custody of the word' in Oaxaca, Mexico; the weekly barter between Misak indigenous people; or the rejection of the highway to the sea by the Afro-descendant communities in Cali, among others, are all initiatives that deepen the philosophical roots of Good Living and are inspired by different Latin American critical paradigms, which all challenge the positivist framework and the unique narrative of an ideal of Westernised development.

Conclusion

In Latin America, two interconnected perspectives – dependency theories from the 1970s and the decolonial turn from the 2000s – have served as critical frameworks for understanding communication, both based on an attempt to overcome the media-centric and developmental approaches and on a complex conception of progress and well-being. From the end of the 20th century, the call to formulate a new ecology of knowledge based on the epistemologies from the South has also opened academia to address the exclusion of indigenous thought in critical tradition. As an emerging theory, indigenous communication invites us to seek equity or 'communicative justice'. This justice can be contextualised from the concept of 'pluriverse', which returns us to the ideals of the 1970s since it calls to promote media diversity, in this case incorporating the voice and communicational needs of indigenous collectives whose communicative forms were excluded from the enunciation of development.

Latin American indigenous communication connects with the paradigm of *Buen Vivir*, which is the aspiration for a sublime life that runs through most Andean and, to a large extent, Amazonian cosmologies. *Buen Vivir* represents a radical critique of developmental conceptions (thus overcoming dependency theory) and challenges colonial thought since it is constructed as a more inclusive 'from within' line within the decolonial turn. This non-developmental and anti-racist option feeds the discourse of many social movements, aligning with the calls for eco-social justice and an intersectional understanding of exclusions. This is significant in Latin America and other knowledge and worldviews of different origins, in Africa or Asia, which offer similar inspiration for the practices of a de-Westernised, local, widespread and fair communication. The challenge might be to face the different regional alternatives, putting them in a dialogue of knowledge that allows the path for a more democratic and less interventionist external communication model.

Note

1 It was translated from Spanish by the authors.

References

Acosta, A. (2015). El Buen Vivir como alternativa al desarrollo: Algunas reflexiones económicas y no tan económicas. *Política y Sociedad, 52*(2), 299–330. https://doi.org/10.5209/rev_POSO.2015.v52.n2.45203

Arcila, C., Barranquero, A., & González Tanco, E. (2018). From media to Buen Vivir: Latin American approaches to indigenous communication. *Communication Theory, 28*(1). https://doi.org/10.1093/ct/qty004

Barranquero, A., & Saez, C. (2015). Comunicación y buen vivir: La crítica descolonial y ecológica a la comunicación para el desarrollo y el cambio social. *Palabra Clave, 18*(1), 41–82. https://doi.org/10.5294/pacla.2015.18.1.3

Butler, A., Teasley, C., & Sánchez-Blanco., C. (2019). A decolonial, intersectional approach to disrupting whiteness, neoliberalism, and patriarchy in Western early childhood education and care. In P. Trifonas (Ed.), *Handbook of theory and research in cultural studies and education: Springer international handbooks of education* (pp. 1–18). Springer.

Castro-Gómez, S., & Grosfoguel, R. (Comps.) (2007). *El giro decolonial: Reflexiones para una diversidad epistémica más allá del capitalismo global*. Siglo del Hombre Editores, Universidad Central, Pontificia Universidad Javeriana.

Comisión Económica para América Latina y el Caribe (CEPAL), & Fondo para el Desarrollo de los Pueblos Indígenas de América Latina y el Caribe (FILAC). (2020). *Los pueblos indígenas de América Latina – Abya Yala y la Agenda 2030 para el Desarrollo Sostenible: Tensiones y desafíos desde una perspectiva territorial*. Documentos de Proyectos (LC/TS.2020/47). United Nations.

Cruz, C., Hidalgo-Capitán, A., Cubillo-Guevara, A., Membreño, A., Romero, J., & Reyes, M. (2018). El buen vivir nahoa en la comunidad de Urbaite – Las Pilas (Altagracia). In A. Hidalgo-Capitan & J. Romero (Eds.), *La concepción de vida deseable de los pueblos indígenas y las comunidades étnicas de Nicaragua*. Universidad de Huelva.

Cubillo-Guevara, A. P., & Hidalgo-Capitán, A. L. (2015a). El buen vivir como alternativa al desarrollo. *Perspectiva Socioeconómica*, 2, 5–27. https://doi.org/10.21892/24627593.223

Cubillo-Guevara, A. P., & Hidalgo-Capitán, A. L. (2015b). El Sumak Kawsay Genuino como fenómeno social amazónico ecuatoriano. *OBETS*, *10*(2), 301–333. https://doi.org/10.14198/OBETS2015.10.2.02

de Sousa Santos, B. (2006). *Epistemologies of the South: Justice against epistemicide*. Routledge.

de la Torre, C. (2015). The streets as examples of "true" democracy? The South-American experience. *Estudos Ibero-Americanos*, *41*(2), 328–350. https://doi.org/10.15448/1980-864X.2015.2.21304

Deneulin, S. (2012). *Justice and deliberation about the good life: The contribution of Latin American Buen Vivir social movements to the idea of justice* (Working Paper No. 17). University of Bath Centre for Development Studies.

Derrida, J. (2004). Versöhnung, Ubuntu, pardon: Quel genre? In B. Cassin, O. Cayla, & P. J. Salazar (Coords.), *Vérité, Réconciliation, Réparation* (pp. 111–156). Seuil.

Dussel, E. (2015). *Filosofías del sur: Descolonización y transmodernidad*. Akal.

Escobar, A. (2007). Worlds and knowledges otherwise. *Cultural Studies*, *21*(2–3), 179–210.

Escobar, A. (2011). *Encountering development: The making and unmaking of the third world* (p. 1). Princeton University Press.

Escobar, A. (2016). Thinking-feeling with the Earth: Territorial struggles and the ontological dimension of the epistemologies of the South. *AIBR: Revista de Antropología Iberoamericana*, *11*(1), 11–32. https://doi.org/10.1080/09502380601162506

Escobar, A. (2018). *Designs for the pluriverse: Radical interdependence, autonomy, and the making of worlds*. Duke University Press.

Escobar, A. (2020). Política pluriversal: Lo real y lo posible en el pensamiento crítico y las luchas latinoamericanas contemporáneas. *Tabula Rasa*, 36, 323–354. https://doi.org/10.25058/20112742.n36.13

Fanon, F. (2008). *Black skin, White masks*. Grove Press.

Forno, F., & Weiner, R. (Eds.). (2020). *Sustainable community movement organisations: Solidarity economies and rhizomatic practices*. Routledge.

Foucault, M. (1971). The order of discourse. *Social Science Information*, *10*(2), 7–30. https://doi.org/10.1177/053901847101000201

Freire, P. (2005). *The pedagogy of the oppressed*. Continuum.

Freire, P. (2011). *The pedagogy of hope*. Bloomsbury Publishing.
Gade, C (2012). What is Ubuntu? Different interpretations among South Africans of African descent. *South African Journal of Philosophy*, *31*(3), 484–503. https://doi.org/10.1080/02580136.2012.10751789
Ghiso, A. (2000). Potenciando la Diversidad (Diálogo de saberes, una práctica hermenéutica colectiva). *Notas para Daniela*, 1–13.
Giraldo, O. F. (2020). El desmoronamiento en la creencia del Estado: Buen vivir y autonomía de los pueblos. In A. I. Mora, A. Oviedo, A. Avella, E. Vega, C. Campuzano, F. Simbaña, J. Helberth, J. Plaza, O. Giraldo, P. Lora, & R. Solano, *Buenos vivires y transiciones: La vida dulce, la vida bella, la vida querida, la vida sabrosa, la vida buena, la vida plenitud: Convivir en armonía* (pp. 55–86). Uniminuto.
González Tanco, E. (2015). *Identidad y empoderamiento para "liberar la palabra": Construcción de un sistema de comunicación indígena en los pueblos originarios del Cauca, Colombia* [PhD thesis, Universidad Complutense de Madrid].
González Tanco, E., & Arcila, C. (2022). Buen Vivir as a critique of communication for development. In Y. Miike (Ed.), *Handbook of global interventions in communication theory* (pp. 324–335). I.C.A.'s Handbook Series. Routledge.
Grosfoguel, R. (2011). Decolonising post-colonial studies and paradigms of political-economy: Transmodernity, decolonial thinking, and global coloniality. *Transmodernity: Journal of Peripheral Cultural Production of the Luso-Hispanic World*, *1*(1), 1–38.
Gudynas, E. (2011). Buen Vivir: Today's tomorrow. *Development*, *54*(4), 441–447. https://doi.org/10.1057/dev.2011.86
Gudynas, E. (2013). Transitions to post-extractivism: Directions, options, areas of action. In M. Lang & D. Mokrani (Eds.), *Beyond development: Alternative visions from Latin America* (pp. 165–188). Transnational Institute, Rosa Luxemburg Foundation.
Gudynas, E. (2016). Alternativas al desarrollo y Buen Vivir En: El Buen Vivir como paradigma social alternativo. In F. García-Quero & J. Guardiola (Eds.), *Dossieres economistas sin fronteras* (Vol. 23, pp. 6–11). Economistas Sin Fronteras.
Habermas, J. (1988). *Theory and practice*. Beacon Press.
Herrera, E., Sierra, F., & Del Valle, C. (2016). Hacia una Epistemología del Sur. Decolonialidad del saber-poder informativo y nueva Comunicología Latinoamericana. Una lectura crítica de la mediación desde las culturas indígenas. *Chasqui*, *131*, 77–105.
Lugones, M. (2008). Colonialidad y género. *Tabula Rasa*, *9*, 73–101. www.revistatabularasa.org/numero-9/05lugones.pdf
Magallanes, B. C, & Ramos, J. M. (Eds.). (2016). *Miradas propias. Pueblos indígenas, comunicación y medios en la sociedad global*. Centro Internacional de Estudios Superiores de Comunicación para América Latina (CIESPAL).
Maldonado, C., Reyes, C., & Del Valle, C. (2015). Emergencia indígena, comunicación-otra y Buen Vivir: Pensar la socio-praxis comunicativa de los pueblos indígenas. *Chasqui*, *128*, 166–183.
Mejía, M. R. (2020). *Educación popular: Raíces y travesías de Simón Rodríguez a Paulo Freire*. Aurora.
Metz, T. (2022). *A relational Moral Theory: African Ethics in and beyond the Continent*. Oxford University Press.
Mignolo, W. (2008). La opción descolonial. *Misceláneo, Estudios Transatlánticos*, *1*, 4–22. https://doi.org/10.30827/rl.v0i1.3555

Mohanty, C. T. (1984). Under Western eyes: Feminist scholarship and colonial discourses. *Boundary 2*, *12–13*, 333–358. https://doi.org/10.2307/302821

Monni, S., & Pallottino, M. (2015). A new agenda for international development cooperation: Lessons learnt from the Buen Vivir experience. *Development*, *58*(1), 49–57.

Montoya, G. P., Quiguanás, A., & Bototo, C. A. (2015). *Poder en espiral: Acción política y gobierno propio en territorios ancestrales de Jambaló y Toribío* [Master's thesis, Universidad del Cauca].

Oñate, M. C. (2016). Ubuntu: Voz palenquera de múltiples colores. Hacia una argumentación metafórica cimarrona. *Discurso & Sociedad*, *10*(4), 559–587.

Orobitg, G., Martínez, M., Canals, R., Celigueta, G., Gil García, F., Gómez, S., Izard, G., López, J., Muñoz, O., Pérez, B., & Pitarch, P. (2021). Los medios indígenas en América Latina: Usos, sentidos y cartografías de una experiencia plural. *Revista de Historia*, *83*, 132–164. https://doi.org/10.15359/rh.83.6

Pedro-Carañana, J., Herrera-Huérfano, E., & Almanza, J. O. (Eds.). (2022). *Communicative justice in the pluriverse: An international dialogue*. Taylor & Francis.

Prashad, V. (2007). *The darker nations: A people's history of the third world*. The New Press.

Quiroz, K. O., Elbirt, A. L., & Burgos, R. (2021). Lo andino como región y expresión comunicacional. *Journal of Latin American Communication Research*, *9*(1–2), 31–52. https://doi.org/10.55738/journal.v9i1-2p.31-52

Rivera Cusicanqui, S. (1987). *Oppressed but not defeated: Peasant struggles among the Aymara and Quechua in Bolivia, 1900–1980*. UNRISD.

Sánchez, J. A. (2021). Buen vivir, Vivir bien o Ubuntu vs. Mal vivir desde una visión afrodescendiente en Ecuador. *NULLIUS: Revista de pensamiento crítico en el ámbito del Derecho*, *2*(1), 84–103. https://doi.org/10.33936/revistaderechos.v2i1.3527

Segato, R. L. (2013). Ejes argumentales de la perspectiva de la Colonialidad del Poder. *Revista Casa de las Américas*, *272*, 17–39.

Shome, R. (2019). Thinking culture and cultural studies – from/of the global South. *Communication and Critical/Cultural Studies*, *16*(3), 196–218. https://doi.org/10.1080/14791420.2019.1648841

Sierra, F., & Maldonado, C. (2017). *Comunicación, decolonialidad y Buen Vivir*. Fragua.

Sierra, F., Maldonado, C., & del Valle, C. (2020). Nueva comunicología latinoamericana y giro decolonial. Continuidades y rupturas. *CIC, Cuadernos de Información y Comunicación*, *25*, 225–242. https://doi.org/10.5209/ciyc.68236

Soto, D. P. (2008). Nueva perspectiva filosófica en América Latina: El grupo Modernidad/Colonialidad. *Ciencia Política*, *5*, 8–35.

Soubbotina, T., & Al-Shawarby, S. (2004). Beyond economic growth: Meeting the challenges of global development. *The World Bank Research Observer*, *19*(2), 211–237.

Terblanché, A. C. (2019). Ubuntu and environmental ethics: The West can learn from Africa when faced with climate change. In M. Chemhuru (Ed.), *African environmental ethics. The international library of environmental, agricultural and food ethics*, *29*. (pp. 93–109). Springer. https://doi.org/10.1007/978-3-030-18807-8_7

Thomson, B. (2011). Pachakuti: Indigenous perspectives, buen vivir, sumaq kawsay and degrowth. *Development*, *54*(4), 448–454.

Unceta, K. (2014). *Desarrollo, postcrecimiento y buen vivir*. Ed Abya Yala.

van Norren, D. (2020). The sustainable development goals are viewed through gross national happiness, Ubuntu, and Buen Vivir. *International Environmental Agreements*, *20*, 431–458. https://doi.org/10.1007/s10784-020-09487-3

Viteri Gualinga, C. (2002). Visión indígena del desarrollo en la Amazonía. *Polis, Revista de la Universidad Bolivariana*, *1*(3), 1–7.

Waisbord, S. (2020). Family tree of theories, methodologies, and strategies in development communication. In J. Servaes (Ed.), *Handbook of communication for development and social change* (pp. 93–132). Springer.

Walsh, C. (2013). *Pedagogías decoloniales: Prácticas insurgentes de resistir, (re)existir y (re)vivir*. Abya Yala.

Wynter, S. (1995). 1492: A new world view. In V. Lawrence & R. Nettleford (Eds.), *Race, discourse, and the origin of the Americas: A new world view* (pp. 5–57). Smithsonian Institution Press.

Wolfson, T. (2012). From the Zapatistas to Indymedia: Dialectics and orthodoxy in contemporary social movements. *Communication, Culture & Critique*, *5*(2), 149–170. https://doi.org/10.1111/j.1753-9137.2012.01131.x

Ziegler, J. (2008). *La Haine de l'Occident*. Albin Michel.

5 The role of indigenous religion in building community resilience

The case of the Karen, an ethnic minority group in the Myanmar-Thailand border region

Hee-Chan Song

Introduction

Approximately five to seven million Karen people have maintained their traditional indigenous culture in Myanmar and western Thailand. However, radical external changes in the political environment have threatened the population. Since the beginning of the 20th century, the Karen people have been severely oppressed and have suffered from a long-standing war with Burmese insurgents and separatists. Over time, political turmoil has forced Karen communities to flee to the border areas of Myanmar and Thailand, where they face complex socio-political issues. Those living outside the refugee camps are even viewed as illegal migrants or painted as pro-communist, which highly compromises their safety.

Studies have found that despite hardships, the Karen communities have long protected their unique ethnic identity and cultural practices (Rangkla, 2014). Many Karen communities continue their traditional practices, such as the wrist-tying ceremony, to remember who they were and what they did (Bird et al., 2016). These practices have enabled communities to forge solid social ties and stave off hostile forces that might threaten their solidarity (Platz, 2003). Scholars have demonstrated that practices such as the wrist-tying ceremony strengthen and reinforce the distinctive ethnic identity of the Karen people (Cheesman, 2002). These studies have revealed how an ethnic minority community adapts to radical external changes while protecting its identity through symbolic cultural ceremonies.

Drawing from the literature review, this chapter asks *what factors, which I call resilience factors, build community resilience among ethnic minority people*? Because the theoretical focus of this chapter is resilience, I adopt resilience theory to identify the resilience factors (Linnenluecke, 2015; Sutcliffe & Vogus, 2003; Williams et al., 2017). Resilience is generally defined as 'the capacity of a system to absorb disturbance and reorganise while changing to retain the same function, structure, identity, and feedback' (Walker et al., 2004, p. 4). In the past two decades, organisational researchers have extensively applied this concept to specific contexts, such as occupation (Kossek &

DOI: 10.4324/9781003358879-5

Perrigino, 2016), human resource management (Lengnick-Hall et al., 2011), corporate sustainability (DesJardine et al., 2019), risk management (Williams et al., 2017), civic community (Rao & Greve, 2018), and long-term strategic tactics of the Roman Empire (Carmeli & Markman, 2011).

In this chapter, I opt for the ecological perspective because the specific focus of this study is to understand the adaptiveness of an ethnic minority community amid radical external changes. System ecologists posit that a macro ecosystem can be resilient by completing a long-term adaptive process that enables a system to keep its identity while simultaneously adapting to external changes (Carpenter et al., 2001; Holling, 1973). Drawing upon this thinking, the scholars ask how a collective system balances the persistence of core identity (i.e., system persistence) and transformation to adapt to external change (i.e., system flexibility) (see also Farjoun, 2010). This adaptive aspect of resilience is central to the ecological perspective, which is missing in the engineering perspective. Using the ecological perspective, this chapter reveals the adaptive process and identifies the resilience factors of ethnic minority communities.

I begin this chapter with a brief review of resilience theory, which compares the engineering and ecological perspectives and explains why the ecological lens is more appropriate for examining community resilience. I then explain why and how the Karen people's religious beliefs may serve as crucial resilience factors. Finally, the implications of this study are described in the discussion section.

Theoretical background

Ecological and engineering perspectives on resilience

The concept of resilience could be more precise. The theoretical approaches adopted to describe resilience thus differ in the relevant literature, including ecology (Holling, 1973; Holling & Gunderson, 2002), psychology (Bonanno, 2004; Fletcher & Sarkar, 2013), engineering (Hollnagel et al., 2006), strategic management (Carmeli & Markman, 2011; Ortiz-de-Mandojana & Bansal, 2016), and organisational studies (Lengnick-Hall et al., 2011; Powley, 2009).

The different approaches are typically divided into two camps: engineering and ecology (Desjardins et al., 2015). Researchers who take the engineering approach mainly investigate how quickly a system returns to equilibrium after a perturbation, often by operationalising resilience as the return time (i.e., the time it takes to bounce back from an external shock) (DesJardine et al., 2019; Maguire & Hagan, 2007). However, researchers who take the ecological approach focus on the adaptive capacity of a system to absorb and tolerate disturbances through adaptation (Adger, 2000; Carmeli & Markman, 2011; Walker et al., 2004). Because the comparison illuminates my choice of the ecological perspective, I further elaborate on the differences in detail.

First, from the ecological perspective, resilience is a *process* of evolution and not an *outcome* of evolution that implies *survival*. For example, Williams et al. (2017, p. 742) define resilience 'as the *process* by which an actor (i.e., individual, organisation, or community) builds and uses its capability endowments to interact with the environment in a way that positively adjusts and maintains functioning prior to, during, and following adversity' (italic added for emphasis). Extending a historical case of the Republic of Rome's resilience to corporate settings, Carmeli and Markman (2011, p. 329) similarly suggest that 'corporate resilience is about neither crisis management nor turnaround programs, but rather about an ongoing bundling and redeployment of capture and governance strategies.' These studies conceptualise resilience from an ecological perspective and suggest that resilience is a long-term process of adapting to changing environments, not necessarily survival or return time (Lengnick-Hall & Beck, 2005). Scholars taking the ecological perspective thus claim that survival is only a necessary condition of resilience, such that a resilient system survives; however, not all surviving systems are resilient if they lose their identity and core functioning.

The second difference between the engineering and ecological perspectives is the resilience mechanism. The distinction goes back to the system ecologist Holling's thesis (1973, 1996), which focused on the different definitions of resilience and the profound differences in theoretical assumptions, mechanisms, and implications. In his thesis, the engineering perspective assumed a form of stability that quickly drives a system to return to a pre-disturbance single equilibrium. However, the ecological perspective pays more attention to evolutionary processes. This is because the ecological perspective does not presume a return to a single equilibrium, which is taken for granted from the engineering perspective. Instead, it emphasises the possibility of multiple equilibria between environmental changes (external change) and organisational responses (internal configuration) (Carmeli & Markman, 2011; Elmqvist et al., 2003; Holling, 1996). Thus, long-term fluctuation between multi-equilibria is considered necessary for a system to buffer and absorb environmental changes (Holling, 1996). However, from the engineering perspective, fluctuation is considered an unstable, inefficient, and abnormal phenomenon (Holling, 1996).

This ecological approach is more suitable for answering the research question. It allows us to determine how an ethnic minority community thrives despite external changes (system flexibility) while maintaining a community identity over an adaptive process (system persistence). This study aimed to identify the resilience factors by examining the adaptive process. I now narrow down the literature review to community resilience, as the context of this study is *community*.

Community resilience from an ecological perspective

The unit of analysis varies in resilience research, mainly conducted at the individual (Fletcher & Sarkar, 2013), organisational (Ortiz-de-Mandojana &

Bansal, 2016), and macro-ecosystem levels (Folke et al., 2010; Walker et al., 2004). The unit of analysis in this study is a community. A community is generally defined as a group of people living in the same geographic area and sharing common values, behavioural patterns, and belief systems (Norris et al., 2008). A community often consists of systemically constructed socio-economic contexts, most leading to formal and informal interactions among its members (Norris et al., 2008).

In this study, I define a resilient community as one in which its members are collectively capable of preserving their community identity, tradition, and practices while adapting to a changing environment. From this perspective, building community resilience means gaining collective knowledge of external threats. Doing so enables community members to understand the external risks, determine where adjustments are required, and search for a collective solution to tackle negative repercussions from the outside (King, 1995). This process is highly related to establishing a strong community culture in which people build shared belief systems, collective prosocial behaviours, and community spirit to work together. This concern can be summarised as a brief question: *What is a community's collective capacity to adapt to external changes while protecting its identity?* In other words, what are the factors that make a community resilient?

Some studies have attempted to answer these questions. For example, Frounfelker et al. (2020) suggested that collective efficacy, inward orientation, and high commitment to religiosity are potential resilience factors. Patel et al. (2017) highlighted the presence of tight social networks within communities. Norris et al. (2008) listed the factors associated with building community resilience: shared values, collective participation, structured role, resources, long-term support, critical reflection, communication, and preparedness. In this study, I focus on an indigenous religion historically shared and recalled among community members. This is partly because, in an indigenous community, traditional religious practices are believed to strengthen the community spirit.

In the following section, I describe the origins and practices of the belief system that shape the identity of the Karen people. I then examine how it is linked to building a resilient community. To this end, I offer an overview of the Karen culture and dig deeper into the vital role of animism in the Karen religion.

Animism as a resilience factor in the Karen community

The Karen are an ethnic minority in Southeast Asia with a shared cultural identity (Moonieinda, 2011). Geographically, they are dispersed across the highlands bordering India, China, Laos, and Thailand and inhabit the lowlands in central and southern Myanmar (Hayami, 1993; Thawnghmung, 2011). Although it is difficult to know the exact number of the Karen people, about 300,000 Karen people are expected to reside in the Myanmar-Thailand border area (Hayami, 1993; Moonieinda, 2011). In 2002, the Royal Thai

Government reported that approximately 438,131 Karens lived in Western Thailand (Buadaeng, 2007).

Researchers have identified the origin of the Karen people, but the evidence is still highly controversial. Some studies reported that they might have travelled from the Middle East and the Gobi Desert (MacLachlan, 2012). Others claimed that the Karen might be one of the long-lost tribes of Israel (Delang, 2003; Petry, 1993). One of the most accepted views may stem from Heppner's (2001) work. In his book *Suffering in Silence: The Human Rights Nightmare of the Karen People of Burma*, Heppner (2001) documented how the Karen migrated from Mongolia in numerous stages around 2,500 years ago and established their communities. He argued that some of them made their way into the hills from the central lowlands, now called the Irrawaddy and Sittaung basins in central Myanmar, which was a largely uninhabited jungle at the time. Overall, researchers seem to agree that the Karen people form a common ethnic community where an individual village is regarded as the most prominent social unit that makes up one socio-political and ritual society, where the social order goes hand in hand with individual order, and personal well-being and communal well-being are inseparable (Hayami, 1993).

Two essential characteristics of the Karen substantially differentiate them from other ethnic minority groups in Southeast Asia. The first is their language, and the second is their religion. Karen's linguistic family comprises 17 to 20 subgroups (Thawnghmung, 2011). Some trace their origins back to the Tibeto-Burmese language branch (Platz, 2003; Hayami, 1996), while others are much closer to the Sino-Tibetan language family (Delang, 2003). The Burmese Census conducted in 1921 recognised 14 dispersed hill tribes using different languages. It characterised them into six tribes: the Sgaw, the Bwe, the Pwo, the Padang, the Karenni, and the Zayin. Based on this, Lewis (1924) categorised the Karen people into three main tribes: the Sgaw, the Pwo, and the Bwe. Danpongpee (2000) later added a fourth tribe: the Toungthu. Although linguistic differences occasionally make communication difficult among the tribes, all spoken languages share the same linguistic structure, referred to as Sgaw Karen, enabling them to communicate and bond together (Thawnghmung, 2011).

The second source that distinguishes them is religion. Religion binds the geographically dispersed Karen people into one ethnic identity. They have long held strong beliefs in animism. The Karen animistic belief system is even viewed by many scholars as a more original element of the Karen identity than their linguistic root (Ikeda, 2012). Ikeda (2012) suggested that the shared belief in animism explains why they still prefer to live together in the mountains, not the lowlands, and resist mingling with outsiders. I now dig deeper into animism in the following section.

Animism as a belief system in the Karen culture

According to Swancutt (2019), animism is a socio-cultural mechanism of how indigenous people respond to other beings, forces of nature, objects, and even technical devices. The Karen people have developed various elements of animism as a belief system. Their animism plays two pivotal roles in their daily routines: (1) shaping a unique worldview of relationships between human and non-human entities and (2) forming a normative basis for their moral code.

First, Karen communities believe that although animals and people have different bodies and characteristics, they possess the same type of soul. For this reason, Karen people believe that nonhumans and humans can form authentic relationships that may resemble the relationships among humans (Steenhuisen, 2020). Hayami (1996) observed that Karens believe in the existence of territorial spirits (e.g., the Lord of Water and Lord of Land) and that the spirits guard against evil spirits lurking in the inhabitable forest. They also believe that good spirits reside in villages in addition to the supreme tutelary spirit (Hayami, 1996). The good spirits are believed to be elderly relatives who can be appeased through respect or small gifts or enraged by social conflicts and moral violations (Moonieinda, 2011). Hayami (1993) further explained that the Karens believe that one's careless, indecent, and anti-community acts can incite good spirits to act against the entire community. This belief in nuanced connectivity with non-human entities essentially mediates between the community and the Lord of Water and Lord of Land, who are believed to govern the mountain (Rajah, 2008). The Karens believe that when harmony between humans and nonhumans is finally established, the harmony brings happiness and health (Hayami, 1993) and the forgiveness needed to appease the enraged spirit (Paul, 2018).

Specifically, each Karen community member is assumed to have 37 *keys*, believed to be vital to a person's health (Hayami, 1993). The head *k'la* is considered the most significant because its permanent loss results in death (Hayami, 1993). Hayami (1993) stated that harmful spirits readily lure k'las or become lost in the forest. However, Rangkla (2014) argued that they freely depart the body and arrive again when shocked or frightened. The ritual of calling and securing k'la by tying cotton threads around one's wrists is practised to protect and facilitate healing from attacks by evil spirits (Hayami, 1993). According to Hayami (2004), this symbolic ceremony primarily aims to initiate collective reflection and honour the triadic link among individuals' well-being, non-human entities' well-being, and the socio-ecological order of the community.

Second, Karen's animistic belief system shapes their daily moral code. For example, according to Po (1928, p. 20), 'marriage is a sacred and solemn act.' White tunic dresses are worn by unmarried women to symbolise strict sexual morality (Hayami, 1996). In Karen's life, sexual misconduct is closely related to animistic punishment. Sex outside marriage is highly discouraged for fear of provoking a spirit that can harm the offending individuals and destroy the entire community (Moonieinda, 2011). Likewise, sexually blasphemous words directed at the spirits are believed to bring about misfortune that harms the entire community's well-being over time.

For this reason, the Karen people try to reach a relaxed, calm, and stable mental state. Coolness is the most desirable condition for a community where harmony is maintained with a good spirit (Hayami, 1993). Creating a calm state in any aspect of Karen's life is morally valued as it creates a harmonious condition (Rajah, 2008). It is assumed that people in a relaxed state seek to promote favourable conditions for their daily routine, crop growth, and even the success of married life (Rajah, 2008). Hayami (1993) concluded that this coolness is the most desirable condition at the community level for the surrounding nature and the individual. Thus, village leaders and male elders engage in several rituals to communicate and negotiate with the tutelary spirit to maintain a good relationship and, thus, a relaxed state (Richthammer, 2020).

Animism as a resilience factor

I build on these previous studies to argue that Karen's unique belief system in animism enables them to be resilient (i.e., protecting their core identity while adapting to extreme external change). To do so, I describe the external changes this study specifically focuses on and explain the socio-cognitive mechanism of how animism plays the role of a resilient factor.

External threats to Karen communities

One of the most compelling external threats to Karen communities originated from the Burmese juntas and insurgents that tried to remove anti-Burmese ethnic groups (Rajah, 2002). Table 5.1 depicts some milestone events and describes how Karen's collective movement shifted in response to political threats. Since the British colonisation of Myanmar, strong antagonism has existed between the Karen and Burmese (Cheesman, 2002; Rajah, 2002). During World War II, the Karen strategically sided with the British, while the Burmese aligned with Japan (Neiman et al., 2008). After the war, the Karen were denied ownership of their territory, and even worse, Burmese authorities took the territory and legitimised their status as the country's leading ethnic group. It has been claimed that they often mistreat Karen and have unfortunately massacred Karen villages (Moonieinda, 2011).

As a result, most Karen people have been at war with the Burmese armies, mainly since the Burmese attained independence in 1948 (Buadaeng, 2007; Cook et al., 2015). In the late 1990s, the violence became even more intense and could have been considered genocidal, according to several reports. Most Karen people who were attacked and displaced faced severe physical and social adjustments for survival. Over the process, long-term relocations were implemented to push the Karen to the periphery of mainstream Burmese society (Cusano, 2001). Unfortunately, the Karen National Union and other guerrilla armies split into various factions, some of which ended up battling each other (Moonieinda, 2011; Rajah, 2002).

Animism as a resilience factor: system persistency

Because of the radical political turmoil that the Karen experienced, Karen communities were required to develop some ideas or practices that could unite them. Their animistic belief system played an essential role in this process. First, their religion united them by supporting the recall of their collective identities. For example, many Karen leaders use wrist-tying ceremonies amid external disturbances to symbolise reunification and togetherness (MacLachlan, 2012). MacLachlan (2012) found that wrist-tying ceremonies played a pivotal role in recalling a sense of oneness that helped mitigate the geographical and potential socio-cultural differences among Karen communities. Specifically, Karen leaders used two narrative strategies to solidify the people. First, they stressed that the belief in Karen animism was already embedded in Karen identity, not something externally given (MacLachlan, 2012). Second, the leaders formed a universal understanding of *Karenness* through ancestral legends, myths, and stories about wrist-tying ceremonies (MacLachlan, 2012). MacLachlan (2012) referred to the wrist-tying ceremony as an 'old and pure Karen practice' passed down to the present Karen communities from the ancestors.

One compelling narrative is the origin of the wrist-tying ceremony. According to a Karen legend, the first Karen immigrants from Southern China to Northern Myanmar started the wrist-tying ceremony. A sandstorm erupted as they crossed the Gobi Desert. Frequent sandstorms eventually scattered all the people. Over time, they settled across the mountainous areas of Southeast Asia. They developed a symbolic ritual to recognise themselves, hoping that they could reunite someday. This ritual was the wrist-tying ceremony. Community members wore white threads on their wrists so that if they were separated again, they would have a standard method of recognising that they belonged to the same ethnic community. Although individual Karen communities' lifestyles, rules, and other ethnological elements might eventually become different, their belief in animism could remain the same. Thus, the ceremony was well accepted among all Karen communities. According to the legend, the sandstorm was a severe threat in the past that drove the people to invent the symbolic wrist-tying ceremony. In the present, the political turmoil triggers the resurrection of the ceremony.

The second role of animism in unifying the Karen people is related to the strong bond between the living space and its surrounding natural environment (Hayami, 1993, 1996). It is important to note that Karens peacefully coexist with their wider environment. As discussed earlier, they place equal value on known and unknown forms of nature, including human, non-human biological species, the land, trees, rocks, and even ghosts (Steenhuisen, 2020). Thus, the Karen people treat nature as a neighbour. Such a strong bond with nature, which originated from animism, formed a spiritual sense of duty to protect the space in which their ancestors lived. This prevented them from abandoning their land or moving to other areas. Thus, it served to keep them in the current space where they settled.

Role of indigenous religion in building community resilience 75

Table 5.1 External political turmoil that directly or indirectly threatened the Karen community and their response to threats

Years	Description	Source
1824–26	The first Anglo-Burmese war took place in Myanmar.	Cheesman, 2002
1881	The Karen National Association (KNA) was established to promote Karen identity, leadership, and education and to secure socio-economic advancement.	Rajah, 2002
1886	As anti-British sentiment emerged in Myanmar, the British recruited Karen armies against the Burmese government.	Rajah, 2002
1939	An attempt to establish an independent Karen state was made, yet it was unsuccessful. As a result, Karen-Burmese hostility increasingly became violent.	Cheesman, 2002
1947	Burmese-dominated government policies had both highlighted and suppressed ethnic distinctions.	Cheesman, 2002
1948	The Karen advocated for independence from the Burmese with the British after WWII. However, following Burmese independence in 1948, the British promise to review Karen independence was suddenly forgotten.	Neiman et al., 2008
1949	One year after Burmese independence, an unyielding Karen separatist movement with a primarily Christian leadership arose.	Rajah, 2002
1962	A Burmese military government took over the parliament, and all people were subject to its jurisdiction.	Cheesman, 2002
1974	The practice of dictatorial authority was codified into law with the 1974 constitution.	Cheesman, 2002
1988	A national movement for democracy took place in Myanmar in 1988. The Karen National Union headquarters became the base of operation for pro-democracy organisations.	Moonieinda, 2011
1994	The Democratic Kayin Buddhist Army was established in December 1994.	Karen Human Rights Group, 1996
2007	The Karen National Union/Karen Liberation Army (Peace Council) was established.	Myanmar Peace Monitor, 2019a, 2019b
2009	The Burmese government announced the Border Guard Forces scheme to suppress any military actions in the border area of Myanmar and Thailand, forcing many minority ethnic groups to move from their territories. This occurred without the promised political discussions.	Myanmar Peace Monitor, 2019, 2019b

Many Karen communities settled in the mountainous areas of Myanmar and northern Thailand and converted the harsh land into rice beds or flower gardens (Santasombat, 2004). They developed knowledge and skills related to mountainous cultivation, which later became significant elements of their way of life (Santasombat, 2004; Trakansuphakorn, 2008). The strong interconnectedness with the land, water, and trees in the wild was developed through cultivation (Hayami, 1993). This means that not only did the spiritual bond with nature form a moral duty to protect their living space, but it also gave them a collective ability to learn how to protect their land. An interdependency was manifested in the Karen's animism and animistic ceremonies, which played an essential role in strengthening their bond with nature. This is one of the reasons they still stick to their original settlement despite the external threat and forced migration.

Perhaps one ideal example of a strong bond with nature is the collective calling 'owners of the water and land,' performed during animistic ceremonies (Paul, 2018). The ritual aims to preserve and restore homes from external invasion (Paul, 2018). Some scholars even found that many Karens still believe that the long-standing war between their armed groups and the Burmese militaries means a glorious fight to protect the region's ecological diversity and the ownership of their land (Trakansuphakorn, 2008). For example, all administrative divisions of the Karen National Union, including the Karen State in Myanmar, are referred to as *Kawthoolei*, 'where control over territories (security), authority over population (governance), and access to resources (development) are being contested and renegotiated as a way to build peace' (Kham, 2021, p. 15).[1] According to Paul (2018), it is a statement about the Karen people's right to reject any development projects that may negatively affect their water, land, and natural resources. He further argued that the Karen's efforts to preserve clean water, natural forests, and endangered species, even in the face of civil war and forced migration, are evidence of the strength of their animistic beliefs. Animism, therefore, is an essential factor in their connection to nature that fuels their desire to maintain their harsh mountainous lifestyle.

Ecological value has been even more prominent in Karen communities. Many Karen communities have recently been recognised for their environmental activism because of their bond with the land and their dedication to protecting it. There is growing re-awareness among the younger generations of the forest that a crucial component of Karen ethnic identity is eco-centrism, as the ecological movement of the Karen strengthens young generations' animistic beliefs in nature and the interdependent relationship between humans and nonhumans (Steenhuisen, 2020). Younger Karen people gain a more profound sense of identity and self-reliance due to the unique sensibility of their intimate bond with and reliance on the forest (Steenhuisen, 2020). For example, some have formed the Karen Environmental and Social Action Network. This community-based, non-governmental, and non-profit organisation strives to increase livelihood security and fights against external agents that threaten the ecological diversity of their living space.

The strong belief in animism compels individual community members to uphold community values rather than pursue individual aims that might conflict with collectivistic values. This internal mechanism of community solidarity helped the Karen people pursue collective goals, thereby preventing potential deviators. For example, Hayami (1993) defined a traditional Karen community as a politico-religious social order that played a watchdog role in monitoring community members. *Thout kyar*, translated as 'being faithful' in English, operated as the Karen community's most fundamental law-like moral quality. Young and older adults see this quality as an essential societal norm to define one another and force themselves to be morally compatible. *Through kyar* means living as a relational being embedded in their family and community rather than an independent being that may conflict with much more significant social units (Chambers, 2019). This reduced internal conflicts among numerous Karen communities and established a pan-Karen identity across Myanmar and Thailand (Kuroiwa & Verkuyten, 2008).

Animism as a resilience factor: system flexibility

The ecological perspective highlights the balance between system persistence and flexibility (Folke et al., 2010; Walker et al., 2004). Indeed, excessive persistence makes a system potentially rigid, whereas too much flexibility can harm a system's core functioning and identity. Therefore, understanding the balance between persistence and flexibility is central to unpacking the adaptive aspects of a resilient system. A relevant question in this context is how Karen communities change aspects of their core practices and cultures that may conflict with ancestral traditions.

One striking aspect of Karen flexibility is adopting external ideas through unique hybridisation with foreign religions. Interestingly, Karen animistic beliefs have been increasingly integrated with Western Christianity and Theravada Buddhism. This has led to institutional and even financial support from Western and mainstream Thai society. Relevant observations are reflected in anthropologists' fieldwork. In the case of Christianity, Ikeda (2012) demonstrated that Karen communities were voluntarily Christianised and willingly embraced Western influence. When Karen people encountered the Baptist missionaries in Myanmar in the early 19th century, they considered potential integration rather than simply rejecting or attacking them. Surprisingly, some Karen religious leaders even viewed themselves as a lost tribe of Israel based on the compelling similarities between several Karen myths and the early books of the Old Testament (Platz, 2003; Delang, 2003). The leaders strategically viewed the Bible as 'the lost book' and treated missionaries to be 'white brothers' that brought the Bible to them (Platz, 2003; Ikeda, 2012). Their traditional values were also highly consistent with Christian notions of morality (Platz, 2003; South, 2007).

The Karen could easily understand Christianity through the connections with their religion. When Christianity reached their communities, many people voluntarily converted to it. The first baptism of a Karen person, Ko Tha Byu, by the American missionary Adoniram Judson in 1828, marked the beginning of the widespread conversion of Karen people to Christianity (Platz, 2003; Ikeda, 2012). After learning about the legend of 'the lost book,' another American missionary, Jonathan Wade, was motivated to create the Sgaw Karen script in 1832 and the Pwo Karen script in 1852 (Platz, 2003; Ikeda, 2012).

The second integration with other religions occurred with Buddhism. Existing sources reveal that by the 18th century, most Karen accepted Buddhism as a legitimate religious belief to stabilise relationships with Thailand (Ikeda, 2012). They were called 'Buddhist Karen' to distinguish themselves from dispersed Karen communities (Ikeda, 2012). For Buddhist Karens, there is no superior religion; all religions are considered the same (Platz, 2003). Since the ancient form of Buddhism also emphasised harmony with nature and ecosystems, Buddhism has historically been much more receptive to animist beliefs and practices (MacLachlan, 2012). Buddhists may differ from Karen animists only in that Buddhists do not practise ancestor worship and instead give offerings to the monks. However, Buddhist Karens often treat elderly monks and the Buddha as their ancestors. Thus, integration with Buddhism does not oblige someone to quit ancestral worship (Platz, 2003). Most Buddhist Karens still respect ancestral traditions and practice spirit cults (Hayami, 2004; Buadaeng, 2003). Even though they openly identify as Buddhist Karens, they combine Buddhist principles and moral codes with animist beliefs in spirits, as indicated by their reliance on Buddhist monks and spirit mediums (Richthammer, 2020).

One may view the current internal strife between Christian and Buddhist Karen as potentially threatening to the sense of oneness that the Karen people have developed (Mang, 2016). However, the changes have not replaced tradition but fostered hybridisation and integration. Traditional animistic rituals such as wrist-tying ceremonies are still practised, and animistic beliefs in powerful spirits remain at the heart of pan-Karen identity. To briefly illustrate, the figurative unification of body and soul and the soul-calling chants still remind all Karen people to recall who they were and what they did (Rangkla, 2014). Regardless of their conversion, all Karen religious leaders urge community members to attend wrist-tying ceremonies (Rangkla, 2014). Platz (2003) points out that despite the rise in ethnic and religious tensions worldwide, the Karen are highly flexible in integrating foreign elements of other religions with their traditional belief system.

Table 5.2 summarises how the Karen's belief system in animism ensures their community's resilience. It plays an essential role in recalling their ethnic identity, making them stick to their living spaces, and offering a normative basis for maintaining community ethics. These functions allow Karen communities to protect their collective identity and maintain their cultural practice against external turmoil (i.e., system persistency). It also serves as an open filter for accepting outside ideas and religions, enabling them to connect to larger entities that may support them (i.e., system flexibility).

Table 5.2 Role of animism in promoting community resilience among the Karen people

Two elements of system resilience	Role of animism
System persistency	• *Recalling collective memories:* Animistic religious ceremonies solidify the oneness of the Karen people by supporting their collective identity through the recall of collective memories. • *Ecological attachment to land:* The Karen's belief in animism promotes a strong bond with their living space and nature, which prevents them from easily moving to other regions and remains in their territories. • *Collective moral norm:* The Karen's collective belief in animism compels each community member to keep shared values through strong community-based ethics.
System flexibility	• Karen communities integrate the foreign thoughts and religions of outside cultures with their traditional belief system by actively searching for commonalities between them.

Discussion

Previous studies on resilience were skewed toward the engineering perspective, which conceptualised resilience as recovery capacity (Gittell et al., 2006; Ortiz-de-Mandojana & Bansal, 2016; Sutcliffe & Vogus, 2003). In their studies, resilience is the ability to bounce back from a specific external disturbance quickly. Scholars have accordingly operationalised the concept based on return time or survival. Deviating from the previous studies, this chapter draws upon an ecological perspective that emphasises a system's dual capacity, namely system persistency and flexibility (Folke et al., 2010; Farjoun, 2010). In doing so, it brings a unique case in which the indigenous belief system, the Karen's animistic beliefs, plays a crucial role as a resilience factor that strengthens ethnic identity in response to external political turmoil. Based on this case analysis, I conclude this chapter by discussing an important implication.

Previous studies have focused on formal rules, practices, and institutions that can improve the resilience of a system, thereby framing resilience factors as formal engagement. However, at the community level, this chapter suggests that a resilience factor can be an ethnocultural and informal element of a community. Among others, my focus was the indigenous religion that has historically been passed down from one generation to the other and is still manifested in the current generation's daily ceremonies. The wrist-tying ceremonies symbolise the sense of pride and togetherness of Karen communities. As discussed, Karen communities consist of diverse religious groups and thus present differences in status, class, and language (Gravers, 2007). The term 'Karen' is inclusive, referring to people who speak one or more Karenic languages and whose ancestors have spread widely across Southeast Asia (Hayami, 2004). However, the wrist-tying ceremonies have aided the Karen people in overcoming the differences within Karens. It serves as a collective recall mechanism for all Karen people to support, unite, and live harmoniously. This brings them together and keeps shaping their identity, demonstrating a sense of oneness and their willingness to protect themselves against external political threats (Rangkla, 2014).

The Karen people who have migrated to North America and Europe are also willing to participate in wrist-tying ceremonies. It takes place in their homes around the August full moon. They ward off evil spirits by tying white threads together. They still wear traditional Karen clothes and relate to each other under the umbrella of Karen identity, even though they now speak different languages. Thus, although the practice is rooted in animism, Christian Karen and Buddhists celebrate this ceremony. By uncovering how such an ethnological element serves as an informal institution that shapes community identity and further strengthens solidarity, this study extends our understanding of community resilience factors.

This discussion and the contributions now lead us to introduce a specific term, 'cultural resilience,' in the context of indigenous communities (Harper, 2016). Cultural resilience refers to the capacity of the indigenous community to rebalance the collective lives of community members in the face of extreme external threats (Harper, 2016). As discussed earlier, the Karen people's ethnic identity evolved into the community's identity amid their resistance to the tyranny they faced (Rajah, 2002). The Karen continues to engage in community-centred exchanges despite significant disruptions (Lewis & Young, 2019). This shows they live as a unique cultural community where people continue their core cultural practices and do not simply survive by compromising with external pressure.

Here, we see that community resilience does not merely mean the community's survival amid external events and disturbances. In organisational literature, survival is merely an outcome variable at the population level (Hannan & Freeman, 1984) that is not related to the process of being culturally resilient. It is measured by the mortality rate (Carroll & Delacroix, 1982) or survival time (Brüderl et al., 1992). A culturally resilient community must retain 'essentially the same function, structure, identity, and feedback' (Walker et al., 2004, p. 4) while surviving. This means that survival is only a necessary condition for community resilience. Not all surviving systems (communities in this case) are resilient if they lose their cultural identity. This chapter suggests that cultural resilience can be ensured, once communities survive and simultaneously protect their unique cultural identities.

Conclusion

In conclusion, this chapter highlights the urgent need to explore community resilience in ethnic minority groups facing diverse external risks, including socio-political, ecological, and moral concerns that threaten human rights. By examining a Southeast Asian minority group's belief system in animism, this research illustrates the potential of endogenous forces, such as cultural and religious practices, to foster community resilience. This research adds to the existing knowledge on community resilience and has significant implications for interventions and policies aimed at supporting vulnerable communities. Further research is needed to expand our understanding of community resilience, particularly in diverse contexts, and to develop practical approaches that build on endogenous strengths. As we face global sustainability challenges, it is crucial to learn from the resilience of marginalised groups and acknowledge their agency and cultural diversity. This requires a collaborative effort between researchers, practitioners, and policymakers to ensure that interventions are context-specific, inclusive, and sustainable.

Acknowledgement

I thank Naw Thein Paw Awar for her assistance in developing this chapter.

Note

1 *Kaw* is a Karen word that refers to 'country.' It also refers to a territory comprising 1 to 10 villages in a particular region. A *kaw* often includes communal forests and highland farming regions. In the Pwo Karen language, *kawthoolei* is often translated as 'green country,' 'land without evil,' or 'land of the cool caves,' although most Karen people would translate the term as 'Karen country' (Thansrithong & Buadaeng, 2017). Additionally, it evokes the idea of an original homeland that the Karen defend and restore (Thansrithong & Buadaeng, 2017).

References

Adger, W. N. (2000). Social and ecological resilience: Are they related? *Progress in Human Geography*, 24(3), 347–364. https://doi.org/10.1191/030913200701540465

Bird, J. N., Brough, M., & Cox, L. (2016). Transnationalism and the Karen wrist-tying ceremony: An ethnographic account of Karen settlement practice in Brisbane. *The Australian Journal of Anthropology*, 27(1), 104–120. https://doi.org/10.1111/taja.12176

Bonanno, G. A. (2004). Loss, trauma, and human resilience: Have we underestimated the human capacity to thrive after extremely aversive events? *American Psychologist*, 59(1), 20–28. https://doi.org/10.1037/0003-066X.59.1.20

Brüderl, J., Preisendörfer, P., & Ziegler, R. (1992). Survival chances of newly founded business organisations. *American Sociological Review*, 57(2), 227–242. https://doi.org/10.2307/2096207

Buadaeng, K. (2003). Khuba movements and the Karen in Northern Thailand: Negotiating sacred space and identity. In H. Yukio & T. Sayavongkhamdy (Eds.), *Cultural diversity and conservation in the making of Mainland Southeast Asia and Southwestern China: Regional dynamics in the past and present* (pp. 262–293). Kyoto University Center for Southeast Asian Studies.

Buadaeng, K. (2007). Ethnic identities of the Karen peoples in Burma and Thailand. In J. L. Peacock, P. M. Thornton, & P. B. Inman (Eds.), *Identity matters* (pp. 73–97). Berghahn Books.

Carmeli, A., & Markman, G. D. (2011). Capture, governance, and resilience: Strategy implications from the history of Rome. *Strategic Management Journal*, 32(3), 322–341.

Carpenter, S., Walker, B., Anderies, J. M., & Abel, N. (2001). From metaphor to measurement: Resilience of what to what? *Ecosystems*, 4(8), 765–781. www.ecologyandsociety.org/vol6/iss1/art14/

Carroll, G. R., & Delacroix, J. (1982). Organisational mortality in the newspaper industries of Argentina and Ireland: An ecological approach. *Administrative Science Quarterly*, 169–198. https://doi.org/10.2307/2392299

Chambers, J. (2019). Towards a moral understanding of Karen state's paradoxical Buddhist strongmen. *Journal of Social Issues in Southeast Asia*, 34(2), 258–289. www.jstor.org/stable/26696413

Cheesman, N. (2002). Seeing "Karen" in the union of Myanmar. *Asian Ethnicity*, 3(2), 199–220. https://doi.org/10.1080/14631360220132736

Cook, T. L., Shannon, P. J., Vinson, G. A., Letts, J. P., & Dwee, E. (2015). War trauma and torture experiences reported during public health screening of newly resettled Karen refugees: A qualitative study. *BMC International Health and Human Rights*, 15(1), 1–13. https://doi.org/10.1186/s12914-015-0046-y

Cusano, C. (2001). Burma: Displaced Karens. Like water on the Khu leaf. In M. Vincent & B. Sørensen (Eds.), *Caught between borders: Response strategies of the internally displaced* (pp. 138–171). Pluto Press.

Danpongpee, E. (2000). *Karen stories of creation*. Regional Theological Seminar-Workshop on "Doing Theology with Creation in Asian Cultures," Program for Theology & Cultures in Asia.

Delang, C. (2003). *Living at the edge of Thai society: The Karen in the highlands of northern Thailand*. Routledge.

DesJardine, M., Bansal, P., & Yang, Y. (2019). Bouncing back: Building resilience through social and environmental practices in the context of the 2008 global financial crisis. *Journal of Management*, 45(4), 1434–1460. https://doi.org/10.1177/0149206317708854

Desjardins, E., Barker, G., Lindo, Z., Dieleman, C., & Dussault, A. C. (2015). Promoting resilience. *The Quarterly Review of Biology*, 90(2), 147–165. https://doi.org/10.1086/681439

Elmqvist, T., Folke, C., Nyström, M., Peterson, G., Bengtsson, J., Walker, B., & Norberg, J. (2003). Response diversity, ecosystem change, and resilience. *Frontiers in Ecology and the Environment*, 1(9), 488–494. https://doi.org/10.1890/1540-9295(2003)001[0488:RDECAR]2.0.CO;2

Farjoun, M. (2010). Beyond dualism: Stability and change as a duality. *Academy of Management Review*, 35(2), 202–225. https://doi.org/10.5465/amr.35.2.zok202

Fletcher, D., & Sarkar, M. (2013). Psychological resilience: A review and critique of definitions, concepts, and theory. *European Psychologist*, 18(1), 12. https://doi.org/10.1027/1016-9040/a000124

Folke, C., Carpenter, S., Walker, B., Scheffer, M., Chapin, T., & Rockström, J. (2010). Resilience thinking: Integrating resilience, adaptability and transformability. *Ecology and Society*, 15(4), 43–53. www.jstor.org/stable/26268226

Frounfelker, R. L., Tahir, S., Abdirahman, A., & Betancourt, T. S. (2020). Stronger together: Community resilience and Somali Bantu refugees. *Cultural Diversity & Ethnic Minority Psychology*, 26(1), 22–31. https://doi.org/10.1037/cdp0000286

Gittell, J. H., Cameron, K., Lim, S., & Rivas, V. (2006). Relationships, layoffs and organisational resilience: Airline responses to the crisis of September 11. *Journal of Applied Behavioral Science*, 42(3), 300–329. https://doi.org/10.1177/0021886306286466

Gravers, M. (2007). *Exploring ethnic diversity in Burma*. NIAS Press.

Hannan, M. T., & Freeman, J. (1984). Structural inertia and organisational change. *American Sociological Review*, 49(2), 149–164. https://doi.org/10.2307/2095567

Harper, S. G. (2016). Keystone characteristics that support cultural resilience in Karen refugee parents. *Cultural Studies of Science Education*, 11(4), 1029–1060. https://doi.org/10.1007/s11422-015-9681-9

Hayami, Y. (1993). To be Karen and to be cool. *Cahiers des Sciences Humaines*, 29(4), 747–762.

Hayami, Y. (1996). Karen tradition according to Christ or Buddha: The implications of multiple reinterpretations for a minority ethnic group in Thailand. *Journal of Southeast Asian Studies*, 27(2), 334–349. www.jstor.org/stable/20062746

Hayami, Y. (2004). *Between hills and plains: Power and practice in socio-religious dynamics among Karen*. Trans Pacific Press.

Heppner, K. (2001). *Suffering in silence: The human rights nightmare of the Karen people of Burma*. Universal-Publishers.

Holling, C. S. (1973). Resilience and stability of ecological systems. *Annual Review of Ecology and Systematics*, 4(1), 1–23. https://doi.org/10.1146/annurev.es.04.110173.000245

Holling, C. S. (1996). Engineering resilience versus ecological resilience. In P. C. Schulze (Ed.), *Engineering within ecological constraints* (pp. 31–44). National Academies Press.

Holling, C. S., & Gunderson, L. H. (2002). Resilience and adaptive cycles. In L. H. Gunderson & C. S. Holling (Eds.), *Panarchy: Understanding transformations in human and natural systems* (pp. 25–62). Island Press.

Hollnagel, E., Woods, D. D., & Leveson, N. (2006). *Resilience engineering: Concepts and precepts*. Ashgate Publishing.

Ikeda, K. (2012). Two versions of Buddhist Karen history of the late British colonial period in Burma: Kayin Chronicle (1929) and Kuyin Great Chronicle (1931). *Southeast Asian Studies*, 1(3), 431–460. https://doi.org/10.20495/seas.1.3_431

Karen Human Rights Group. (1996). *Inside the DKBA*. Karen Human Rights Group, Documenting the Voices of Villagers in Rural Burma. www.khrg.org/1996/03/khrg96b23/inside-dkba

Kham, K. K. M. (2021). *The quest for peace in Kawthoolei: The strategies, outcomes, and sustainability of peacebuilding in Southeastern Myanmar, 2012–2020* [Master's thesis, University of Oslo].

King, A. (1995). Avoiding ecological surprise: Lessons from long-standing communities. *Academy of Management Review*, 20(4), 961–985. https://doi.org/10.5465/amr.1995.9512280032

Kossek, E. E., & Perrigino, M. B. (2016). Resilience: A review using a grounded integrated occupational approach. *Academy of Management Annals*, 10(1), 729–797. https://doi.org/10.5465/19416520.2016.1159878

Kuroiwa, Y., & Verkuyten, M. (2008). Narratives and the constitution of a common identity: The Karen in Burma. *Identities: Global Studies in Culture and Power*, 15(4), 391–412. https://doi.org/10.1080/10702890802201685

Lengnick-Hall, C. A., & Beck, T. E. (2005). Adaptive fit versus robust transformation: How organisations respond to environmental change. *Journal of Management*, *31*(5), 738–757. https://doi.org/10.1177/0149206305279367

Lengnick-Hall, C. A., Beck, T. E., & Lengnick-Hall, M. L. (2011). Developing a capacity for organisational resilience through strategic human resource management. *Human Resource Management Review*, *21*(3), 243–255. https://doi.org/10.1016/j.hrmr.2010.07.001

Lewis, D. C., & Young, S. S. (2019). Powerful in flight: Cambodian and Karen refugee narratives of strength and resilience. *Migration Letters*, *16*(3), 379–387. https://doi.org/10.33182/ml.v16i3.639

Lewis, J. L. (1924). *The Burmanization of the Karen people: A study in racial adaptability* [Doctoral dissertation, The University of Chicago].

Linnenluecke, M. K. (2015). Resilience in business and management research: A review of influential publications and a research agenda. *International Journal of Management Reviews*, *19*(1), 4–30. https://doi.org/10.1111/ijmr.12076

MacLachlan, H. (2012). Creating pan-Karen identity: The wrist tying ceremony in the United States. *Asian and Pacific Migration Journal*, *21*(4), 459–482. https://doi.org/10.1177/011719681202100402

Maguire, B., & Hagan, P. (2007). Disasters and communities: Understanding social resilience. *Australian Journal of Emergency Management*, *22*(2), 16–20.

Mang, P. Z. (2016). The Karen and the politics of conversion. *Church History and Religious Culture*, *96*(3), 325–345. https://doi.org/10.1163/18712428-09603001

Moonieinda, V. (2011). *The Karen people: Culture, faith and history*. The Karen Buddhist Dhamma Dhutta Foundation. www.karen.org.au/karen_people.htm

Myanmar Peace Monitor. (2019a). *Karen national union/Karen liberation army (peace council) KNU/KNLA PC (KPC)*. Myanmar Peace Monitor. www.mmpeacemonitor.org/1568/kpc/

Myanmar Peace Monitor. (2019b). *Border guard force scheme*. Myanmar Peace Monitor. www.mmpeacemonitor.org/border-guard-force-scheme

Neiman, A., Soh, E., & Sutan, P. (2008). *Karen's cultural profile*. http://ethnomed.org/culture/karen

Norris, F. H., Stevens, S. P., Pfefferbaum, B., Wyche, K. F., & Pfefferbaum, R. L. (2008). Community resilience as a metaphor, theory, set of capacities, and strategy for disaster readiness. *American Journal of Community Psychology*, *41*(1–2), 127–150. https://doi.org/10.1007/s10464-007-9156-6

Ortiz-de-Mandojana, N., & Bansal, P. (2016). The long - term benefits of organisational resilience through sustainable business practices. *Strategic Management Journal*, *37*(8), 1615–1631. www.jstor.org/stable/43898026

Patel, S. S., Rogers, M. B., Amlôt, R., & Rubin, G. J. (2017). What do we mean by "community resilience"? A systematic literature review of how it is defined in the literature. *PLoS Currents*, *9*.

Paul, A. L. (2018). *With the Salween peace park, we can survive as a nation: Karen environmental relations and the politics of an indigenous conservation initiative* [Master's thesis, York University].

Petry, J. L. (1993). *The sword of the spirit: Christians, Karens, colonialists, and the creation of a nation of Burma* [Doctoral dissertation, Rice University].

Platz, R. (2003). Buddhism and Christianity in competition? Religious and ethnic identity in Karen communities of northern Thailand. *Journal of Southeast Asian Studies*, *34*(3), 473–490. https://doi.org/10.1017/S0022463403000432

Po, S. C. (1928). *Burma and the Karens*. Elliot Stock.

Powley, E. H. (2009). Reclaiming resilience and safety: Resilience activation in the critical period of crisis. *Human Relations*, 62(9), 1289–1326. https://doi.org/10.1177/0018726709334881

Rajah, A. (2002). A nation of intention Burma: Karen ethno-nationalism, nationalism and narrations of nation. *The Pacific Review*, 15(4), 517–537. https://doi.org/10.1080/0951274021000029413

Rajah, A. (2008). *Remaining Karen: A study of cultural reproduction and the maintenance of identity*. ANU E Press.

Rangkla, P. (2014). Karen ethno-nationalism and the wrist-tying ceremony along the Thai – Burmese border. *Journal of Southeast Asian Studies*, 45(1), 74–89. https://doi.org/10.1017/S002246341300060X

Rao, H., & Greve, H. R. (2018). Disasters and community resilience: Spanish flu and the formation of retail cooperatives in Norway. *Academy of Management Journal*, 61(1), 5–25. https://doi.org/10.5465/amj.2016.0054

Richthammer, M. K. (2020). Buddhist and animist non-state authority in a legal plural setting in Karen State. In H. M. Kyed (Ed.), *Everyday justice in Myanmar* (pp. 137–161). NIAS Press.

Santasombat, Y. (2004). Karen cultural capital and the political economy of symbolic power. *Asian Ethnicity*, 5(1), 105–120. https://doi.org/10.1080/1463136032000168925

South, A. (2007). Karen nationalist communities: The "problem" of diversity. *Contemporary Southeast Asia*, 29(1), 55–76.

Steenhuisen, B. (2020). *Karen perceptions of the forest – and its potential for future conservation* [Master's thesis, Wageningen University and Research].

Sutcliffe, K. M., & Vogus, T. J. (2003). Organising for resilience. In K. Cameron, J. E. Dutton, & R. E. Quinn (Eds.), *Positive organizational scholarship* (pp. 94–110). Berrett-Koehler.

Swancutt, K. A. (2019). Animism. In *The Cambridge encyclopedia of anthropology* (pp. 1–17). Cambridge University Press.

Thansrithong, B., & Buadaeng, K. (2017). Refugee camps on the Thailand-Myanmar border: Potential places for expanding connections among Karen Baptists. *ASR: CMU Journal of Social Sciences and Humanities*, 4(2), 89–109. https://doi.org/10.12982/CMUJASR.2017.0006

Thawnghmung, A. M. (2011). *The "other" Karen in Myanmar: Ethnic minorities and the struggle without arms*. Lexington Books.

Trakansuphakorn, P. (2008). Space of resistance and place of local knowledge in Karen ecological movement of Northern Thailand: The case of Pgaz K'Nyau villages in Mae Lan Kham River Basin. *Japanese Journal of Southeast Asian Studies*, 45(4), 586–614. https://doi.org/10.20495/tak.45.4_586

Walker, B., Holling, C. S., Carpenter, S. R., & Kinzig, A. (2004). Resilience, adaptability and transformability in social-ecological systems. *Ecology and Society*, 9(2), 5–14. www.ecologyandsociety.org/vol9/iss2/art5/

Williams, T. A., Gruber, D. A., Sutcliffe, K. M., Shepherd, D. A., & Zhao, E. Y. (2017). Organisational response to adversity: Fusing crisis management and resilience research streams. *Academy of Management Annals*, 11(2), 733–769. https://doi.org/10.5465/annals.2015.0134

6 Disability, inclusion, and Gross National Happiness
The complex case of Bhutan

Seyda Subasi Singh and Matthew J. Schuelka

Introduction

Bhutan is a small country of about 800,000 residents, tucked in the Himalayas between China and India. While rich in culture and community, this constitutional monarchy is also identified as one of the least developed countries by the United Nations (2017) and has a mainly agrarian economy. *Drukpa Kagyu* [Mahāyāna] Buddhism is the state religion of Bhutan, but it is a diverse country that allows freedom of religion (Preece et al., 2022). Gross National Happiness (GNH) shapes most of the reforms in the country. It targets transparency in governance, cultural and environmental preservation, economic equity, and the nation's general well-being (Walcott, 2011). Since the first 5-year plan in 1959, and with a commitment to GNH since the 1970s that shapes its development philosophy, Bhutan has gone through a modernisation process in the school system, which was an aspect of a more comprehensive transformation and modernisation process of the entire country (Schuelka, 2012). In essence, Bhutan built its secular 'modern' school system entirely in the last 60 years. It now has nearly 200,000 students – a quarter of the Bhutanese population (Ministry of Education, 2022).

In this chapter, we describe the understanding of disability through the lens of Buddhism in Bhutan and later discuss the political and public response to the newly and rapidly introduced 'Westernised' educational goals of inclusiveness. Bhutan relies on four pillars of GNH, which are good governance, sustainable socio-economic development, cultural preservations, and environmental conversation; education holds an essential role in the success of these pillars. Nevertheless, education is open to the shaping effect of dominant beliefs and culture in the country where Buddhism and Buddhist philosophy play a rudimentary role in daily life and in more structural layers of policy and governance. Transcending the classical tension between economic and human development parameters suggested by the West and its cultural conservation philosophy, Bhutan targets educational improvement at all levels, and including students with disabilities in the school system is one of the goals, which is also promoted at the international level. Although attending to the needs of students with disabilities and developing inclusive

DOI: 10.4324/9781003358879-6

school systems is relatively new in the country, including students with 'special needs' is already accepted as a critical educational ideal (Ministry of Education, 2012). In line with the current efforts, since the movement toward 'modern' education in the 1960s, Bhutan has declared its readiness to follow the latest guidelines, such as Education for All and the Sustainable Development Goals.

After adopting the modernisation of its education system, Bhutan has gone through a (re)defining process of educational policies. Several policy documents have been developed, and strategies have been formulated. Moving from the traditional education system introduced flexible and modern academic curricula (Subba et al., 2019). In theory, the context of the education system has been localised, and community participation has been encouraged, which promoted an educational programme that offers culturally and socially appropriate content (Chhoeda, 2007). According to Denman and Singye Namgyel (2008), the long way Bhutan has come has brought together the academic necessities of modern education and traditional values promoted by the monastic educational system. However, the experience in practice is that Bhutan's educational curriculum still needs to be centralised, secular, inflexible, and not culturally relevant or locally driven (Schuelka et al., 2019; Schuelka & Kezang Sherab, 2022).

As in other areas of the education sector, education for children with disabilities has gone through modernisation. Bhutan has put much effort into keeping up with international developments for a more inclusive schooling and education system. The steps taken to implement the international trends are mainly guided by Sustainable Development Goals (Kamenopoulou & Dawa Dukpa, 2018). However, implementing inclusive policies and strategic planning is vulnerable to the ethos of schools, support systems, and public acceptance (Graham & Slee, 2008). Hence, examining studies that hint at the public acceptance of inclusive education is essential. A study of 575 households in Bhutan has shown that attitudes towards children with disabilities present a high level of homogeneity and are shaped by 'the paternalistic assumptions of incapacity and dependence' (Preece et al., 2022, p. 46). Whereas low vision or poor hearing are not considered disabilities, severe disabilities' connection to *karma* and their effect on what children with severe disabilities can achieve play an essential role in the attitudes toward including children with disabilities in education. These public attitudes are accompanied by a lack of specialised teachers and inadequate resources in the country (Subba et al., 2019). According to a study conducted with teachers by Kamenopoulou and Dawa Dukpa (2018), there needs to be a holistic understanding of inclusion, and the medical model perspective is predominant among teachers. Furthermore, the willingness for parental involvement in special education needs and inclusive education is found to be very low (Preece et al., 2022). The disability models and concepts introduced by the Western understanding seem to penetrate the policy documents in the country quicker than at the public level.

In our discussion of inclusive education, we explicitly discuss disability inclusion in this chapter. However, we acknowledge that 'inclusive' education should be a broader term to describe education's access, quality, and utility for *all* children in the same educational spaces. We will also note in this chapter that 'disability' is socio-culturally constructed and, in many ways, produced by the act of schooling itself (Schuelka, 2018). The categorisation of 'disability' in Bhutan can be fluid and shift from societal institution to institution and even within institutions themselves. As such, we are defining 'disability' in the Bhutanese context as any characteristic of an individual teen as socially marginalising or divergent from the homogeneity enforced by school pedagogy and curriculum.

Buddhist conceptualisation of disability in Bhutan

Buddhism does not have a central text like the Abrahamic religions, and its meanings and practices are interpreted widely in different regions of Asia. In Bhutan, Buddhism is primarily of Tibetan origin, which includes the *Mahāyāna* branch of Buddhism and incorporates many elements of *vajrayāna*, or Tantric Buddhism. This form of Buddhism, especially in Bhutan, has also borrowed many beliefs and spiritual practices – called *Bön* – that predate the spread of Buddhism in the Himalayas. As a result of this syncretic historical development and the complex nature of human thought and belief, the Buddhist conceptualisation of 'disability' in Bhutan is also complex and full of paradoxes.

One of the central beliefs in Bhutanese Buddhism is *karma*, or the birth and rebirth of all sentient beings through *samsāra*, cycles of life and death until the being is liberated from suffering and attachment, *nirvāna*. The concept of karma plays a significant role in the Buddhist conceptualisation of 'disability' in that the presence of a 'disability' is thought to have been caused by misdeeds or transgressions in a previous life (Kamenopoulou & Dawa Dukpa, 2018; Schuelka, 2015). This causes mistrust and stigma towards the individual with a disability. There are also many instances in Bhutanese Buddhist belief and practice in which an individual, not deemed 'pure' or 'whole', is viewed as ineligible from practising *dharma*, or the 'right way of living' (Schuelka, 2015).

Bhutanese Buddhism also offers significant beliefs and opportunities to practise compassion – *karunā*, another central tenet of *Mahāyāna* Buddhism – and embrace all sentient beings' interconnectedness. There are also complex beliefs and understandings around notions of 'pity' and 'suffering' towards a person with a disability in Bhutan, like the complexities found in other culturally-Buddhist countries such as Thailand (Naemiratch & Manderson, 2009) and Myanmar (Ware & Schuelka, 2019). These beliefs motivate a more applied social justice approach towards conceptualising 'disability' in Bhutan – sometimes as an act of charity and as a basis to construct a vision of equity and justice via a Gross National Happiness-based society.

Disability, education, and Gross National Happiness

Gross National Happiness (GNH) is a holistic approach to identifying the progress toward sustainable development. The concept calls for attention to economic aspects of well-being and multiple domains of well-being. The Gross National Happiness Index uses 33 indicators categorised under nine domains using a multidimensional methodology. The four pillars of GNH are good governance, sustainable socio-economic development, cultural preservation, and environmental conversation. These pillars are classified into nine domains: ecological diversity, psychological well-being, health, good governance, education, time use, cultural diversity and resilience, community vitality, resilience, and living standards. The term 'well-being' holds a significant meaning for the GNH concept; it refers to fulfilling a good life in line with the values and principles spread on the pillars of GNH. The GNH Index, therefore, was developed by the Centre for Bhutan Studies with the help of Oxford University researchers as a measurement tool that includes traditional and non-traditional aspects in 2011. The index does not rank 'happiness' as a subjective and individualistic psychological concept, but rather it concentrates on the community's general well-being (Karma Ura et al., 2012a).

The declaration of GNH as the guiding developmental and governance philosophy by the 4th *Druk Gyalpo* [King] of Bhutan, Jigme Singye Wangchuck, 1972, was an invitation to all countries to pay attention to non-economic aspects of well-being. When Bhutan embraced democracy as a constitutional monarchy in 2007, ensuring the nation's general well-being became a vital part of the constitution, and the commitment to GNH was declared by Article 9 in the constitution. Since then, it has substantially affected Bhutan's social and economic policy, and its impact has crossed the county's borders. When the Bhutanese prime minister introduced the concept of GNH during a United Nations forum in 1998, the concept captured the attention of many. The General Assembly of the United Nations on 19 July 2011 invited national governments to give more importance to happiness and well-being in determining how to achieve and measure social and economic development. The declaration of World Happiness Day by the United Nations, the UN Conference on Happiness, the World Happiness Summit (WOHASU), and the release of World Happiness Reports show the recognition of happiness as a global concept. The effect of Bhutan in terms of making happiness a human development goal is also appreciated in the UN 'The World Happiness Report', and much of the growing international interest in happiness exists thanks to Bhutan (Helliwell et al., 2022, p. 3).

As a pioneer in making 'happiness' the priority of social and economic policy, Bhutan does not hold a high ranking in the World Happiness Ranking. In the 2016 World Happiness Report, the ranking of the country for the years 2012–2014 was 75 (Helliwell et al., 2015). In the World Happiness Report 2019, Bhutan was ranked the 95th happiest country in the world and second in South Asia after Pakistan, based on the survey data collected in

2015 (Helliwell et al., 2019). Since 2015, no comprehensive survey has been conducted in the country, but the resonance of the unexpected ranking in the World Happiness Reports is still felt. The English-language newspaper *Daily Bhutan* explains this situation as a discrepancy in the methodology to collect data (Daily Bhutan, 2019). The criteria used by the Centre for Bhutan Studies and GNH in 2015 to assess differs from the criteria of the World Happiness Report. If the World Happiness Report had used the criteria used in Bhutan with 2000 Bhutanese, the rank of Bhutan was expected to be 20 (Phuntsok Tashi, 2004). According to the claims, the low happiness score of Bhutan can also be a result of the integration of Gross Domestic Product in the assessment, which refers to the still existing effect of the Western liberal capitalist perspective on happiness in the world (McCarthy, 2018).

As a country that made 'happiness' an essential aspect of sustainable development in the global arena, Bhutan emphasises the positive outcomes of its approach but, on the other hand, is challenged by the pressure of globalisation and modernisation. Some critics believe that the fourth pillar of GNH, economic growth, needs to be addressed, and the increase in consumption levels is overshadowed by the principles such as ecological worldview or cultural heritage (Brooks, 2013).

Gross National Happiness and education in Bhutan

While Buddhist monastic education has existed in Bhutan for over a thousand years (Zangley Dukpa, 2016), 'modern' secular education began as a state-run institution with the first Five-Year Plan in 1959. Today, monastic education is incorporated into the state as one of the three main elements of education: secular, monastic, and non-formal education. According to the constitution, schooling is offered free for children between 6 and 16 years old and facilitated by the Royal Government of Bhutan (RGoB) to reach gender parity (Ministry of Education, 2014). Recently, the RGoB announced that free higher secondary schooling (ages 16–18) would be expanded to all eligible students (Phurpa Lhamo, 2022). Of course, students' eligibility is predicated on successful results from the Bhutan Certificate of Secondary Education (BCSE) exam. Whilst schooling in Bhutan is available for free, it is not mandated, and many students drop out at various stages because of exam failure and grade repetition (Schuelka, 2018).

The ambition to become a 'happy' State increases practices by which the State offers happiness by guiding and educating the citizens (Karma Ura et al., 2012b). Such a commitment was stated by the former Prime Minister of Bhutan, Jigmi Y. Thinley: 'happiness is far too important to be left as a purely individual responsibility without the state having a direct role' (Jigmi Y. Thinley, 2007, p. 3). According to GNHG, all citizens in Bhutan should be enjoying their rights in economic, social, political, cultural, and aspects equally. Here the State has an essential role in providing basic human needs, which can be compared to the idea of the Welfare State in the West. As in other areas, GNH informs the educational policy of the government in Bhutan (Powdyel, 2014; Jigmi Y. Thinley, 2016). The Bhutanese legislation and policy highlights ensures access to quality and accessible education policy. As a signatory to the Convention of the Rights of the Child (CRC) since 1990, Bhutan states the commitment to education for all in the Bhutanese Constitution as well (2008, p. 19):

> The State shall endeavour to provide education to improve and increase the knowledge, values, and skills of the entire population, with education being directed towards the full development of the human personally.

The commitment to ensuring access to education for all in Bhutan aligns with the emphasis that Bhutan puts on human rights (Kamenopoulou & Dawa Dukpa, 2018). The unique concept of GNH, which is central to several national strategies, calls for an education system that is available and inclusive to all. According to the GNH philosophy, the State must educate citizens to achieve its goal. Strategies and policies have been developed to do this, and strategies for schools, principals, and teachers have been defined (Lund & Chemi, 2015). Jigmi Y. Thinley (2009, p. 216) explains the necessity of abiding by the GNH principles in education by referring to the target of the Bhutanese education system:

> Graduates who are genuine human beings realising their full and true potential, caring for others – including other species, ecologically literate, contemplative as well as analytical in their understanding of the world, free of greed and without excessive desires – knowing, understanding, and appreciating entirely that they are not separate from the natural world and others.
>
> (Jigmi Y. Thinley 2009, p. 214)

To eliminate the threat of materialism, the infusion of GNH in education and the school system was valued by all in Bhutan. Education has become vital to achieving national happiness, creating social cohesion and integration, and establishing a distinctive Bhutanese identity (Lund & Chemi, 2015). As highlighted by GNH, the holistic education approach has been adopted, and the education domain includes four indicators: literacy, educational qualifications, knowledge, and values.

Disability, inclusion, and Gross National Happiness

The philosophy of GNH can be inferred to have direct meaning for persons with disabilities. For example, GNH supports a capability approach toward allowing citizens to realise their full capability and freedom (Pema Tshomo, 2016). Elements of GNH such as education, health (which explicitly mentions 'disability' as an indicator), psychological well-being, living standards, and community vitality are all related – and interrelated – to an understanding of 'disability' in society. However, these GNH indicators can only reflect what currently exists as a snapshot and is not necessarily prescriptive or applicable.

Beyond 'disability' alone, GNH also affects the understanding of inclusive education in Bhutan. As argued earlier, education for GNH is a holistic education endeavour that promotes a more eco-systemic view of the children. Schuelka (2015, 2018) found in his ethnographic fieldwork in Bhutan that students, parents, and students all believed that children with disabilities should be cared for and educated because of Bhutanese and GNH societal values. What this care and education looked like in practice was much more varied, but the relationship to GNH was undoubtedly present. GNH and inclusive education are also complicated by a complex system of education that needs to be aligned in terms of inclusive values (Schuelka & Kezang Sherab, 2022).

On the one hand, GNH, education, and inclusion are socio-culturally compatible. On the other hand, the pedagogy and curriculum in the school system promote competition, failure, rigidity, fixed knowledge, and homogeneity, above all else. In other studies on GNH, Buddhism, and inclusive education, Dawa Dukpa et al. (2022) and Rinchen Dorji et al. (2019) found that teachers in Bhutan believed that the values of 'acceptance', 'helping', 'harmony', and 'compassion' synonymous with GNH and inclusive education as a single concept. As Dawa Dukpa et al. (2022, p. 307) conclude

> Our findings on the connections between GNH, Buddhism, and inclusive education reveal that GNH – informed policies and initiatives support inclusive education. Therefore, the government should continue prioritising GNH education in schools, emphasising the conceptual links between the GNH approach and inclusive values.

Again, there is no disconnect between conceptualising inclusive education, disability, and GNH. However, there needs to be more alignment between various elements of the school system when it realises inclusive values (Schuelka & Kezang Sherab, 2022). As other Bhutanese researchers have also found (Dawa Dukpa et al., 2022; Rinchen Dorji et al., 2019), teachers want to espouse GNH values in their classrooms but are stymied by an education system that has historically and culturally been pulled into a more exclusive and segregated direction. In the next section, we will explore this further.

Implementing inclusive education in Bhutan: from theory to practice

Upon the declaration of the Salamanca Statement in 1994, many countries have changed their perspectives toward special education and committed to shift to inclusive education. The aim has been to make quality education accessible to all children, including the most marginalised groups such as students with disabilities, students from migrant backgrounds, female students, or students in rural areas. Inclusive education eases the direct participation of persons with disabilities who face other disadvantages in education, training, and employment/self-employment opportunities. This international shift from special needs education to inclusive education could also be observed in Bhutan. In the following sections, we discuss how special needs education and the shift to inclusive education have occurred at the policy and practice levels.

Developments at the policy level

In line with the philosophy of GNH, Bhutanese legislation and policy ensure the commitment to improving the health, education, and welfare of all, including children with disabilities. Bhutan followed the international efforts to include children with disabilities in the education system by signing the Convention on the Rights of People with Disabilities (CRPD) in 2010. However, Bhutan is now one of the few countries left to ratify the CRPD. Two years later, and through other efforts at the national level, Bhutan developed a Draft National Policy on Special Educational Needs for a more caring, inclusive, and enabling society in 2012. Moreover, the Ministry of Education set up a separate division in 2011 for Special Education Needs that supports 12 pilot schools in their endeavour to accommodate children with disabilities (Ministry of Education, 2012). The number of 'SEN Schools' is now over 20. The Child Care and Protection Act (Parliament of the Kingdom of Bhutan, 2011) and the Draft National Policy on Special Educational Needs (Ministry of Education, 2012) served as a framework for conceptualising inclusive education in Bhutan. However, these are not official policies, and as of this chapter, no official legislation enshrining inclusive education into law has been enacted.

As a part of the national agenda of ensuring universal access to education, in recent years, Bhutan has experienced this shift toward a more inclusive education perspective by introducing a new concept of schools for students with special needs and by launching the Standards for Inclusive Education in 2017. The Standards for Inclusive Education to support schools in Bhutan towards becoming more inclusive for all children were developed with several national and international organisations (Ministry of Education, 2017). The aim of these standards (Ministry of Education, 2017, p. 3) is explained as

> The Standards for Inclusive Education is a tool to support schools in Bhutan towards becoming more inclusive for all children. The standards aim to guide schools in reflection, planning and actions. Schools with SEN programmes will initially use this tool with SEN programs, but it is available for all schools in Bhutan to use as a guideline for

school improvement and development. Inclusive education is everyone's responsibility and is the best means to ensure education for all children in Bhutan.

Following the launch of the standard, the collaboration between the Ministry of Education Division for Early Childhood Care and Development & Special Education Needs and Save the Children created the 'Ten-Year Roadmap for Inclusive and Special Education in Bhutan'. This roadmap aims 'to understand and bridge the current gaps identified in the service delivery of inclusive and special education. The gaps identified are categorised into four main areas – cross-cutting or organisational gaps, gaps specifically in providing early interventions, school-based education and the transition into post-school life for children with disabilities' (Ministry of Education, 2019).

The initiative of the Bhutanese Ministry of Education to standardise education principles with inclusiveness (National Standards for Inclusive Education), the 'Ten-Year-Roadmap for Inclusive and Special Education in Bhutan', and the support of the Royal Government through a Royal Decree and the National Policy for Persons with Disabilities (GNH Secretariat, 2019) show the support for this endeavour at the governmental level. Several other policy documents, as Rinchen Dorji and Schuelka explain (2016), refer to the commitment to inclusion as a component of the Bhutanese education system. The efforts and the achievements of the Bhutanese Government are summarised in the Ten-Year-Roadmap (Ministry of Education, 2019, p. 4) as follows:

> There have been several achievements towards improving inclusive and special education in Bhutan recently, which have influenced the direction of this roadmap. The Standards for Inclusive Education provide schools with guidelines on improving the inclusive culture, policy and practices at the school level. In contrast, the Guidelines on Assessment, Examination, Promotion and Transition for Children with Disabilities have strengthened the education system's ability to support students' individual needs. The reviewed Teachers' Handbook for Disaster Risk Management and Planning demonstrates the awareness of the Ministry of Education that children with disabilities must be considered in all aspects of school life.

The Royal *Kasho* [Decree] on Education Reform granted in 2020 decrees that a time-bound Council for Education Reform will prepare a visionary and workable roadmap for the 21st century to support the Royal Government of Bhutan. The Bhutanese Ministry of Education's initiation to develop this new national education policy, the '21st Century Education Roadmap' (Ministry of Education, 2021), is another hint of the intention to make inclusive education a key component of Bhutanese education.

Attitudes at the school level

Participation in inclusive education has gained momentum in Bhutan in the last decade. As Subba et al. (2019) discuss, some progress has been recorded in schools in their journey to be more inclusive. School is still viewed as a place for competition, elitism, and discipline. However, at the same time, the school's role has been changing due to new discourses such as capital development, inclusion, and globalisation (Schuelka et al., 2019). The number of students with disabilities has grown in number at schools (Rinchen Dorji, 2015), and the profile of students has become more diverse (Karma Jigyel et al., 2018; Rinchen Dorji & Schuelka 2016).

On the other hand, the pilot project Child-Friendly School Initiative of the Ministry of Education promoted inclusiveness as one of its five aspects (Kamenopoulou & Dawa Dukpa, 2018). As of 2019, 16 public schools are designated as 'Special Educational Needs' schools (Rinchen Dorji et al., 2019), and this number has now grown to 22 with more planned. In practice, this is at least one 'SEN school' in every *Dzongkhag* [district], but this also means that all the inclusion and special educational needs resources are *only* at one school in a district, and children with disabilities living in remote regions do not have access to these schools. On the other hand, most of the teachers working in these schools are under-trained and under-supported (Schuelka, 2013). Hence, the success of inclusive education in Bhutan is discussed mainly within the discourse of teacher preparation. Preparing schools for the inclusion of all children from various backgrounds (e.g. disability, learning difficulties, gender, poverty, rural areas, and ethnicity) cannot take place without quality teaching and teacher training. Therefore, teacher education is expected to develop their capacities to cultivate the required teacher force for new educational standards. The lack of teacher preparation at the pre-service and in-service levels in Bhutan is well-documented and is aggravated by the lack of resources (Karma Jigyel et al., 2021; Rinchen Dorji, 2017).

The emphasis on the need for inclusive learning and teaching structures – curriculum, materials, teacher education, and assessment – has become more visible through newly made policies and declarations. Like national standards, the Royal *Kasho* calls for improvement in teacher education and teacher education structures at the tertiary level. In addition, the Standards for Inclusive Education (Ministry of Education, 2017) emphasise the need for professional development to ensure that all teachers can respond to diversity and call for a structural change in teacher preparation. Therefore, teacher preparation and attitudes of teachers remain central issues in Bhutan (Rinchen Dorji et al., 2019).

However, the research that tackles these issues is limited and stays at a minimum level. The study by Rinchen Dorji and his colleagues (2019) revealed that teachers have mainly positive attitudes towards inclusive education and support, including children with special education needs in mainstream schools. These findings are attributed to the altruism and compassion that the

Bhutanese share. The Buddhist belief in *karma* is discussed as the reason for the unconditional feelings of compassion and empathetic behaviour among the Bhutanese. However, the positive attitudes of teachers and acceptance of inclusive education as doing a good deed contradict the persistent bullying at the schools. A report by UNICEF (2021) highlights the increasing marginalisation and discrimination against children with disabilities in Bhutan. Bullying and lack of academic learning exist in the school environment, and children with disabilities are confronted with adverse behavioural problems.

Similarly, several studies and reports point to more understanding of inclusiveness among other teaching staff, school principals, and parents (Karma Jigyel et al., 2018; Schuelka et al., 2019). The media report on negative attitudes towards people with disabilities across Bhutanese society is another non-empirical document contradicting the supportive attitude of the general public towards people with disabilities (Bhutan Broadcasting Service Corporation, 2016). Similarly, the study of Schuelka and his colleagues (2019) demonstrated that inclusivity is a new concept for the Bhutanese education system, and teachers associate inclusivity with low academic achievers or children with disabilities. Furthermore, the same study showed that efforts to promote social inclusivity at the school level are bound to the individual initiation of teachers and school principals and not governmental policy.

Attitudes of parents

Parental involvement has been identified as a challenge for inclusive education and all Bhutanese schools. Bhutanese parents are fond of their children's education, especially in rural areas (Karma Jigyel et al., 2018). This reluctance can be attributed to the belief of parents that teachers know the best, and parents may hesitate that they are knowledgeable enough to be involved (UNICEF, 2014). The same UNICEF report (2014) also discusses the unwillingness for parental involvement can be because of gratefulness to teachers, and parents may not be willing to seem ungrateful. On the other hand, communication between the schools and parents is not at the required level. Communication occurs mainly as one-way communication where the schools inform parents about what to do. This is explained by the novelty of inclusive education in the country (Rinchen Dorji, 2015) and the lack of trained human resources and teachers who can achieve fruitful two-way communication between parents and schools (Kamenopoulou & Dawa Dukpa, 2018).

With the understanding that education can be successful only through a partnership between stakeholders (Epstein, 2010), there have been several studies to reach the attitudes of parents toward inclusive education, special needs education, and the pilot programs for special education needs in Bhutan. As the number of students with disabilities increases in schools and more specially designated programmes, the research investigates parental experiences. Including children with special education needs in pilot programs designed for special education needs is welcomed among parents. Parents are content with the physical support their children get in these schools, and they find the school environment very supportive (Karma Jigyel et al., 2018).

In their study, Karma Jigyel and his colleagues (2021) researched the expectations of parents with children with disabilities. Three key areas emerged. Firstly, parents highlighted the problem of school resources to support their children's learning. The need for resources forms an intransigent challenge for the Bhutanese context. Secondly, both physical facilities and human resources at schools are concerns for the parents. Parents' expectations focus on inclusive education facilities in terms of developing the social skills of children with disabilities for an independent future. Thirdly, parents wish their children to benefit from the social skills and speech development offered by the special needs education programs so that they can have an independent future and secure employment.

Concluding remarks

Responding to the diverse needs of diverse students is a crucial component of achieving an inclusive society. Hence, education systems should be able to cater to diverse needs. Achieving an inclusive education system is a process that embeds valuing diversity, providing support, accessibility, and equal opportunity for achieving one's full potential (Subba et al., 2019). With the steps taken, Bhutan shows that the country understands inclusive education is required for an inclusive society, social participation, and GNH. At the nexus of adopting the modern way of education, responding to international initiatives for inclusion, and preserving socio-cultural values, Bhutan has issued several documents and policy papers accompanied by standards, roadmaps, strategies, and plans concerning inclusive education and special needs education. However, the commitment to a more inclusive education system is accompanied by challenges to its implementation. The gap between the development of policies and implementation remains intact (Kamenopoulou & Dawa Dukpa, 2018). The Bhutan Education Blueprint 2014–2024 (Ministry of Education, 2014) points to some challenges in implementing inclusive education. The causes of the challenges are mainly the need for more adequate resources, support services, and expertise. The UNICEF-Bhutan Report from 2021 points similarly to an increase in gender inequality, dropouts, and bias against boys in the country (UNICEF, 2021). As Preece et al. (2022) discuss, those who need to implement policies and bring change are mainly left behind, and there is a general lack of understanding of disability, inclusion, and appropriate support systems. As discussed previously, the positive attitudes to people with disabilities are mainly attributed to the empathetic behaviour and compassion that Bhutanese people show; however, there are contradictions at the practice level where people with disabilities are still marginalised. Apart from the challenges at the practice level, another challenge discussed by Karma Jigyel and his colleagues (2018) is the concept of borrowed policies. The policies borrowed from other countries with a different socio-cultural context than Bhutan require a smooth transition and contextualisation. Among all the developments at the policy level, the country still faces challenges at the teacher preparation, school, and parental involvement levels.

While Bhutan faces significant gaps between aspirational policy and actual practice when it comes to inclusive education – as do most countries across the Global North and Global South – what Bhutan can teach the rest of the world is how inclusive education can represent an extension of both Buddhism and of Gross National Happiness. Some aspects of Buddhism negatively conceptualise 'disability', such as *karma* and the emphasis on body and mind purity to receive the *dharma*. However, Buddhism also features many positive conceptualisations, such as *karuna* [compassion] and a more complex understanding of pity and suffering that transcends the absolutist Westernnotion of these terms. As Shogo (2015) highlights, *karuna* is imperfectly translated into English and can mean simultaneously suffering. Shogo also astutely reminds us that 'compassion' means 'with passion', pointing out the original Latin meaning of the word 'passion': the suffering of pain. One of the central pillars of Buddhism is that all sentient beings 'suffer', and so it is in that way that we can think of a person with a disability as being on a continuum on which we all suffer. This is not dissimilar to prevailing disability theory, which also presents the notion of disability as a continuum of ability seen in education, health care, and even in disability re-conceptualisation in statistics as a matter of functional capability. In other words, Western philosophies of mind and body only return to more ancient notions of the interconnected dialectic of dis/ability that Buddhist philosophy has espoused for thousands of years.

In practice, the development philosophy of GNH continues Buddhist philosophical traditions not just in terms of disability and inclusion but also in thinking about happiness not as an individual heuristic but as an interconnected community endeavour in which all sentient beings must be considered. In Dzongkha, the Bhutanese national language, GNH is expressed as *Gyalyong Gakid Pelzom* ['happiness and peace for all nations for the realisation of all things good and virtuous']. This understanding is far removed from Western notions of happiness such as 'life, liberty, and the pursuit of happiness' – a line from the United States Constitution with an explicitly individualistic meaning. What Bhutan can teach us all is that a development philosophy rooted in GNH, with its meaning of 'happiness' rooted in the Buddhist understanding of interconnected communities and beings, that disability inclusion is not an 'extra' or 'add-on' or 'in addition to' proposition, but rather a moot point because we are all *inter*connected at the very core of existence. To make matters even more poignant, Buddhists also believe in *anātman*, or 'non-self', and argue that there is no such thing as permanent existence or static forms of essence. GNH, rooted in this notion as well, offers up a unique possibility to conceptualise 'disability' in terms of a continuum of ability interconnected with the collective suffering of the community, as well as a belief that any perceived state of 'being disabled' is an illusion within the actual reality of impermanence.

The possibilities of reconceptualising disability inclusion through Buddhism and GNH do not belie the current realities of exclusion and marginalisation of persons with disabilities in Bhutan or elsewhere. Bhutan is a land of contradictions and paradoxes when it realises happiness. However, Buddhism and GNH demonstrate that realising happiness and accurate continual attainment process involving attainment that involves numerous life cycles [*samsāra*]. Gross National Happiness is a call to action to think about humanity beyond capitalistic terms, beyond *dis*ability, and towards a more inclusive and sustainable future.

References

Bhutan Broadcasting Service Corporation Ltd. (2016). *ABS conducts grassroots level awareness on disability*. Accessed December 27. http://www.bbs.bt/news/?p=65067

Brooks, J. S. (2013). Avoiding the limits to growth: Gross national happiness in Bhutan as a model for sustainable development. *Sustainability, 5*, 3640–3664.

Chhoeda, T. (2007). Schooling in Bhutan. In A. Gupta (Ed.) *Going to school in South Asia*, pp.53–65. Greenwood Press.

Daily Bhutan. (2019). *Known as The Kingdom of Happiness, why is Bhutan ranked 95th in the World Happiness Report 2019?* Retrieved from https://www.dailybhutan.com/article/known-as-the-kingdom-of-happiness-why-is-bhutan-ranked-95th-in-the-world-happiness-report-2019

Dawa Dukpa, Carrington, S., Mavropoulou, S. & Schuelka, M. J. (2022). Exploring the congruence between Bhutanese teachers' views about inclusion, Gross National Happiness, and Buddhism. In M. J. Schuelka & S. Carrington (Eds.), *Global directions in inclusive education: Conceputalizations, practices, and methodologies for the 21st century* (pp. 293–311). Routledge.

Denman, B. D. & Singye Namgyel. (2008). Convergence of monastic and modern education in Bhutan? *International Review of Education, 54*(3), 475–491.

Epstein, J. L. (2010). School/Family/Community Partnerships: Caring for the children we share. *Phi Delta Kappan, 92*(3), 81–96.

Graham, L., & Slee, R. (2008). An illusory interiority: Interrogating the discourses of inclusion. *Educational Philosophy and Theory, 40*(2), 277-293.

Gross National Happiness Commission Secretariat. (2018). *National policy for persons with disabilities. Final Draft – May 2019*. https://www.gnhc.gov.bt/en/wp-content/uploads/2019/06/1.-Final-Draft_NPPWD_May_2019.pdf

Helliwell, J. F., Layard, R. & Sachs, J. D. (2015). *World Happiness Report 2015*. https://s3.amazonaws.com/happiness-report/2015/WHR15_Sep15.pdf

Helliwell, J. F., Layard, R. & Sachs, J. D. (2019). *World Happiness Report 2019*. https://s3.amazonaws.com/happiness-report/2019/WHR19.pdf

Helliwell, J. F., Layard, R. Sachs, J. D., De Neve, J., Aknin, L. B., & Wang, S. (2022). *World Happiness Report 2022*. https://happiness-report.s3.amazonaws.com/2022/WHR+22.pdf

Jigmi Y. Thinley. (2007). What is Gross National Happiness? In the centre for Bhutan studies, *Rethinking Development*, pp. 3–11. The Centre for Bhutan and GNH Studies. https://www.bhutanstudies.org.bt/rethinking-development/

Jigmi Y. Thinley. (2009). *Educating for gross national happiness workshop*. 7–12 December 2009, Thimphu, Bhutan. Retrieved from http://www.gpiatlantic.org/pdf/educatingforgnh/educating_for_gnh_proceedings.pdf

Kamenopoulou, L. & Dawa Dukpa. (2018). Karma and human rights: Bhutanese teachers' perspectives on inclusion and disability. *International Journal of Inclusive Education*, 22(3), 323–338. https://doi.org/10.1080/13603116.2017.1365274

Karma Jigyel, J. Miller, S. Mavropoulou & J. Berman. (2021). Expectations of parents of children with disabilities in Bhutan inclusive schools. *International Journal of Disability, Development and Education*, https://doi.org/10.1080/1034912X.2020.1869189

Karma Jigyel, J. A. Miller, S. Mavropoulou & J. Berman (2018). Benefits and concerns: parents' perceptions of inclusive schooling for children with special educational needs (SEN) in Bhutan. *International Journal of Inclusive Education, 24(10), 1064–1080*. https://doi.org/10.1080/13603116.2018.1511761

Karma Ura, Alkire, S. & Tshoki Zangmo. (2012). *GNH and GNH Index*. https://ophi.org.uk/wp-content/uploads/GNH_and_GNH_index_2012.pdf

Karma Ura, Alkire, S., Tshoki Zangmo & Karma Wangdi. (2012). *An Extensive analysis of GNH Index*. https://ophi.org.uk/wp-content/uploads/Ura_et_al_Extensive_analysis_of_GNH_index_2012.pdf

Lund, B. & Chemi, T. (2015). *Dealing with Emotions: A pedagogical challenge to innovative learning*. Brill.

McCarthy, J. (2018). *The birthplace of 'Gross National Happiness' is growing a bit cynical*. Retrieved from https://www.npr.org/sections/parallels/2018/02/12/584481047/the-birthplace-of-gross-national-happiness-is-growing-a-bit-cynical?t=1656239148610

Ministry of Education. (2012). *National policy on special educational needs*. Thimphu: Royal Government of Bhutan.

Ministry of Education. (2014*). Bhutan education blueprint, 2014–2024: Rethinking education*. Thimphu: Royal Government of Bhutan.

Ministry of Education. (2017). *Standards for inclusive education*. http://www.education.gov.bt/wp-content/downloads/publications/publication/Standards-for-Inclusive-Education-in-Bhutan.pdf

Ministry of Education. (2019). *Ten-year roadmap for inclusive and special education in Bhutan*. http://www.education.gov.bt/wp-content/uploads/2022/01/Ten-Year-Roadmap.pdf

Ministry of Education. (2021). *Education Roadmap*. http://www.education.gov.bt/?p=8533

Ministry of Education. (2022). *Annual education statistics 2021*. Policy and Planning Division, Ministry of Education, Royal Government of Bhutan. http://www.education.gov.bt/wp-content/uploads/2022/03/AES-2021-Final-Version.pdf

Naemiratch, B. & Manderson, L. (2009). Pity and pragmatism: understandings of disability in northeast Thailand. *Disability & Society*, 24(4), 475–88. https://doi.org/10.1080/09687590902879106

Parliament of the Kingdom of Bhutan. (2011). *Child Care and Protection Act*.

Pema Tshomo. (2016). Conditions of happiness: Bhutan's educating for gross national happiness initiative and the capability approach. In M. J. Schuelka & T. W. Maxwell (Eds.), *Education in Bhutan: culture, schooling, and Gross National Happiness* (pp. 139–151). Springer.

Pema Thinley. (2016). Overview and 'heart essence' of the Bhutanese education system. In M. J. Schuelka & T. W. Maxwell (Eds.), *Education in Bhutan: culture, schooling, and Gross National Happiness* (pp. 19–37). Springer.

Phuntsok Tashi. (2004). The role of Buddhism in achieving Gross National Happiness. In Karma Ura & Karma Galay (Eds.), *Gross National Happiness and Development* (pp. 483–495). https://www.bhutanstudies.org.bt/gross-national-happiness-and-development/

Phurpa Lhamo. (2022, 28 April). *Government stops scholarship to private schools this year. Kuensel.* https://kuenselonline.com/government-stops-scholarship-to-private-schools-this-year/

Powdyel, T. S. (2014). *My green school: An outline supporting the Educating for Gross National Happiness initiative.* Kuensel Corporation, Ltd.

Preece, D., Murray, J., Rose, R., Zhao, Y., & Garner, P. (2022). Public knowledge and attitudes regarding children with disabilities, their experience and support in Bhutan: a national survey. *Early Child Development and Care, 192*(1), 36–50. https://doi.org/10.1080/03004430.2020.1730432

Rinchen Dorji. (2015). Exploring disability and inclusive education in the context of Bhutanese education. *Bhutan Journal of Research & Development 4*(1), 1–16.

Rinchen Dorji. (2017). *An Investigation of attitudes and experiences of implementing inclusive education in Bhutan: perspectives of teachers, principals and past students.* Unpublished doctoral thesis, University of New England, Armidale NSW Australia.

Rinchen Dorji, Bailey, J., Paterson, D., Graham, L. & Miller, J. (2019). Bhutanese teachers' attitudes towards inclusive education. *International Journal of Inclusive Education, 25*(5), 545–564. https://doi.org/10.1080/13603116.2018.1563645

Rinchen Dorji & Schuelka, M. J. (2016). Children with disabilities in Bhutan: Transitioning from special needs education to inclusive education. In M. J. Schuelka & T. W. Maxwell (Eds.), *Education in Bhutan: culture, schooling, and Gross National Happiness* (pp. 181–198). Springer.

Schuelka, M. J. (2012). Inclusive education in Bhutan: a small state with alternative priorities. *Current Issues in Comparative Education, 15*(1), 145–156. https://www.tc.columbia.edu/cice/pdf/26007_15_01_Schuelka.pdf

Schuelka, M. J. (2013). Education for youth with disabilities in Bhutan: past, present, and future. *Bhutan Journal of Research & Development Spring 2*, 65–74.

Schuelka, M. J. (2015). The evolving construction and conceptualisation of 'disability' in Bhutan. *Disability & Society, 28*(4), 500–513. https://doi.org/10.1080/09687599.2015.1052043

Schuelka, M. J. (2018). The cultural production of the 'disabled' person: Constructing difference in Bhutanese schools. *Anthropology and Education Quarterly, 49*(2), 183–200. https://doi.org/10.1111/aeq.12244

Schuelka, M. J., Kezang Sherab & Tsering Yangzome Nidup. (2019). Gross National Happiness, British values, and non-cognitive skills: the role and perspective of teachers in Bhutan and England. *Educational Review. 71*(6), 748–766. https://doi.org/10.1080/00131911.2018.1474175

Schuelka, M. J. & Kezang Sherab. (2022). Educational values in complex systems: an introduction to the educational values evaluation and design framework and a case study of inclusivity in Bhutan. *Current Issues in Comparative Education, 24*(1), 114–131. https://doi.org/10.52214/cice.v24i1.8773

Schuelka, M. J., & Maxwell, T. W. (Eds.). (2016). *Education in Bhutan: culture, schooling, and Gross National Happiness.* Springer. https://doi.org/10.1080/09687599.2015.105204

Shogo, W. (2015). Compassion (*Karunā*) and pity (*Anukampā*) in Mahāyāna Sūtras. *Journal of International Philosophy, 4*, 267–272. https://www.toyo.ac.jp/uploaded/attachment/15446.pdf

Subba, A. B., Chokey Yangzom, Karma Dorji, Sangye Choden, Ugyen Namgay, Carrington, S. & Nickerson, J. (2019). Supporting students with disability in schools in Bhutan: perspectives from school principals. *International Journal of Inclusive Education, 23*(1), 42–64. https://doi.org/10.1080/13603116.2018.1514744

The Constitution of the Kingdom of Bhutan. (2008). https://www.nab.gov.bt/assets/templates/images/constitution-of-bhutan-2008.pdf

UNICEF. (2014). *Meeting the educational needs of children with disabilities in South Asia: a gap analysis covering Bhutan and the Maldives.* Kathmandu: UNICEF Regional office of South Asia (ROSA).

UNICEF. (2021). *UNICEF Bhutan Country Office annual report 2021.* https://www.unicef.org/reports/country-regional-divisional-annual-reports-2021/Bhutan

United Nations. (2017). *World population prospects: The 2017 revision.* United Nations Department of Economic and Social Affairs, Population Division.

Walcott, S. M. (2011). One of a kind: Bhutan and the modernity challenge. *National Identities, 13*(3), 253–265. doi: https://doi.org/10.1080/14608944.2011.585633

Ware, H. & Schuelka, M. J. (2019). Constructing 'disability' in Myanmar: Teachers, community stakeholders, and the complexity of disability models. *Disability & Society, 34*(6), 863–884. https://doi.org/10.1080/09687599.2019.1580186

Zangley Dukpa. (2016). The history and development of monastic education in Bhutan. In M. J. Schuelka & T. W. Maxwell (Eds.), *Education in Bhutan: culture, schooling, and Gross National Happiness* (pp. 39–55). Springer.

Authors' note

There is no presence of surnames or family names in Bhutanese names. The naming convention in Bhutan is for an individual to have one or two non-gendered and non-ordered names given to them by a Lama or other community religious official. Therefore, to be culturally appropriate and follow the arguments for referencing and citation of Bhutanese names by Schuelka and Maxwell (2016), we cited them fully and alphabetised by the first letter of their first given name.

7 Philosophical and practical challenges of *Ubuntu*

Application to decolonial activism and conceptions of personhood and disability

Maria Berghs

Introduction

In much of the literature on decolonisation and decolonial thinking, there has been a focus on epistemic violence that can occur when we do not take the ontological and epistemological positions of differing life-worlds (Mignolo, 2011; Mignolo & Escobar, 2013; de Sousa Santos, 2015) seriously. However, Gopal (2021) has argued that we also need to learn from activist histories of anti-colonialism to understand the priorities that would shape decolonialism, which are about more than creating intellectual spaces and diverse freedoms. The priorities of anti-colonial activism were the issues of social justice and freedoms for all (Gopal, 2021), which can set them at odds with the aims of racialised capitalism (Virdee, 2019). However, some of the critical tenants of epistemologies and ontologies from the Global South are the grounds that can elucidate activism and decolonial practice in the present.

In keeping with the idea of rethinking ontological and epistemological positioning (de Sousa Santos, 2015), this chapter focuses on the concept of *Ubuntu*. An explanation of the concept of *Ubuntu* or *Unhu* is a Southern African humanist and ethical worldview. From the Zulu language, it is often translated as 'a person is a person through other persons' and, as such, is both a description of diversity and a normative ethical claim about how we should live. In popular consciousness, people associate *Ubuntu* with South Africa's Truth and Reconciliation Commission (TRC). However, it has been gaining ground in decolonial activism and has a rich African history.

Despite this history, there have been present issues with *Ubuntu*'s philosophical and practical application and its acceptance. This chapter examines why and tries to find an answer for how *Ubuntu* could become part of efforts of activism linked to understanding broader and more diverse conceptions of 'rights' and ecology. Using a case study approach, it examines how decolonial activism has been put into practice on the African continent in the fields of 1) education, 2) justice and rights, 3) disability and 4) climate justice. The chapter is not meant to be exhaustive, but using these four case studies it tries to find a framework of *Ubuntu* that illustrates its practical application

DOI: 10.4324/9781003358879-7

as ethics and what this could teach us about decolonial practices. It begins by defining *Ubuntu* and explaining how it becomes correlated to what restorative justice means.

Ubuntu

Ubuntu means personhood, humanity or humanness, and the concept is often associated with South African history, particularly the nation's TRC after the apartheid era. *Ubuntu* became a part of discourses of transitional and restorative justice in the post-apartheid state due to the theological influence of Archbishop Desmond Tutu. In the TRC, an essential part of restorative justice was the idea of the perpetrator asking the victim for forgiveness to be accepted back into the community to promote collective healing. *Ubuntu*'s humanist philosophy lay at the TRC's foundations, which promoted healing through confrontation with the painful 'truth' of the past. Marx (2002) argues that the idea of 'truth' was not just forensic but also encompassed three differing types of truth – a) personal, b) social and c) healing truth – as part of *Ubuntu* or what it means to be human through others and ensure collective peace. As such, Desmond Tutu personifies the idea of *Ubuntu* as an ethical stance towards others, emphasising interdependence, diversity and forgiveness for peaceful coexistence (Otieno, 2020).

Furthermore, Desmond Tutu illustrates those three ideas of truth (Swanson, 2007), encompassing how the personal becomes part of the social and collective to allow healing. He was an *Ubuntu* in living practice, showing how *Ubuntu* should be understood as a method for praxis. He illustrated a generosity of spirit and humanity bound up with the well-being of others that scholars and popular press have identified as a uniquely African philosophy (Gathogo, 2008).

While *Ubuntu* is associated with South Africa, it is an indigenous African philosophical and religious concept and is found across the African continent:

> It is called *Unhu* among the Shona people of Zimbabwe; *Ubuntu* among the Nguni speakers of Southern Africa; *Utu* among the Swahili speakers of East Africa, and *Umundu* among the Kikuyu of Kenya, among others. It is a philosophical and religious concept that defines individuals' relationships with others.
>
> (Gathogo, 2008, p. 5)

In the Zulu language, *Ubuntu* is expressed as *umuntu ngumuntu ngabantu*, which translates as 'a person is a person through other persons' (Shutte, 1993; Berghs, 2017). A human being can only become human through the diversity and otherness of other human beings (Louw, 1998; Eze, 2008; Berghs, 2017). This entails that it is the acceptance of the diversity of others that allows us to become human. Ewuoso and Hall (2019, p. 96) explain that in the Nguni-Bantu tradition, *'ubu'* means 'potency or an enfolded being', and *'ntu'* means 'being in actuality or unfolded being'; thus, *Ubuntu* is a state of becoming human.

Thus, Van der Merwe (1996) and Metz (2011; 2022) argue that *Ubuntu* is not just a theology or ontology but also a normative claim about how we should live or become human. It means to be concerned with the diversity of what personhood could imply and understand that it is connected to my being human. The concept of personhood in Western cultures is often bounded, individual and teleological in that you are expected to become a person. The idea of personhood in *Ubuntu* is one where a person only becomes a person through a community or the diversity of others. It sees humanness as being interdependent and hospitable to others (Gathogo, 2008).

While a strength of *Ubuntu* has been its association with the TRC and South Africa, that has also been where most discontent has been levered. Criticisms of the TRC have focused on the lack of choice for the individual victims in the function of the collective symbolic good and especially how little was done materially for the population to ensure healing and restorative justice (Fox, 2011). Metz (2011, p. 532) argues that *Ubuntu* has often been neglected for a variety of reasons: firstly, because its conception of what it means to be human is too 'vague' to be able to actualise; secondly, it does not acknowledge the importance of human freedom with its focus on the collective; and thirdly, as a traditional indigenous philosophy, it is not associated with post-industrial and urban societies. Other people have tended to be critical of Africans, noting issues of nationalism, tribalism, the patriarchal nature of society and patrimonial and other forms of corruption (Gathogo, 2008). While such criticisms of the TRC and parts of African societies are justified, answers to criticisms of *Ubuntu* can be found in decolonial activism.

Practical applications decolonial activism

Scholars have argued that instead of focusing on what *Ubuntu* has meant in the past, we must focus on what it could mean in the present (Metz, 2011; Mutanga, 2023). *Ubuntu* has been endorsed as a way to achieve decolonisation in that it embodies an African ontology and normative ethical stance for action. de Sousa Santos (2015) argues that we commit a cognitive injustice if we do not recognise differing ontological and epistemological positions in the Global South. Taking *Ubuntu* seriously in guiding decolonialism illustrates how we *should* be with others as an ethical maxim.

Africans from across the continent have revealed how *Ubuntu* is not about nationalism, tribalism, patriarchy or corruption, but this past and present legacy has often been neglected (Berghs, 2017). Misgivings about *Ubuntu* have tended to focus on how *Ubuntu* has been used and exploited by present-day leaders to ensure political and economic power, how they have implemented it tokenistically and why it has failed, due to issues like patrimonialism. Nevertheless, just as there are many negative examples, there are many positive examples, and we have those Africans who, through their present-day activism, illustrate what the ethics of *Ubuntu* could entail for decolonial practice. In what follows, four examples of decolonial activities using *Ubuntu* from education, justice, disability and environment are presented.

Education

Despite all the emphasis on decolonising the curriculum in the Global North, for instance, in countries like the United States and the United Kingdom, very few of those processes actively engage in rethinking the very ontological and epistemological foundations of the process of decolonisation in what kind of 'person' that the universities should produce (Gopal, 2021). Saini and Begum (2020) note some of the foils of the processes of decolonisation in the academy, in that it does not focus on anti-racist practices, address institutional whiteness nor question the very foundations of the decolonial practices and how they pander to the institutions.

This is because universities have tended to take a 'soft' approach to decolonisation by including scholars and texts from the Global South and questioning the role of colonialism and empire (de Sousa Santos, 2018). Even if they engage in social justice (Gopal, 2021), they have yet to think critically about the ethical norms of decolonisation or what type of student (and, by proxy, knowledge of the world) decolonisation should produce. This would entail taking a 'hard' approach to decolonisation, and such a need for changing not only the neoliberal values of universities but also the forms in which education is delivered can be found in the 'radical' student movements. Examining the South African student protests in 2015's #Feesmustfall movement, where students objected to the raising of university fees, reveals a range of issues linked to understanding *Ubuntu*, such as inequalities in access to education and lack of social and economic transformation for the majority Black population. Griffiths (2019) argues that there were two correlated issues that students were explicitly protesting for – 1) the need to decolonise the higher education system and 2) the rise of fees – but ultimately, implicitly, what they wanted was social transformation through access to university.

In the #Feesmustfall student protests, I argue that you can note the frustration with how the principles of *Ubuntu* as social healing have not been achieved in South African society. The social transformation has been for the elites and not the collective. Taking *Ubuntu* seriously means understanding that it entails 'becoming' human through other human beings through recognition of diversity (Ewuoso & Hall, 2019). Neoliberal universities have not been transformational spaces nor acted and spoken out against the government, ruling classes and those in power to ensure a better life for their fellow human beings (Cini, 2019). If we are to learn about the core principles of *Ubuntu*, they point to social transformation through access to education which should be partially socialised so that fees are affordable. It also notes that the university's space should be an ethical forerunner in illustrating decolonisation, which is more than about teaching texts but also about leading by example in understanding why anti-racism, reparations or restorative justice is essential. If I am human through other humans, their lives, wellbeing, futures and diversity are at stake. If we are interconnected, the university should strive for that interconnectedness, and champion embodied social justice. This leads to my next point.

Justice and rights

At its heart, *Ubuntu* is a normative claim; it tells us about how we should act, and as such, it has been vital in South African transitional justice. However, too often, *Ubuntu* has been used as a political tool for nation-building or developing a national consciousness in South Africa rather than focusing on what ethical tools *Ubuntu* could give the populace to understand not only justice but how to progress as human beings (Marx, 2002). Libin (2020) notes how *Ubuntu* successfully illustrated restorative justice and understood the role of affect in being human for forgiveness and empathy. While criticisms have been countered towards the emphasis on the collective healing in the function of individual victims, as was noted earlier, I argue that this has been considering the present embodied inequalities in South African society, as student activism has shown.

In participating in the TRC, victims who told their painful truths revealed the past because they were assured of healing in the promise of a better 'restorative' future. As previously stated, there were three ideas of truth: a) personal, b) social and c) restorative (Marx, 2002). From a Western perspective, individual rights could triumph and outweigh the collective. However, in *Ubuntu*, the victim's rights and truth are bound with the rights of the society and thus become restorative for all. This is not a utilitarian perspective where the rights of the many triumphs over those of the few (Ewuoso & Hall, 2019). That restorative process is part of a human becoming, and the TRC is a moment in a long-term transition. As Desmond Tutu would argue, *Ubuntu* was meant to be healing (Libin, 2020) in that it had to involve human actions for individual and collective social change (Swanson, 2007). Those human actions personified *Ubuntu* in that they acted to restore the dignity of the victims and the collective through a peaceful transition to democracy. One could argue that some victims (individuals) and society (society) at large might feel that the sacrifices for truth have not been worth it if truth has not been restorative in upholding that dignity and respect in a democracy.

As related earlier, this relationship between the individual and collective rights in *Ubuntu* has sometimes been perplexing for outsiders to understand. It seems to require the sacrifice of the individual for the collective if you examine the present history of the TRC. However, if we take the South African Treatment Action Campaign (TAC) as an example, the relationship founded on interdependency should hopefully become clear (Zivi, 2014). The TAC was an activist organisation started in 1998 to advocate for treatment access to antiretrovirals for people with the human immunodeficiency virus (HIV). This virus can cause acquired immunodeficiency syndrome (AIDS), for which there is no cure. In the 1990s, South Africa had some of the highest incidences of HIV/AIDS worldwide. Although there were effective antiretrovirals to prevent the transmission of HIV and prevent AIDS, those were only accessible through payment and private healthcare.

What was unusual about TAC was the political role of South African patients (some wealthy) who were involved in campaigning for treatment access for the collective who could not pay for those drugs (Sabi & Rieker, 2017). Zackie Achmat, an anti-apartheid activist, played a crucial role in the TAC by revealing his sexuality and his positive HIV status and forgoing access to antiretroviral drugs until other HIV-positive people in South Africa could gain access (Mbali, 2005). One of the critical issues TAC campaigned for was preventing mother-to-child HIV transmission. However, when the government refused to act even after mass demonstrations, Berger and Kapczynski (2009) noted how in 2001, the TAC mounted one of the world's most successful socio-economic human rights cases. They took the South African government to court for violating the constitution, arguing that fundamentally its citizens had a right to health (Berger & Kapczynski, 2009).

In the TAC, *Ubuntu* is the individual African fighting for the collective. However, the individual's stories and pain only become a political force thanks to the work and embeddedness in an interdependent collective. Secondly, it is that embodied action within a collective that allows the individual to regain a sense of dignity and respect which is restorative. TAC was also fighting for each right to health and, as such, protects individual human rights within a collective. Lastly, that action to protect the individual was symbolic or performative and required socio-economic action to ensure that everyone got access. In this way, *Ubuntu* can become very radical but also simple in rethinking what decolonisation could mean when we think about access to rights.

Disability: Rethinking the human

> When you ask people in Sierra Leone who have an impairment what that means for them, they will typically not use the term 'disability' or 'disabled' but say something linked to explaining feelings of moral abjection . . . or abandonment, like stating, 'I am useless'. This is related to the importance of the performance of obligations of kinship as embodied, for example, so that others accept their caring roles or work and value this as a contribution to the group's well-being.
> (Berghs, 2018, p. 164)

This quote points to the importance of the individual to inclusion in the group and how that is fundamentally moral. The activism of students and the TAC points to a problem of how we view socio-economic and other forms of access and what we do if inclusion is denied, which is more than just a discourse on rights but also one of moral solidarity and ethical action.

At the heart of *Ubuntu* is also an understanding of the human and respect for human diversity. However, that respect and understanding can include uncomfortable relationships, emotions and effects (see Livingston, 2005), which are also a part of *Ubuntu* and becoming human. *Ubuntu* offers a model of the human that respects disability and views impairment as cognitive, sensory, mental, physical and spiritual. The spiritual dimension of being human should be addressed. However, disablement can occur if a person is viewed as not entitled to inclusion, for instance, if their identity or personhood in some way threaten the social order. The social order encapsulates ideas of kinship, belonging and acceptance of the diversity of the other.

One way in which to comprehend this is through the Shona concepts of *Ukama*, which is very similar to *Ubuntu* in meaning interdependence, as it stems from the word *hama* meaning relative (Le Grange, 2012; Murove, 2004; Ndofirepi & Maringe, 2020). However, Ndofirepi and Maringe (2020, p. 223) also note how the stem *kama* means 'to milk an animal', so our interdependence, status and survival are not just linked to our interdependence as humans but also the wider non-human environment, which gives us nourishment and life. Murove (2004, 2012) has argued that *Ubuntu* is also a spiritual interdependence and has connected *Ukama* to environmental ethics. Le Grange (2012) also argues that *kama* does away with the distinction between the anthropocentric and ecocentric, which oppose each other. Instead, *Ukama* points to a spiritually diverse ecology that we are all a part of. *Ukama* understands that the natural world can be spiritual too; for instance, in totemic animals, the role of the ancestors or spirits is found in the natural and supernatural world (Chibvongodze, 2016). In *Ubuntu* and *Ukama*, disablement can also encapsulate this diversity of how we are part of a broader ecology that has somehow been disturbed through oppressive or exploitative actions.

In disability studies, the anti-apartheid movement, Black consciousness and student movements in the 1960s, 1970s and 1980s played a critical role in inspiring the history of disability activism globally. Alongside Paul Hunt's experiences in institutional settings in the U.K., it was Vic Finkelstein's anti-apartheid activism and inclusion in prison as a person with disabilities that lay at the foundations of the social model of disability in making a distinction between having an impairment and the process of oppression as disablement (Berghs, 2017). I think we can see that same impetus in *Ubuntu* as a model to understand disability, in how African disability studies scholars are taking up this concept of *Ubuntu* and using it to rethink our theory and methods in ensuring more inclusive understandings of what it means to be human and what type of ecology we live in. While not perfect due to underfunding and lack of political support, one example would be the Zimbabwean context, where the school curriculum is premised on *Ubuntu* to try and ensure inclusive education. Musengi (2021) uses *Ubuntu* for a more pedagogically just teaching practice and as a postcolonial philosophical framework that has exposed how colonialism caused the schism between hearing and d/Deaf society in Shona culture. In such work, we note how *Ubuntu* is an ethic that can be put into practice but also functions as a theoretical model to understand the past and reorientate oppressions that turn off the present.

Climate justice: rethinking ecology as a right

Thinking further about decolonial practices, *Ubuntu* connects closely to climate justice and how we must rethink ecology to encapsulate ecological diversity and rights. Africans like Saro-Wiwa and Maathai have been at the forefront of environmental activism, and we can learn a lot from how they pursued climate justice. Saro-Wiwa fought against the environmental destruction of the indigenous Ogoni people's homelands by the Shell oil company in Nigeria, and Maathai started the Green Belt Movement (GBM) planting trees to combat deforestation and thus empowering women in Kenya (Berghs, 2017). Both situated the human as part of the environment and realised that by protecting the environment, they also acted to ensure their intergenerational, cultural and spiritual futures. They illustrated how activists in the Global South have answers to environmental destruction and misappropriation of resources often perpetuated by large multinationals from the Global North, sadly with the collusion of those in power. They fought for the rights of their homelands and people's futures by arguing that environmental destruction was illegal and broader in scope than was understood in the Global North.

The role of African activists and civil society was to speak out against environmental destruction and offer practical solutions, which international frameworks like the United Nations (U.N.) Sustainable Development Goals (SDGs) only sometimes provide (van Norren, 2022). The U.N. SDGs lack legislative 'teeth' and do not offer any concrete ways to counter climate justice nor give us a moral framework on how we should live and behave. *Ubuntu* illustrates how people, animals and the land are spiritually and culturally interwoven, broadening our understanding of what it means to be human to one of ecological interdependence (*kama*). This counters typically Western values of individualism found in neoliberalism and instead gives us an ethical framework in which we must act to protect humanity (Terblanché-Greeff, 2019). As such, Brás (2021) argues that it is an ecopolitical alternative to some of humanity's challenges due to the climate crisis.

In current climate justice activism, African youth activists can be marginalised and overlooked despite their critical contributions (Barnes, 2021); they give an added dimension to discourses on what climate justice means as ethics and what the link is to understanding rights. As illustrated in climate justice, *Ubuntu* illustrates how indigenous concepts of humanity, ecology and even rights are more comprehensive in scope than typically understood by the Global North and thus illustrate ways neoliberal capitalism and frameworks must change to be more inclusive. It also gives us an understanding that activism means bringing change and showing the path people should travel – and that Africans will lead the way through *Ubuntu*.

Ubuntu as a decolonial ethical practice

In the four case study examples, I have noted how activism from the African continent has been at the vanguard of decolonial movements to ensure progressive social change. This is because informing such activists is an understanding of a moral, ethical code of practice that is wider in scope than what we would typically understand in the Global North. In illustrating the importance of the TRC and *Ubuntu*, it was noted that a triad exists at the heart of *Ubuntu* (not a dyad) and that *Ubuntu* was a practice. To show *Ubuntu* was to act humanly, with a spirit of generosity (Ewuoso & Hall, 2019), because my humanity is understood through the diversity of what makes us human. However, for *Ubuntu* to exist between the individual and the collective, there needs to be restorative truth (actions), as shown in Figure 7.1, which will allow for healing.

Figure 7.1's illustration is very different from Eurocentrism or ideas in the Global North that posit what is human against another' as unfavourable, as found, for instance, in the work of Edward Said's *Orientalism*, where the 'West' is superior and defined itself against the Middle East (Mignolo, 2011; Mignolo & Escobar, 2013; de Sousa Santos, 2015). Instead, a human's becoming and healing are deeply entwined with their recognition of the diversity of many others and their actions together. In this chapter, four examples of activism have illustrated *Ubuntu* in action but have also shown how delicate the balance is between individual, collective and restorative truth. For *Ubuntu* to be successful in decolonisation, they all have to be present.

Ubuntu begins with a moral feeling

The examples in this chapter highlight how *Ubuntu* begins from a moral moment where dignity and respect for the other/s must be shown. *Ubuntu*

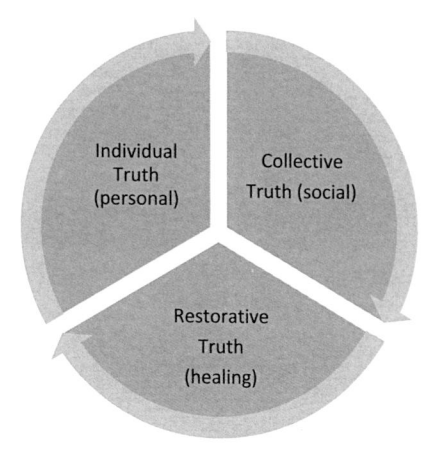

Figure 7.1 Ubuntu as a practice

is upheld when a human being shows a spirit of generosity and acts ethically towards others (Ewuoso & Hall, 2019), and this becomes critical when there are inequalities and injustice. In their overview of African philosophy, Metz and Ukpokolo (2017) note that when we consider African ethical positions, this has a normative focus on explaining how we should act. Nevertheless, I argue that before that imperative to act morally towards the other, there is an emotion – a spirit of generosity – in understanding that a common good for us as individuals is tied up to the well-being of others we encounter.

Ubuntu are performative actions for individual and collective

In African philosophy, Metz (2017) argues that such an ethic is found in communitarian or vitalist approaches where emotions should be followed with performative actions in illustrating hospitality, obligations of kinship, caring actions and the generosity of character that typify *Ubuntu*. For *Ubuntu* to succeed, actions are needed, and such actions would typically involve both the individual and the collective. Suppose the individual acts, but the group does not uphold *Ubuntu*. In that case, that is when injustice happens, or individuals feel a burden or sacrifice is being created in obligations of kinship or caring practices. Many Africans will recognise the responsibilities of kinship and the patrimonial system as sometimes feeling like a burden, but this is not *Ubuntu*. *Ubuntu* is a stance of generosity that must be reciprocated and buffered by restorative action. The individual must be supported by the collective and the collective by the individual; when these are not in balance, we note that protests are engaged. For *Ubuntu* to function for individuals and collectives, both must ensure performative actions. Those actions for the collective should be the assurances of the well-being of the individuals within *Ubuntu*.

Ubuntu means to protest the status quo to restore the truth of who we are

If the individual or the collective is not acting to uphold justice, then *Ubuntu* means to protest and ensure that the world becomes a more just place. *Ubuntu* revolts against oppression, violence and the past and present legacy of colonialism, racism, ableism and sexism. *Ubuntu* is not just performative but also engaged in protest actions for social actions, especially when the rights and dignity of the individuals or collective are not upheld. Restorative actions (truth) will lead to healing and finding a balance between individual and collective. Rights within such a system are broader than understood in the Global North (Bowsher, 2022), as they are linked to humans and the broader ecosystem in which we live. As such, this is a tool for decolonial praxis in that *Ubuntu* overtly links to more diverse perspectives of personhood and connects that diversity to the broader ecosystems in which we live (Berghs, 2017, 2021).

Ubuntu is ecological and spiritual

Ubuntu is not anthropocentric but instead views diversity through a wider lens of what it means to be communitarian or vitalist (Metz, 2017). Those philosophical understandings consider the differing ontological and epistemological understandings of the world and its ecology, which can also include the spiritual. In such a way, *Ubuntu* also becomes a guide to see the individual and collective as part of a restorative visible and invisible ecology that is fundamentally healing if upheld.

Conclusion

When examining *Ubuntu*, it has tended to be viewed within the lens of the TRC with many limitations, especially when considering the rights of the victims and the legacy of colonialism, violence, oppression and inequalities in South African society. However, I have shown that *Ubuntu* is a complex philosophy that is very radical in connecting individual and collective to healing. Decolonial activism, as we have noted, has a history of protest and sometimes violence that must be condoned. The process of decolonisation, in coming to terms with the inequalities of past and present, is very uncomfortable, can be painful, and will upset boundaries of power and ensure change, but it is fundamentally necessary if healing and dignity of the other/s as human becoming are to be achieved. *Ubuntu* is viewed as an ethic, and normative ethics tells us how to act for restorative actions. Let us take *Ubuntu* seriously as a decolonial practice. We can ask why the social responsibilities of ethical actions are enabled or hindered individually or socially by the state or structurally. How can we ensure that individual and collective rights are upheld to protect the broader ecology and understanding of the world?

References

Barnes, B. R. (2021). Reimagining African women youth climate activism: The case of Vanessa Nakate. *Sustainability*, 13(23), 13214. https://doi.org/10.3390/su132313214

Berger, J. M., & Kapczynski, A. (2009). The story of the TAC case: The potential and limits of socio-economic rights litigation in South Africa. In D. R. Hurwitz, M. L. Satterthwaite, & D. B. Ford (Eds.), *Human rights advocacy stories* (pp. 1–30). Foundation Press.

Berghs, M. (2017). Practices and discourses of Ubuntu: Implications for an African model of disability? *African Journal of Disability*, 6(1), 1–8. https://doi.org/10.4102/ajod.v6.292

Berghs, M. (2018). Ethical (dis) enchantment, afflictive kinship and ebola exceptionalism. In G. Thomas & D. Sakellariou (Eds.), *Disability, normalcy and the everyday* (pp. 160–182). Routledge.

Berghs, M. (2021). An African ethics of social well-being: Understanding disability and public health. In T. Falola & N. Hamel (Eds.), *Disability in Africa: Inclusion, care, and the ethics of humanity* (pp. 75–90). Boydell & Brewer.

Bowsher, J. (2022). *The informational logic of human rights*. Edinburgh University Press.

Brás, J. G. V. (2021). For an epistemic decolonisation of education from the Ubuntu philosophy. *Pedagogy, Culture & Society*, 1–16. https://doi.org/10.1080/1468136 6.2021.2011386

Chibvongodze, D. T. (2016). Ubuntu is not only about the human! An analysis of the role of African philosophy and ethics in environment management. *Journal of Human Ecology*, 53(2), 157–166. https://doi.org/10.1080/09709274.2016.11906968

Cini, L. (2019). Disrupting the neoliberal university in South Africa: The# FeesMustFall movement in 2015. *Current Sociology*, 67(7), 942–959. https://doi.org/10.1177/0011392119865766

de Sousa Santos, B. (2015). *Epistemologies of the South: Justice against epistemicide*. Routledge.

de Sousa Santos, B. (2018). *Decolonising the university: The challenge of deep cognitive justice*. Cambridge Scholars Publishing.

Ewuoso, C., & Hall, S. (2019). Core aspects of Ubuntu: A systematic review. *South African Journal of Bioethics and Law*, 12(2), 93–103. http://doi.org/10.7196/SAJBL.2019.v12i2.679

Eze, M. O. (2008). What is African communitarianism? Against consensus as a regulative ideal. *South African Journal of Philosophy*, 27(4), 386–399. https://doi.org/10.4314/sajpem.v27i4.31526

Fox, G. (2011). Remembering Ubuntu: Memory, sovereignty and reconciliation in post-apartheid South Africa. *PlatForum*, 12, 79–79.

Gathogo, J. (2008). African philosophy is expressed in the concepts of hospitality and Ubuntu. *Journal of Theology for Southern Africa*, 130, 39.

Gopal, P. (2021). On decolonisation and the university. *Textual Practice*, 35(6), 873–899. https://doi.org/10.1080/0950236X.2021.1929561

Griffiths, D. (2019). # FeesMustFall and the decolonised university in South Africa: Tensions and opportunities in a globalising world. *International Journal of Educational Research*, 94, 143–149. https://doi.org/10.1016/j.ijer.2019.01.004

Le Grange, L. (2012). Ubuntu, kama, environment and moral education. *Journal of Moral Education*, 41(3), 329–340. https://doi.org/10.1080/03057240.2012.691631

Libin, M. (2020). "Revealing is healing": Ubuntu, the TRC hearings, and the transmission of affect. In M. Libin (Ed.), *Reading affect in post-apartheid literature* (pp. 61–103). Palgrave Macmillan.

Livingston, J. (2005). *Debility and the moral imagination in Botswana*. Indiana University Press.

Louw, D. J. (1998). Ubuntu: An African assessment of the religious other. *The Paideia Archive: Twentieth World Congress of Philosophy*, 23, 34–42. https://doi.org/10.5840/wcp20-paideia199823407

Marx, C. (2002). Ubu and Ubuntu: On the dialectics of apartheid and nation building. *Politikon: South African Journal of Political Studies*, 29(1), 49–69. https://doi.org/10.1080/02589340220149434

Mbali, M. (2005). *TAC in the history of rights-based, patient-driven HIV/AIDS activism in South Africa*. M Publishing.

Metz, T. (2011). Ubuntu as a moral theory and human rights in South Africa. *African Human Rights Law Journal*, 11(2), 532–559. www.scielo.org.za/pdf/ahrlj/v11n2/11.pdf

Metz, T. (2017). An overview of African ethics. In T. Metz & I. Ukpokolo (Eds.), *Themes, issues and problems in African philosophy* (pp. 61–75). Palgrave Macmillan.

Metz, T. (2022). *A relational Moral Theory: African Ethics in and beyond the Continent*. Oxford University Press.

Metz, T., & Ukpokolo, I. (Eds.). (2017). *Themes, issues and problems in African philosophy*. Palgrave Macmillan.

Mignolo, W. D. (2011). *The darker side of Western modernity: Global futures, decolonial options*. Duke University Press.

Mignolo, W. D., & Escobar, A. (Eds.). (2013). Globalisation *and the decolonial option*. Routledge.

Murove, M. F. (2004). An African commitment to ecological conservation: The Shona concepts of Ukama and Ubuntu. *Mankind Quarterly, 45*(2), 195. https://doi.org/10.46469/mq.2004.45.2.3

Murove, M. F. (2012). Ubuntu. *Diogenes, 59*(3–4), 36–47. https://doi.org/10.1177/0392192113493737

Musengi, M. (2021). Ubuntu for disability-inclusive pedagogy: Illustrations from deaf education in Zimbabwe. In J. Mukuni & J. Tlou (Eds.), *Understanding Ubuntu for enhancing intercultural communication* (pp. 189–201). IGI Global.

Mutanga, O. (ed). (2023). *Ubuntu Philosophy and Disabilities in Sub-Saharan Africa*. Routledge.

Ndofirepi, A. P., & Maringe, F. (2020). Ukama ethic in knowledge production: Theorising collaborative research and partnership practices in the African university. In A, P. Ndofirepi & F. Maringe (Eds.), *Rurality, social justice and education in Sub-Saharan Africa* (Vol. II, pp. 215–238). Palgrave Macmillan.

Otieno, S. A. (2020). Ethical thought of Archbishop Desmond Tutu: Ubuntu and Tutu's moral modelling as transformation and renewal. In N. Wariboko & T. Falola (Eds.), *The Palgrave handbook of african social ethics* (pp. 589–604). Palgrave Macmillan.

Sabi, S. C., & Rieker, M. (2017). The role of civil society in health policy making in South Africa: A review of the strategies adopted by the treatment action campaign. *African Journal of AIDS Research, 16*(1), 57–64. https://doi.org/10.2989/16085906.2017.1296874

Saini, R., & Begum, N. (2020). Demarcation and definition: Explicating the meaning and scope of "decolonisation" in the social and political sciences. *The Political Quarterly, 91*(1), 217–221. https://doi.org/10.1111/1467-923X.12797

Shutte, A. (1993). *Philosophy for Africa*. UCT Press.

Swanson, D. M. (2007). Ubuntu: An African contribution to (re) search for/with a "humble togetherness". *Journal of contemporary issues in Education, 2*(2), 53–67. https://doi.org/10.20355/C5PP4X

Terblanché-Greeff, A. C. (2019). Ubuntu and environmental ethics: The West can learn from Africa when faced with climate change. In M. Chemhuru (Ed.), *African environmental ethics* (pp. 93–109). Springer.

Van der Merwe, W. L. (1996). Philosophy and the multi-cultural context of (post) apartheid South Africa. *Ethical Perspectives, 3*(2), 1–15. https://doi.org/10.2143/EP.3.2.563038

van Norren, D. E. (2022). African Ubuntu and sustainable development goals: Seeking human mutual relations and service in development. *Third World Quarterly*, 1–20. https://doi.org/10.1080/01436597.2022.2109458

Virdee, S. (2019). Racialised capitalism: An account of its contested origins and consolidation. *The Sociological Review, 67*(1), 3–27. https://doi.org/10.1h177/0038026118820293

Zivi, K. (2014). The practice and the promise of making rights claims: Lessons from the South African treatment access campaign. In O. Onazi (Ed.), *African legal theory and contemporary problems* (pp. 173–198). Springer.

8 Decolonising gender and development

The influence of *Ubuntu* philosophy on the articulation of African feminism

Nyamwaya Munthali and Thomas Kitinya Kirina

Introduction

A current discourse within development studies is the decolonisation of the field (Cummings et al., 2022), based partly on the existence of epistemological dominance and ideological asymmetries in development practice and knowledge production processes (Istratii & Lewis, 2019; Schöneberg, 2019). In the sub-field of gender and development, mainstream gender theory and feminist approaches often emerge from Global North perspectives, neglecting indigenous religious influence and cultural relativism (Istratii, 2020; Vaditya, 2018). Addressing this Northern hegemony, this chapter engages with two tenets of decolonisation to contribute to decolonising gender and development, specifically regarding feminism. These tenets relate to positioning marginalised epistemologies and applying a culturally sensitive approach to understanding the interpretation of feminism. Applying these tenets, the chapter analyses African feminism through the lens of *Ubuntu* philosophy, engaging with the issue of cultural relativism in interpreting feminism. This analysis contributes insights into the potential influence of *Ubuntu* philosophy on articulating African feminism(s) within the sub-field of gender and development.

Decolonisation of gender and development studies

Development is 'the process of improving the quality of all human lives and capabilities by raising people's levels of living, self-esteem, and freedom' (Todaro & Smith, 2020, p. 2). Development studies, as a field, analyses the historical trajectory of development and presents approaches to this process. Gender[1] and development studies is based on the assertion that development processes affect men and women differently. For instance, they experience different access to education, capital, and other resources. Further, their ability to access opportunities in the employment market and related labour burdens vary. These gender-based disparities have high economic costs and lead to wasted human resources and missed opportunities for

DOI: 10.4324/9781003358879-8

economic development (Senders et al., 2012). Given this, gender and development studies are concerned with understanding gender relations to provide development practitioners with valuable insights to enhance gender equality (Momsen, 2010). A part of this response is supporting the feminist movement that advocates for bridging gender gaps.

Decolonisation is derived from post-development theories hinged on critiquing the modernisation theory of development. Post-development theories of development constitute two perspectives: post-modernist and postcolonial perspectives that were popularised from the 1980s and onwards. Post-modernist development problematises assumptions that the Global South populace was/are homogenous and that the Global North's development path was/is the blueprint for development (Willis, 2011). Postcolonial approaches, on the other hand, are centred on coloniality that survives colonialism. Colonialism refers to a political and economic relation in which a nation's sovereignty is determined by another nation's power – making such a nation an empire (Potter et al., 2018).

In comparison, coloniality refers to long-standing patterns of power that emerge from colonialism and define culture, labour, intersubjective relations, and knowledge production well beyond the bounds of a nation's era of colonisation (Torres, 2007). For example, the recognition of English as an official language in former colonies or the recognition of British Law as the official and paramount law in these territories. Therefore, decoloniality perspectives recognise the importance of social diversity and the influence of power relations in the formulation and diffusion of development concepts (Schöneberg, 2019). Decolonisation then aims to disrupt world views based on Northern assumptions (Eurocentrism), including concepts of 'development' that have been transferred as part of the colonial process. The disruption of Eurocentrism involves accounting for social and cultural differences, particularly in the context of former colonies still experiencing colonialism's legacies (Willis, 2011). Decoloniality of knowledge particularly relates to "processes and actions that intentionally dismantle the entrenched, unequal patterns of knowledge creation and use that emanate from our colonial past; it is a process full of complexities, tensions and paradoxes" (de Oliviera Andreotti et al., 2015, p. 22).

Because of this relationship between former colonies and colonists, postcolonial scholars such as Amartya Sen advocate for making developing countries' views widely known and more influential. They have taken steps to decolonise gender and development studies. Sen (1999) mainly has engaged with this agenda by reframing the focus and meaning of development through the capability approach. Sen argues that we cannot adequately measure poverty solely by looking at income or even traditional notions of utility. Instead, the true measure of poverty lies in understanding what a person is capable of being and doing. Rather than just tallying material possessions or emotional experiences, it's vital to assess the opportunities and freedoms a person can access and realise (Todaro & Smith, 2020).

Further, Gita Sen and colleagues formed the Development Alternatives with Women for a New Era (DAWN) Network in the Global South. This network advocated for the 'women and development' approach to empowerment.[2] This approach requires that colonial effects on gender relations be considered to enhance gender equality (Momsen, 2010). In line with these considerations, Nkealah (2016) asserts that coloniality plays a role in exacerbating gender discrimination and its subsequent effects.

Concerning this assertion, Nzegwu (1994) points at colonial systems, through epistemic dominance, replacing dual-sex systems perspectives on gender equality with mono-sex systems perspectives in former colonies. The first perspective puts forward that Western feminism focuses on sameness, i.e., women aspiring to be men as a goal for gender equality. Therefore, the mono-sex system takes men's position as the yardstick of empowerment and considers gender equality as a situation where women take men's position(s) in society (Nzegwu, 1994). The dual-sex system conceives women and men as social complements in terms of gender equality. This perspective of gender equality expresses that social roles and responsibilities that define gender identity are acknowledged, valued, and validated by both men and women for society's benefit (effective functioning) (Nzegwu, 1994). African feminists critique the first perspective as being an individualistic and unbalanced model for gender equality that is in tension with and inappropriate to assess or engage with the non-individualistic and balanced mono-sex systems associated with African society (Ahikire, 2006; Coetzee, 2018; Nzegwu, 1994). More specifically, the dual-sex system, for which the sameness of men and women is a goal of gender equality, is criticised along two lines. Firstly, for excluding women from the aforementioned social gender identity (pitting them against men) to the end of marginalising women and, in effect, creating the sexist structures that (Western) women fight and, at the same time, paradoxically seek inclusion (Ahikire, 2006; Nzegwu, 1994). According to Nzegwu (1994), this situation shows the depth of structural inequalities in Western societies. Secondly, the mono-sex system is criticised for devaluing women's position and roles (e.g., motherhood) in African society and epitomising men's circumstances, as this reduces the value of difference in men and women that positions them to engage in mutually beneficial roles that maintain the effective functioning of society (McQuaid & Plastow, 2017; Nkealah, 2016).

Concerning Nzegwu's (1994) sentiments, the decolonisation discourse in the sub-field of gender and development presents as mainstream gender theory and feminist approaches being articulated from the Global North perspective, i.e., using secular logic – mute to religious influence and cultural relativism (Istratii, 2020). The central issue of the discourse is that the universality of what is understood as gender relations and feminism is not shared by everyone. Therefore alternative notions of feminism should be made salient (Nkealah, 2016). Because of the Northern hegemony articulated, this chapter engages with two Southern tenets of decolonisation to contribute to decolonising gender and development studies. These tenets relate to centring marginalised epistemologies and cultural relativism. 'Epistemology is the practice of perceiving knowledge and what is constructed as legitimate knowledge' (Vaditya, 2018, p. 1). Further, epistemic marginalisation refers to situations in which individuals and social groups are subject to exclusion in processes of knowledge production or not considered a valid source of knowledge based on long-standing biases related to factors that include race, sex, location, or based on the intersection of such factors (Vaditya, 2018).

Regarding the other tenet, cultural relativism, this concept considers that human values are not universal and depend on the culture and religion of a society (Brown, 2008). Therefore, any culture can be evaluated on its principles, not so-called universal ones (Brown, 2008). However, these tenets relate to excluding specific knowledge from the base of valid knowledge. Given this, it is necessary to articulate alternative and culturally sensitive interpretations of aspects of knowledge (e.g., feminism).

Mainstream (Western) feminism perspective

Three waves of feminism are mainly documented in the existing literature: the first wave (liberal), second wave (socialist), and third wave (radical). In this chapter, popularised views of feminism are ingrained in second and third-wave feminism that builds on and is a critique of the first wave (Pilcher & Whelehan, 2004). These waves of feminism are largely conceptualised by authors from the Global North, hence popularised due to epistemic dominance.

The second wave of feminism relates to an era that responded to the limitations of the first wave of feminism. This wave emerged in the late 1960s and was/is characterised by activism and militancy (Aikau et al., 2003). This era shifted from the first waves' focus on political issues such as legal and social barriers to voting rights, access to education, or property ownership to the motivation to liberate women from the oppressive patriarchy through a revolution that pushed women to enter or claim historical male-dominated spaces (Pilcher & Whelehan, 2004).

In true Marxist style, the second wave mobilised women into groups to engage in consciousness-raising, direct action, and demonstrations as part of what came to be identified as the 'women's liberation movement' (Hoggart, 2000). Through this movement, the women's liberation movement gained momentum and immense support and shaped popularised prominent feminism. However, the movement also received pushback from cohorts of society as 'women's libbers' that were no-deodorant or no-bra wearing, armpit hair and leg hair growing, man-haters (Pilcher & Whelehan, 2004).

The third wave of feminism was propelled by the limitations of the second feminist wave (Pilcher & Whelehan, 2004). These limitations include that despite the women's liberal movement claiming to be inclusive of lesbians, women of colour, and working-class women, it remained a movement that was dominated by a white middle-class heterosexual women's view and only provided token representation for the sub-communities aforementioned

(Nnaemeka, 2003). Another limitation of the second wave cited is its reference to gender at all, and related to this are third wavers views that the feminist agenda has shifted, i.e., the historical and political conditions in which second-wave feminism emerged are non-existent (Aikau et al., 2003; Snyder, 2008).

It is essential to consider that women of colour, including African feminists, form a section of society that contribute to third wavers perspectives. However, there are also points of departure for African feminists on the aspect of radical and even socialist feminism. These are discussed further in the chapter.

African feminisms – 'We should all be feminists'

Scholars like Alkali et al. (2013) put forward that Western feminists have fallen short in recognising that the black community has been excluded from the gender justice discourse – a situation that has implored this community to mobilise beyond ethnic and geographical boundaries and define their feminism. This strand of feminism considers that, unlike Western feminists, African women face unique discrimination based on interacting and influencing factors, including colonialism, patriarchy, poverty, and cultural practices. More specifically, Western feminists are mute to African women's experiences of racism and neo-colonialism. They are limited in their sensitivity to African cultural artefacts such as tradition, norms, and values. They also fail to zoom into African women's specific struggles on their track empowerment trajectory (Ezenwa-Ohaeto, 2019; Pindi, 2020). These specific struggles include genital mutilation, early (child) marriage and marriage conventions, and oppression by other women and not only men. As such, Western feminism pays limited attention to and is none or partially responsive to African women's empowerment needs, foci, or goals. Western feminists cannot relate to African women's empowerment goals considering that they are at a higher level of freedom regarding certain aspects of women's empowerment and their gender equality trajectory based on them enjoying a certain level of privilege above African women (Pindi, 2020). White women's privilege is exemplified by their role in slave-owning societies and their position in racist institutions.

Based on this backdrop, African feminism is a movement that seeks to address gender inequality in the African context, with a focus on the unique experiences of African women (Coetzee, 2018; Roth, 2003). African feminism has a long history that dates to the colonial era when women began to resist the oppression of colonial powers (McFadden, 2007). The first wave of Africa feminism emerged in the 1960s and 1970s, as African countries gained independence from colonial powers (Roth, 2003). During this period, women's organisations were formed to fight for women's rights and challenge the patriarchal structures imposed by colonialism. The feminist movements were inspired by organisations in the West, but they adapted feminist theories to the African context. One of the key features of African feminism is its intersectional approach, which recognises that women's experiences are

Table 8.1 Subcultures/various forms of African feminism

African feminisms	Description
African womanism	'Situates the feminist vision within black women's confrontation with culture, colonialism and many other forms of domination that condition African women's lives' (Nkealah, 2016, p. 62).
Stiwanism	'Is in favour of an understanding that equality for women in society can only be found when common cause is made with the oppression suffered by all in society, including men' (McQuaid & Plastow, 2017, unpaginated).
Motherism	A maternal form of feminism that sees rural women as performing the necessary task of nurturing society (Nkealah, 2016).
Femalism	"Puts the woman's body at the centre of feminist conversations. . ... It projects the female body as a sign by linking 'the freedom of woman to that of the African nation', and woman thus becomes 'Mother Africa susceptible to various manipulations and intrigues'" (Opara, 2005, p. 193).
Snail-sense feminism	'Women should adopt snail-like patience and efficiency in negotiating their ways around and over boulders, rocks, thorns, crags and rough terrains littered along their ways when dealing with men in the very hash patriarchal environment which they find themselves in' (Ezenwa-Ohaeto, 2019, p. 1).
Nego-feminism	Calls for negotiation with men and their inclusion in discussions and advocacy for feminism – from the standpoint that men's involvement is essential for female empowerment (Nnaemeka, 2003).

shaped by their race, class, and other social identities or multiple factors, which cannot be separated from each other (Basu, 2018).

African women's responses to the blind spots of Western feminism have influenced the conceptualisation of alternative feminisms that are iterated from an African cultural perspective, an African geopolitical position, and an African ideological viewpoint (McQuaid & Plastow, 2017; Pindi, 2020) (see Table 8.1). These diverse yet related notions of feminism that have primarily emerged from West Africa, particularly Nigeria, have shifted the foci of the feminist agenda in Africa (Nkealah, 2016). These perspectives challenge Western feminism approaches by calling for collaboration and involvement of both men and women to advance the feminist agenda while maintaining women's femininity.

These African feminisms have three similarities. Firstly, they challenge 'feminism' as a term, considering its origins and definition by and within Western cultures, i.e., because they fall short in capturing African women's experiences (Alkali et al., 2013). Secondly, they are indigenously defined, as they are based on the African historical context and cultures to create the basis for appropriate interventions to empower women and re-socialise men (Nnaemeka, 2003). Thirdly, they are not based on individualism but place community (well-being) over the individual and incorporate gender inclusion, collaboration, and accommodation to foster that both women and men contribute to improving the material conditions of women (Adichie, 2014; Nkealah, 2016).

In her book, Adichie (2014) illustrates and touches on the relevance or provokes thought on these three African feminism principles by sharing her experiences as a Nigerian woman. With regards to the first assertion of African feminism, through the excerpts from her book that follow, Adichie provokes commentary on how Western feminism is challenged by and has an antagonistic relationship with African culture. By reflecting on this antagonist relationship, she, in essence, validates the necessity for the formulation of African feminism(s).

> Then an academic, a Nigerian woman, told me that feminism was not our culture and that feminism was un-African, and I was only calling myself a feminist because Western books had influenced me. Which amused me because much of my early reading was decidedly unfeminist: I must have read every single Mills & Boon romance published before I was sixteen. And each time I try to read those books called 'classic feminist texts', I get bored, and I struggle to finish them . . . Anyway, since feminism was un-African, I decided I would now call myself a Happy African Feminist.
>
> (Adichie, 2014, unpaginated)

> Then a dear friend told me that calling myself a feminist meant that I hated men. So, I decided I would now be a Happy African Feminist Who Does Not Hate Men. At some point, I was a Happy African Feminist Who Does Not Hate Men And Who Likes To Wear Lip Gloss And High Heels For Herself And Not For Men. Of course, much of this was tongue-in-cheek, but what it shows is how that word feminist is so heavy with baggage, negative baggage: you hate men, you hate bras, you hate African culture, you think women should always be in charge, you don't wear make-up, you don't shave, you're always angry, you don't have.
>
> (Adichie, 2014, unpaginated)

On the second premise of African feminism, she highlights relevant African experiences through the excerpts that follow. The excerpts from her book point to (1) the need to engage both women and men in critical reflection on their historical understanding of and the underpinnings of gender-based division of labour in the present-day, and (2) the need for ideas of women empowerment to emerge from logical reasoning on what values and capabilities should be considered and guide people's fair access to opportunities to benefit society ultimately.

So, in a literal way, men rule the world. This made sense – a thousand years ago. Because human beings lived then in a world in which physical strength was the most important attribute for survival, the physically stronger person was more likely to lead. Moreover, men, in general, are physically stronger. (There are, of course, many exceptions.) Today, we live in a vastly different world. The person more qualified to lead is not the physically stronger person. It is the more intelligent, the more knowledgeable, the more creative, more innovative. Furthermore, there are no hormones for those attributes. A man is as likely as a woman to be intelligent, innovative, and creative. We have evolved. But our ideas of gender have not evolved very much.

(Adichie, 2014, Unpaginated)

Other [African] men might respond by saying, 'Okay, this is interesting, but I don't think like that. I don't even think about gender.' Maybe not. And that is part of the problem. That many men do not actively think about gender or notice gender. Men say, like my friend Louis did, that things might have been bad in the past, but everything is fine now.

(Adichie, 2014, unpaginated)

Some people will say a woman is subordinate to men because it's our culture. But culture is constantly changing. I have beautiful twin nieces who are fifteen. If they had been born a hundred years ago, they would have been taken away and killed. Because a hundred years ago, Igbo culture considered the birth of twins to be an evil omen. Today that practice is unimaginable to all Igbo people. What is the point of culture? Culture functions ultimately to ensure the preservation and continuity of a people. In my family, I am the child who is most interested in the story of who we are, in our ancestral lands, in our tradition. My brothers are not as interested as I am. But I cannot participate because Igbo culture privileges men, and only the male members of the extended family can attend the meetings where major family decisions are taken. So, although I am the one who is most interested in these things, I cannot attend the meeting. I cannot have a formal say. Because I am female.

(Adichie, 2014, unpaginated)

Culture does not make people. People make culture. If it is true that the full humanity of women is not our culture, then we can and must make it our culture.

(Adichie, 2014, unpaginated)

My own definition of a feminist is a man or a woman who says, 'Yes, there's a problem with gender as it is today, and we must fix it; we must do better.' All of us, women and men, must do better.

(Adichie, 2014, unpaginated)

On the last and final position of African feminism, Adichie motivates, also through the earlier excerpts, that both men and women should be feminists. This reasoning relates to the shortcomings of individualistic feminist approaches and brings into focus the benefits African feminist approaches present for the progress or well-being of society. This relates well to *Ubuntu*'s philosophy, as discussed in the next section.

Ubuntu philosophy

Ubuntu is an African moral philosophy loosely associated with African humanism. These humanistic perspectives centre on linking spirituality (religion), African traditional values of collectivism and community, and democratic values with socio-economic development requirements (Willis, 2011). African humanism includes Zambian humanism, Tanzania's *ujamaa*, Ghana's conscientism, and Kenya's *harambee* (Hailey, 2008).

Ubuntu as a philosophy and social ethic is based on the African aphorism '*Umuntu ngumuntu ngabantu*' (Zulu language) or '*Motho ke motho ka batho*' (Sotho language) (Louw, 1998). In English, this aphorism is commonly translated as and exemplified by the phrase 'I am because we are' or 'a person is a person through other persons' or 'I am because of others' (Tomaselli, 2004, p. 243). *Ubuntu* philosophy not only describes how humans are inherently bound to each other but also prescribes how individuals self-actualise through communal relationships that are harmonious, cohesive, and reciprocal (Tavernaro-Haidarian, 2018). It also involves communal engagement favouring relational governance and communication approaches (Metz, 2011; 2022).

Ubuntu as a word, and its underpinning aphorism, as previously seen, have varying definitions that render it challenging to grasp (Mabovula, 2011; Hailey, 2008). Various definitions of *Ubuntu* partly stem from the difficulty of precisely translating the concept into Western languages (Hailey, 2008; Louw, 2006). For instance, Louw (2006) describes *Ubuntu* as 'humanity', 'humanness', or 'humaneness'. Tomaselli (2004) put forward it is translated as 'humanity toward others'; whilst for Mabovula (2011), *Ubuntu* represents 'the collective consciousness of the people of Africa'. Nonetheless, Hailey (2008), Tomaselli (2004), and Louw (1998) point to three positions on personal identity, rational choice, and justice that define the philosophy[3] (see Figure 8.1). These positions are applied in this chapter to operationalise the *Ubuntu* philosophy.

Regarding the first position, *Ubuntu*'s philosophy reflects that identity formation is more relational. More specifically, that personal identity is formed between how we see ourselves and how those around us see us (Forster, 2010). Therefore, personal identity has an internal and external relational component. Non-relational views of personality do not consider the latter in identity formation. With the second position, rational choice, *Ubuntu*'s philosophy puts forward that part of self-interest is to consider community well-being (Mutanga, 2023). Therefore, rational choice involves considering others' welfare because our well-being and value are tied to how we value others' well-being (Eliastam,

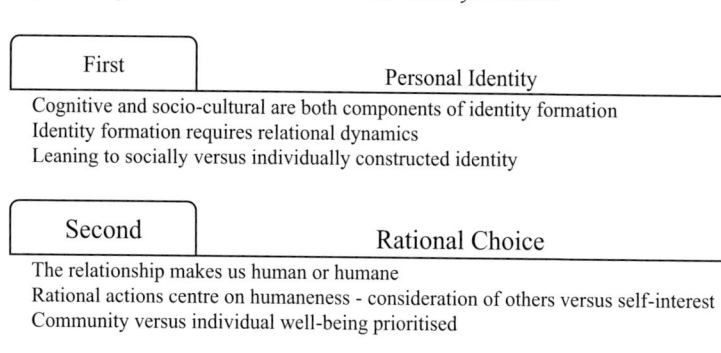

First	Personal Identity

Cognitive and socio-cultural are both components of identity formation
Identity formation requires relational dynamics
Leaning to socially versus individually constructed identity

Second	Rational Choice

The relationship makes us human or humane
Rational actions centre on humaneness - consideration of others versus self-interest
Community versus individual well-being prioritised

Third	Justice

Oppressing or exacting revenge reduces our humanity or humanness
Retributive justice is harmful to the formerly oppressed and the oppressor
Reconciliation makes use of human
Restorative versus retributive justice advocated

Figure 8.1 *Ubuntu*'s philosophical positions
Source: (Hailey, 2008; Louw, 1998; Tomaselli, 2004)

2015). On the last position, justice, *Ubuntu* philosophy favours restorative justice over retributive justice. The philosophy describes retributive justice as a cycle of revenge that harms both the former oppressor and the oppressed. This is based on the notion that retributive justice can lead to tipping power scales to the point of the oppressed becoming the oppressors instead of creating a stable, balanced, and fair society (Niekerk, 2013; Udo, 2020).

Reflecting on African feminism through the lens of *Ubuntu* philosophy

At its core, feminism is the belief in full social, economic, and political equality for women or even equality of the sexes, freedom from oppression, and gender equality (Pilcher & Whelehan, 2004). However, the specific goals embedded in these broad goals vary for different categories of women and fail to represent an entire gender of different cultures. This is a current discourse within feminism, specifically concerning intersectional feminism and cultural relativism in feminism (Istratii, 2020).

In the subsequent sections, each *Ubuntu* philosophical position is discussed with regards to African feminism. This discussion aims to highlight how the cultural manifestation premised on *Ubuntu* philosophy reflects in and/or potentially shapes African feminism.

Personal identity

Identity formation is influenced by several individual and societal factors (Forster, 2010). Further, these factors of identity formation include cognitive, scholastics, socio-cultural, cyber-socialising, and parenting. Central to the discussion in this paper is the cognitive and socio-cultural aspects that represent the two components of identity formation.

Ubuntu's philosophy includes and leans towards the notion that identity formation is relational. Therefore, it is a social process, i.e., individuals form a self-concept of whom they are due to interaction with other members of society (Forster, 2010). Similarly, Nzegwu (1994, p. 73) said, 'we begin life and form our relational identity in the nexus of caring, sharing, family and society'. Therefore, regarding gender identity, it may follow that this is also a relational identity (not shaped in isolation) such that relational dynamics are crucial to understanding and redefining these identities. Concerning African feminism, this could explain the basis of the dual-sex system that advances gender equality and associated gender identity based on the complementarity and equally assigned values of gender roles in societal contexts.

Furthermore, African feminism challenges culture to mitigate the stronghold of the patriarchy – considered a central feature of African society and a structural barrier to women's empowerment. In order to achieve this goal, it is implied that a desired gender identity comes into focus and 'this' desired identity guides an empowerment/feminist approach. Based on the notion that African feminists see gender identity as more relational, it is further implied that if an individual's idea of an empowered self or even a project's idea of an empowered person (based on, for instance, a mono-sex perspective) is misaligned with societies views of an empowered person (e.g., a dual-sex systems perspective) then a conflict of identity goals may occur (Nzegwu, 1994). This conflict between the individual or a project and the community could then hinder an individual's empowerment efforts or foster community resistance to a project's efforts. Given this, relational identity as a feature of African identity formation requires understanding in formulating empowerment interventions to enhance their chances of success (Senders et al., 2012). 'Mitigating resistance by building on tradition' is an empowerment strategy that resonates with manoeuvring the tensions between Western feminist and African feminist perspectives and their implications mentioned earlier.

Rational choice

Among the critiques of Western feminism is that it is individualistic. It removes women from their social identity, which renders them to seek a stronger position in society that is complementary to men and instead focuses women on displacing or fighting men to advance a self-serving empowerment agenda (Ahikire, 2006). More specifically, Western feminism includes exclusionary practices founded on gender, i.e., radical feminist views exclude men (and transgender women) from actively engaging in feminist social movements (Ezenwa-Ohaeto, 2019; Koyama, 2003). This exclusion is based on two arguments. Firstly, men vis a vie the patriarchy are labelled the aggressors and the focus of the fight for gender equality; hence, they cannot be fully or logically incorporated as feminists. Secondly, men or transgender women cannot purport to be privy to women's experiences to empathise with them and ultimately identify with the feminist cause.

This critique implies that this form of feminism conflicts with more community-oriented cultures. From a cultural relativism position, African societies are considered more community-oriented (Mabovula, 2011). Therefore, it is a natural progression that African feminism draws from this cultural manifestation that (1) calls for both men and women to be concerned about and involved in the gender equality movement as opposed to engaging men and women in a non-progressive competitive and antagonist relationship in order to foster women's empowerment; and (2) that is more inclined to a dual-sex system perspective of gender equality where both roles of women are valued and are elevated in this context for both parties to contribute to the well-being of society (Nzegwu, 1994). These perspectives run congruent to *Ubuntu's* philosophy that purports that rational choice is not based on self-interest but on community well-being which has a bearing on individual well-being. This view on rational choice conflicts with the mainstream notions of rational choice – a term predominant in economics and for all intent and purposes centred on self-interest being human beings' primary mode of operation (Potter et al., 2018).

Justice

With justice, specifically, the preference for restorative or distributive justice also motivates engagement concerning the relationship of *Ubuntu* philosophy to African feminism and African feminists' critique of Western feminism. This engagement is necessary considering Western feminism relates to Marxist principles and specifically notions of revolution – tipping the societal scale of privilege with women's activity overthrowing the patriarchy to occupy male spaces (Hoggart, 2000; Pilcher & Whelehan, 2004). This view of feminism resonates with concerns associated with retributive justice. This is because this form of feminism could lead to the oppression of men as opposed to a balanced and fair society for the sexes to function optimally, and both contribute to the advancement of society (Nzegwu, 1994). Therefore, African feminism, potentially influenced by *Ubuntu* philosophy, rejects this approach and opts for a more Gandhian feminist approach[4] that reflects aspects of restorative justice.

A stance on an empowerment approach that responds to the concerns of aforementioned retributive justice (often enshrined in Western feminism) reflects in the African feminisms of Nego-feminism and Snail-sense feminism (Nnaemeka, 2003). The Nego-feminist branch puts forward the idea that regardless of gender (and race or class), collaboration, negotiation, and compromise, as well as balance, are required in the gender equality movement. Snail-sense feminism, similarly, ascribes to feminists avoiding a confrontational and combative approach to the patriarchy (Ezenwa-Ohaeto, 2019). Hence, feminists in this context negotiate their way around the patriarchy, withstanding sexist men while collaborating with those who are not sexist and applying diplomatic principles in their interface with the patriarchy and broader society.

Conclusion

Referencing Chimamanda Adichie's (2014) book *We should all be feminists*, this chapter sought to highlight plausible influences of *Ubuntu* philosophy on the formulation of African feminism(s), with the broader goal of engaging with cultural relativism in the interpretation of feminism in the gender and development sub-field while promoting marginalised knowledge. Based on the three positions of *Ubuntu* philosophy discussed – personal identity, rational choice, and justice – we identified points of convergence between these positions and aspects of African feminism. The study finds that African feminism relates to *Ubuntu* philosophy in terms of personal identity being a more social than individualistic process, opposition to self-interest above community well-being, and preference for retributive justice over restorative justice. In decolonising the sub-field of gender and development, these insights point to three reflections for development scholars. First, scholars should consider their understanding of desirable gender identities, explore the actual context of operation, and use this reflection to formulate culturally appropriate feminist approaches. Second, given African societies' inclination to communality, addressing gender inequality could benefit from engaging both men and women in the feminist movement and emphasising the societal benefits of gender equality as motivation for women's empowerment. Lastly, development scholars involved in feminist interventions should exercise reflexivity to prevent their interventions from creating new power imbalances or gravely fracturing the balance and functioning of society.

Notes

1 According to Momsen (2010, p. 2.) Gender is 'the socially acquired notions of masculinity and femininity by which women and men are identified' while gender relations are 'socially constructed forms of relations between women and men.'
2 World Conference in Mexico City the feminist approaches of predominantly white women from the North aimed at gender equality were rejected by many women in the South who argued that the development model itself lacked the perspective of developing countries. They saw overcoming poverty and the effects of colonialism as more important than equality, (Momsen, 2010 p. 13).
3 Carneades.org https://www.youtube.com/watch?v=E_naFb_kdCQ&t=9s, point to these three positions we use to operationalise Ubuntu Philosophy and build on from the work of other authors in academic literature.
4 A situation where '[…] there is no centralization of authority of a violence. Gandhi preached non-violence. He was impressed by the famous line from Mahabharat […] meaning non-violence is the supreme virtue. The concept of non-violence is based on the faith in human goodness and assumption that human nature is essentially one that responds to love, (Xaxa & Mahakul 2009, p. 47).

References

Adichie, C. N. (2014). *We should all be feminists*. Fourth Estate.

Ahikire, J. (2006). African feminism in context: Reflections on the legitimation battles, victories and reversals. *Feminist Africa*, 7–23.

Aikau, H., Erickson, K., & Moore, W. L. (2003). Three women writing/riding feminism's third wave. *Qualitative Sociology, 26*(3), 397–425. https://doi.org/10.1023/A:1024022427568

Alkali, M., Talif, R., Yahya, W. R. W., & Jan, J. M. (2013). Dwelling or duelling in possibilities: How (Ir)relevant are African feminisms? *GEMA Online Journal of Language Studies, 13*(3), 237–253.

Basu, A. (Ed.). (2018). *The challenge of local feminisms: Women's movements in global perspective*. Routledge.

Brown, M. F. (2008). Cultural relativism 2.0. *Current Anthropology, 49*(3), 363–373. https://doi.org/10.1086/529261

Coetzee, A. (2018). Feminism ís African, and other implications of reading Oyèrónké Oyěwùmí as a relational thinker. *Gender and Women's Studies, 1*(1), 1–16. https://doi.org/10.31532/GendWomensStud.1.1.001

Cummings, S., Munthali, N., & Shapland, P. (2022). A systemic approach to the decolonisation of knowledge: Implications for scholars of development studies. In D. Ludwig, B. Boogard, P. Macnaghten, & C. Leeuwis (Eds.), *The politics of knowledge in inclusive development and innovation* (pp. 65–79). Routledge.

de Oliviera Andreotti, V., Stein, S., Ahenakew, C., & Hunt, D. (2015). Mapping interpretations of decolonisation in the context of higher education. *Decolonisation: Indigeneity, Education & Society, 4*(1), 21–40.

Eliastam, J. L. B. (2015). Exploring Ubuntu discourse in South Africa: Loss, liminality and hope. *Verbum et Ecclesia, 36*(2), 1–8. https://doi.org/10.4102/ve.v36i2.1427

Ezenwa-Ohaeto, N. (2019). Reflections on Akachi Adimora-Ezeigbo's "snail-sense feminism": A humanist perspective. *Preorejah, 4*(2), 1–11.

Forster, D. A. (2010). African relational ontology, individual identity, and Christian theology: An African theological contribution towards an integrated relational ontological identity. *Theology, 113*(874), 243–253. https://doi.org/10.1177/0040571X1011300402

Hailey, J. (2008). *Ubuntu: A literature review*. The Tutu Foundation. http://citeseerx.ist.psu.edu/viewdoc/download?doi=10.1.1.459.6489&rep=rep1&type=pdf

Hoggart, L. (2000). Socialist feminism, reproductive rights and political action. *Capital & Class, 24*(1), 95–125. https://doi.org/10.1177/030981680007000105

Istratii, R. (2020). *Adapting gender and development to local religious contexts: A decolonial approach to domestic violence in Ethiopia*. Routledge.

Istratii, R., & Lewis, A. (2019, September). *Applying a decolonial lens to research structures, practices and norms in higher education: What does it mean and where to next?* Conversation Event Report. https://lidc.ac.uk/applying-a-decolonial-lens-to-research-structures-practices-and-norms-in-higher-education-what-does-it-mean-and-where-to-next/

Koyama, E. (2003). The transfeminist manifesto. In *Catching a wave: Reclaiming feminism for the twenty-first century* (pp. 161–173). Routledge.

Louw, D. J. (1998). Ubuntu: An African assessment of the religious other. *The Paideia Archive: Twentieth World Congress of Philosophy, 23*, 34–42. https://doi.org/10.5840/wcp20-paideia199823407

Mabovula, N. (2011). The erosion of African communal values: A reappraisal of the African Ubuntu philosophy. *Inkanyiso: Journal of Humanities and Social Sciences*, 3(1). https://doi.org/10.4314/IJHSS.V3I1.69506

McFadden, P. (2007). African feminist perspectives of post-coloniality. *The Black Scholar*, 37(1), 36–42. https://doi.org/10.1080/00064246.2007.11413380

McQuaid, K., & Plastow, J. (2017). Ethnography applied theatre and Stiwanism: Creative methods in search of praxis amongst men and women in Jinja, Uganda. *Journal of International Development*, 29(7), 961–980. https://doi.org/10.1002/jid.3293

Metz, T. (2011). Ubuntu as a moral theory and human rights in South Africa. *African Human Rights Law Journal*, 11(1), 532–559. www.scielo.org.za/pdf/ahrlj/v11n2/11.pdf

Metz, T. (2022). *A relational Moral Theory: African Ethics in and beyond the Continent*. Oxford University Press.

Mutanga, O. (ed). (2023). *Ubuntu Philosophy and Disabilities in Sub-Saharan Africa*. Routledge.

Momsen, J. (2010). *Gender and development*. Routledge.

Niekerk, J. V. (2013). *Ubuntu and moral value* [Doctoral thesis, University of Witwatersrand]. http://hdl.handle.net10539/13638

Nkealah, N. (2016). (West) African feminisms and their challenges. *Journal of Literary Studies*, 32(2), 61–74. https://doi.org/10.1080/02564718.2016.1198156

Nnaemeka, O. (2003). Nego-feminism: Theorising, practising, and pruning Africa's way. *Journal of Women in Culture and Society*, 29(2), 357–385. https://doi.org/10.1086/378553

Nzegwu, N. (1994). Gender equality in a dual-sex system: The case of Onitsha. *Canadian Journal of Law & Jurisprudence*, 7(1), 73–95. https://doi.org/10.1017/s0841820900002575

Opara, C. (2005). On the African concept of transcendence: Conflating nature, nurture and creativity. *Melintas*, 21(2), 189–200.

Pilcher, J., & Whelehan, I. (2004). *50 key concepts in gender studies*. Sage.

Pindi, G. N. (2020). Beyond labels: Envisioning an alliance between African feminism and queer theory for the empowerment of African sexual minorities within and beyond Africa. *Women's Studies in Communication*, 43(2), 106–112. https://doi.org/10.1080/07491409.2020.1745585

Potter, R., Binns, T., Elliot, J. A., Nel, E., & Smith, D. W. (2018). *Geographies of development: An introduction to development studies*. Routledge.

Roth, B. (2003). Second wave Black feminism in the African diaspora: News from new scholarship. *Agenda: Empowering Women for Gender Equity*, 17(58), 46–58. https://doi.org/10.1080/10130950.2003.9674493

Schöneberg, J. (2019). Imagining postcolonial-development studies: Reflections on positionalities and research practices. In I. S. A. Baud, E. Basile, T. Kontinen, & S. von Itter (Eds.), *Building development studies for the new millennium* (pp. 97–118). Springer.

Sen, A. (1999). *Development as freedom*. Oxford University Press.

Senders, A., Lentink, A., Vanderschaeghe, M., & Snelde, R. (2012). *Gender in value chains: Practical toolkit to integrate a gender perspective in agricultural value chain development*. Royal Tropical Institute.

Snyder, R. C. (2008). What is third-wave feminism? A new directions essay. *Chicago Journals*, 34(1), 175–196. www.jstor.org/stable/10.1086/588436

Tavernaro-Haidarian, L. (2018). A relational model of public discourse: The African philosophy of Ubuntu. In L. Tavernaro-Haidarian (Ed.), *A relational model of public discourse*. Routledge.

Todaro, M. P., & Smith, S. C. (2020). *Economic development*. Pearson.

Tomaselli, K. G. (2004). First and third person encounters Ecquid Novi, theoretical lances and research methodology. *South African Journal for Journalism Research, 25*(2), 210–234. https://doi.org/10.3368/ajs.25.2.210

Torres, N. (2007). On the coloniality of being: Contributions to the development of a concept. *Cultural Studies, 21*(2), 240–270. https://doi.org/10.1080/09502380601162548

Udo, E. J. (2020). The dialogic dimension of Ubuntu for global peacebuilding. In E. Essien (Ed.), *Handbook of research on the impact of culture in conflict prevention and peacebuilding* (pp. 302–322). IGI Global.

Vaditya, V. (2018). Social domination and epistemic marginalisation: Towards methodology of the oppressed. *Social Epistemology, 32*(4), 272–285. https://doi.org/10.1080/02691728.2018.1444111

Willis, K. (2011). *Theories and practices of development*. Routledge.

Xaxa, J., & Mahakul, B. (2009). Contemporary relevance of Ghandhism. *The Indian Journal of Political Science, 70*(1), 41–54.

9 Neozapatista decolonial pedagogy

An approach to the disruptive conceptualisation of the learner

Jon Igelmo Zaldívar, Gonzalo Jover, and Patricia Quiroga Uceda

Introduction

In the last two decades of the 20th century, the decolonial shift can be an epistemic break or opening in the ecology of knowledge that emerges with its force in social sciences and the humanities. The starting idea is that a type of knowing can be developed from sideline positions of modernity, i.e., from subaltern sectors that modern conventional conceptions have traditionally pushed away. This shift may be studied as a development of post-structuralist cultural studies related to continuity (Grünner, 1998).

In the third decade of the 21st century, the decolonial shift is noticeably present in gender studies, demographics, ecology, anthropology, political and cultural studies, sociology, and education. Many academic departments at prestigious universities are now devoted to this study dimension. Even social movements that have had considerable impact in the media in the last decade, such as *Black Lives Matter* and *Me Too*, bear clear continuity with the decolonial perspective (Abraham, 2021). These movements have consolidated in the wake of others with more prolonged backgrounds, such as anti-racism, anti-sexism, and pro-LGTB rights. The notoriety these fundamentally decolonial movements have gained in the academic and social field has been answered back from conservative sectors by the so-called 'anti-woke culture war'. Those who have articulated this reply aim to 'engage in borderline discourses by buying into and actively propagating the culture war discourse with a view of undermining and reneging social justice struggles' (Cammaerts, 2022, p. 12).

Decolonial studies call for reclaiming their link to practices historically confronting modern logic. From historicist lines, concerning Latin America, it is considered that

> Decolonial practices join the decolonial shift, and the latter have always existed; they are a resistance to the order imposed in 1492 upon Spain's arrival in the continent of Abya Yala, the year Columbus was able to

dominate the indigenous people and make off with their lands, thereby starting a new age worldwide: coloniality.

(Rodríguez Reyes, 2016, p. 153)

Dussel's studies strongly influence this historicist line in the 1970s. One of the key books is his *Historia de la iglesia en América Latina: Coloniaje y liberación 1492/1973* (History of the Church in Latin America: Colonialism and liberation 1492/1973), published by the Argentinian liberation theologist in 1974. In that book, Dussel explores the juxtaposition of domination and liberation based on their geopolitical, erotic, and pedagogic ramifications (Dussel, 1974). From this juxtaposition emerges a theory whose anchor resides in reflecting on the praxis of the liberation of the oppressed. This theory is articulated from the margins and periphery of the system. Hence the importance of the liberating praxis of the poor (geopolitical), of the female as a sexual object (erotic), and of the alienated son (pedagogical).

Beyond its historicist dimension, which is crucial, it is essential to note that, especially in Latin America, 'the decolonial shift becomes a form of alternate thought, critical and self-critical, that facilitates an understanding of reality, the identity processes and phenomena of the indigenous movement' (Sandoval Forero & Capera Figueroa, 2017, p. 18). It starts by identifying an epistemicide, a concept referring to the phenomenon of imposing Eurocentric forms of knowledge as the only possible ways to understand reality and the phenomena in which individuals participate in society. The impact of this epistemicide has been effective and continued and has not yet stopped. Attending to this phenomenon, Boaventura de Sousa Santos (2014) concludes that global justice cannot be accessible without global cognitive justice.

This chapter explores the Zapatista movement that came to light in the state of Chiapas, Mexico, in 1994. In recent decades, the indigenous Zapatists have become a beacon and an alternative in articulating decolonial political and social configurations. Our analysis focuses on the educational alternatives the Zapatista communities have constituted within the movement itself, such as the Sistema Educativo Rebelde Autónomo Zapatista de Liberación Nacional (Zapatista Rebel Autonomous Educational System of National Liberation) (SERAZ-LN). At the same time, other organisations, in clear continuity with the Zapatista rebel experience, have taken up educational projects that address the theoretical underpinnings of decolonial pedagogy, such as the Universidad de la Tierra (University of the Earth) (Unitierra) and the Universidad Intercultural (Intercultural University). In this study, we try to answer two questions: What pedagogical underpinnings are taken up by indigenous communities to start their alternative vision of education? What conceptualisation of the learner is found in decolonial pedagogy based on the Zapatista experience in Mexico?

Decolonial studies have also been subject to criticism from the academic world. Some of these critical elements have been highlighted by authors such as Inclán (2016), who has called attention to how decolonial approaches have failed to analyse the internal contradictions of the subaltern groups or the relationship marginal groups establish with the hegemonic dynamics based on complex historical relationships. Another critical focus is on consolidating a 'white/western postcolonial' theory as an offshoot of racialisation in the production and consumption of knowledge. As Cumes and Íñigo (2017, p. 5) note, 'the word and thought of postcolonial, decolonial, and decolonial whites and mestizo theoreticians relies on a context of colonial hegemony in which they have and are granted authority over the indigenous people'.

The chapter begins with a contextualisation of the Zapatista movement within the framework of the events that define its history as a social movement. Particular emphasis is placed on the educational initiatives that the Zapatistas have launched almost 40 years since their emergence in 1994. Later, the educational experience is placed within the discursive line of decolonial pedagogy, referring to how the Zapatistas have inspired other educational projects in different parts of Mexico. In the final part of the chapter, we delve into the conceptualisation in a disruptive perspective of the learner in these alternative initiatives from four general lines of analysis.

The Zapatista army of national liberation uprising

On January 1, 1994, the top echelons of power in the nation, with President Carlos Salinas de Gortari at the head, celebrated Mexico's joining the North American Free Trade Agreement (NAFTA). The same day, in another corner of Mexico, in the state of Chiapas, on the Guatemalan border, the Zapatista Army of National Liberation (EZLN) rose in arms. The protesters' primary demand was to provide land and fundamental rights for the indigenous communities of Chiapas. The indigenous people had a long history of protests, usually followed by the repressive response of government troops (Inclán, 2021). Twelve days of direct armed confrontation between the EZLN and the Mexican army followed. On January 12, the Zapatistas set aside their armed struggle to solve the situation of the indigenous peoples of Mexico:

> For some time now, the Zapatistas no longer used shotguns but words to call for dignity and justice. They have transformed the way of arms into a way of communication with the other indigenous people of Chiapas, the indigenous peoples of the entire nation, Mexico's civil society, and people of goodwill the world over. They make their voice heard in newspapers, radio, television, the internet, and at gatherings organised in Mexico and abroad.
>
> (De Vos, 2001, p. 193)

When they burst onto the political stage, the Zapatistas were generating a fundamentally disruptive movement that defended the indigenous people's history of resistance but were now employing such postmodern channels of communication as the internet. The insurgency coincided with the negotiations of Mexico's political forces for the democratisation of the country after more than 60 years of uninterrupted rule of the *Partido Revolucionario Institucional* (Institutional Revolutionary Party) (PRI) and the federal elections that year. However, the Zapatists rejected the institutional mechanics of political parties. The revolution they sought was of another sort. What they had in mind was an authentic alternative community-based political project that, unlike the usual political confrontation between the market and the State, 'would represent an attempt to displace the economy from the centre of social life, subordinating it to politics and ethics and re-engaging it in culture' (Esteva, 1994, p. 195). Badiou (2003) has underscored how the uprising questioned traditional discourse and politics. 'The Zapatista uprising in Chiapas draws a line for the Mexican State. It shows that the traditional State can be identified and limited by a new form of political action' (Badiou, 2003, p. 13, as quoted by Giarracca, 2008, p. 12). For Holloway (2002), the point that made the EZLN's struggle now, at the height of neoliberalism, was the effect of 'dissonance' it represented. Indeed, it is worth recalling that Fukuyama, in his book *The End of History and the Last Man*, announced the end of history understood as an ideological struggle (Fukuyama, 1992). Ideologies were no longer necessary because the economy had replaced them.

The Zapatistas' demands were crystalised in accords signed in the town of San Andrés Larrainzar in February 1996, by which the federal government promised to recognise the rights and autonomy of the indigenous people. Real progress, however, was scant. A new opportunity arose in 2001 when the constitutional reform recognised indigenous rights. However, the Zapatistas deemed it a watered-down version of the 1996 accords since it did not state all the promises, including recognising the indigenous people and communities as legal entities (Bailón Corres, 2019). They felt the Mexican government had betrayed them once again.

Consequently, in 2003 they began to focus their protest efforts by building their autonomous local authorities, the *Juntas de Buen Gobierno* (Councils of Good Government), despite lacking legal recognition (Inclán, 2021). Furthermore, Inclán (2021) wonders about the reasons for this limited political result from a movement that at first seemed bound to succeed, given the national and international projection it gained and the period in which it arose, overlapping with the open debate among the nation's legislative elites to make electoral processes more plural and transparent. In her view, the reason must be sought precisely in that overlap and in the fact that negotiations with the EZLN and those regarding making the country more democratic were taking place simultaneously but separately. As a result, any progress made in the latter was at the expense of closing off opportunities for the former, as if they were sliding doors.

The Zapatista movement in Chiapas, in any case, remains today a worldwide symbol for those seeking alternatives to the status quo. On the national level, it influenced other insurgency initiatives, such as the one in the state of Oaxaca in 2006. In May of that year, the State's elementary teachers staged a strike that lasted several months and gave rise to the so-called 'Oaxaca commune.' At first, the protest had little effect on the population. The communities distrusted the teachers and their professional interests. The state government tried to repress the protests by force, riding on that distrust, but what they got was the opposite effect; so what began as an event specific to teachers ended up funnelling protests and demands that brought together different social and political movements, including the indigenous communities. The social structure itself of Oaxaca collaborated, being the most culturally diverse in Mexico and the only one with an indigenous majority.

For Gustavo Esteva, one of the main ideologists of the Chiapas and Oaxaca uprisings, the protests represent a questioning not only of colonisation and its institutions but of the process itself of capitalist modernity and its rationalities (González Gómez, 2019). Esteva believes capitalism is dead, but this does not mean it is no longer active since it is still the source of effects from its twitching, like a zombie. In the face of this dead reality, which is Western modernity, these Mexican peoples' movements represent real hope, 'the possibility that we are in the midst of the first social revolution of the 21st century, the revolution of the new realms of community' (Esteva, 2008, p. 40).

The configuration of an alternative education system

The failure to comply with the San Andrés accords of 1996, or the limited response given in the constitutional reform of 2001 to the promises made, did not halt the Zapatista's claims but did bring about a change in strategy. This consisted of rebelliously implementing the main points of the signed accords. This was a resounding response to the practice of domination exerted by the governmental powers. As Forbis notes, 'refusal as a practice is not simply about rejecting material aid from the government, but also about rejecting the attendant practices of domination' (Forbis, 2016, p. 370). At the same time, in their process to organise as a social movement, the Zapatistas have widened the political framework of their demands, such that they 'have been actively engaged in a process designed not only to unify the indigenous movement but to connect it with organisations and social movements in other sectors and to build up a broad coalition' (Veltemeyer, 2000, p. 98). This all positions the Chiapas indigenous struggle on the theoretical plane of decolonial theory. As Boaventura de Sousa Santos (2020, p. 580) underscores,

> Particularly after the Zapatista uprising (1994) and the World Social Forum (2001) . . . the idea of abstract hierarchy among social struggles has undergone significant changes . . . [this idea] is being replaced by the idea of situated and contextualised hierarchies and time frames.

The Zapatista movement started up a practice of resistance whose backbone is the autonomy of the indigenous people and in which education constitutes an essential element. Indeed, one of the discussion topics in the accords between the EZLN and the federal government of Mexico in 1996 was the 'promotion of intercultural bilingual education'. Gutiérrez Narváez's (2006, p. 296) interpretation of that is vital to understanding what was at stake:

> For the first time [in the San Andrés Larrainzar accords], the Zapatistas called for a differentiated education that addressed the sociocultural characteristics of the groups it was directed at and made it clear that they were not demanding only an increase in the coverage of education; that in addition to quantitative actions, they demanded qualitative changes from the government in the field of indigenous education, and with no arguments against it, the government negotiators signed a set of accords that outlined significant changes.

Since the absence of sufficient governmental redress, different educational initiatives have been configuring the Zapatista Rebel Autonomous Educational System of National Liberation (SERAZ-LN). This network of schools came about from the need detected by the Zapatistas to confront what they characterise as the 'society of power'. As noted by the movement's intellectual leader, Subcomandante Marcos,

> We call 'society of power' the collective group of leaders who have displaced the political class from fundamental decision-making . . . This group controls financial organisations (and thus entire countries), the media, industrial and commercial corporations, schools, armies, and public and private police.
>
> (Subcomandante Marcos, 2003)

SERAZ-LN proposes to meet the demand for proper education for the indigenous people. This demand already appeared in the first document made public by the EZLN on January 1, 1994, the day of the uprising, the 'First Declaration of the Lacandona Jungle'. In this document, the Zapatistas denounced their situation in the following terms:

> We have been refused the most elementary preparation so that they can use as cannon fodder and sack our patria of its riches, without caring that we are dying of starvation and curable diseases, without caring that we have nothing, absolutely nothing, no decent roof above our heads, no land, no jobs, no health, no food, no education, and no right to choose our authorities freely and democratically.
>
> (EZLN, 1994)

From that initial declaration, the search for educational alternatives has been constant for the Zapatistas and has led to the consolidation of their education system. In 2004, 10 years after their emergence as a movement, Subcomandante Marcos stated:

> Concerning education, it proceeds as it should proceed in politics: from bottom to top. Schools are being built in every community (this year more than 50 in the whole area and more a needed) and existing schools are being equipped (this year around 300), education promoters are trained (and take courses in actuation), secondary schools are being built (where they will teach the historical roots of Mexico) and technical schools.
>
> (Subcomandante Marcos, 2004)

Tamayo Flores-Alatorre and Olivier Téllez (2019) reported that at some point, SERAZ-LN had '62 primary schools distributed in the region, with 3300 students, and 135 in secondary, as well as the teaching work done with adults, and 300 promotors' (Tamayo Flores-Alatorre & Olivier Téllez, 2019, p. 65). These figures are impressive, especially considering that this is a self-organised system. As Baronnet (2010, p. 255) notes, the Zapatista's education system 'addresses pragmatic logics of local innovation that derive from the Zapatista rejection of all the governmental social programs, including education, if the State fails to live up to the agreements signed in San Andrés in February 1996'. This policy also has obvious shortcomings, as noted by Stahler-Sholk (2007, p. 52), who pointed out: 'Rejecting official aid in order to expose government hypocrisy implied shorter sacrifice for a longer-term political ideology-resistance in the Gramscian sense of developing counter-hegemonic ideology in a war of position'.

For Baronnet (2015, p. 712), the axial pedagogic idea that runs through Zapatista alternative education is what he calls 'situated learning processes'. This is a model of teaching in which community discovery and cooperation among learners 'arise as tools of troublesome education that tend to politicise campesino and political identities following the need to strengthen and renew a social movement able to forge critical subjectivities of reality and their congruence'. Without a doubt, it consists of an idea that has its resonances for the history of education and features clear influences from the work of Paulo Freire and his proposal for emancipation, as will be shown further.

The alternative education system created by the Zapatistas, with thousands of students and hundreds of schools, faces the problem of its institutionalisation. This is a complex and particularly delicate phenomenon in an organisation that maintains a military hierarchy, the EZLN, while promoting a horizontal political organisation among the indigenous communities. The education system itself plays a crucial role in this 'control' process of institutionalisation since 'education politicised the new generations not only by teaching the principles behind the movement but also by the organisational practice: much of the schoolwork is assembly-based and with positions of authority' (Andrade & Antonio, 2017, p. 36). Quite possibly, the feasibility of their educational project in the mid-term lies in the extent to which the Zapatista communities can settle this problem in the future.

Zapatista decolonial pedagogy: its theoretical underpinnings and its potential to inspire other educational projects

What are the theoretical underpinnings of Zapatista decolonial pedagogy? An observation by De Lissovoy (2010, p. 289) takes a first step toward articulating an answer:

> A decolonial reconceptualisation of social relationships has important implications not only for understandings of curriculum content, knowledge, and ideology but also importantly for pedagogy understood as the ethical problem of the form of the relationships between students and teachers and between students and global society generally.

Decolonial pedagogy has ethical implications of resistance to traditional models of authoritarianism and places care as crucial to recognising the human relationships established in all educational practices.

Several curricular implications can be found based on this ethical dimension that characterise decolonial pedagogy. In practice, this pedagogy upsets the dominant narratives and amplifies the voices and experiences the students embody in their stories of family and community life. The notion itself of knowledge production is challenged. What is proposed is an attitude of disobedience toward the geopolitics and biopolitics of knowledge that shaped an idealised and universalised view of the modern individual projected from Europe for centuries. Following Mignolo (2009), this makes it an epistemic disobedience. It entails giving value to the indigenous criticism of the Western world's universalist aspirations that can be opposed by ways of producing knowledge independent of political and economic interests, mindful of the natural environment, and that is contingent to action from a logic of proportionality.

In the end, the decolonial alternative involves a change in viewpoint, a new perception of reality that impregnates the educational experience. Subcomandante Marcos himself reflected on this change in viewpoint. At a talk he gave at the Universidad Iberoamericana de Puebla as one of the events of the so-called 'La Otra Compaña' (the Other Company), he noted that 'if you look at it from above, the world is small and dollar green. It fits perfectly in a Stock Market's price and trading index . . . because it does not need people. However, if we change our point of view and look at it from below, 'the world grows so wide, it cannot be taken in at a glance, but will need many glances to understand it' (Subcomandante Marcos, 2006).

The Zapatista experience has inspired other decolonial-based educational projects in Mexico, such as the University of the Earth and the Intercultural University. The University of the Earth (Unitierra) project started in 2002 in clear continuity with the indigenous movements in southeast Mexico. It reclaims the ideas of Ivan Illich. Its pedagogic principles need to conceive study to scale the meritocratic pyramid of training programs, academic courses, attendance certificates, and accredited diplomas. As a principle, learning on its premises is done without needing teachers, curricula, students, textbooks, or diplomas (Carlin, 2014).

The University of the Earth is directly connected to the region's indigenous communities. It was founded in Oaxaca by Gustavo Esteva, who died in March 2022. Several years earlier, in 2008, one of the authors of this paper had to interview him and Raymundo Sánchez Barraza, coordinator of the *Centro Indígena de Desarrollo y Capacitación Integral – Universidad de la Tierra- Chiapas: Ivan Illich* (Indigenous Center for Integral Training – University of the Earth: Ivan Illich) (CIDESI – Unitierra Chiapas). In the interview, Esteva remarked that the University of the Earth had been created from

> the roots of the uneasiness/yearnings felt in indigenous communities when they wonder what to do when the young people, who have never been to school, have learned everything they can from a community and still want to keep learning more.
> (Igelmo Zaldívar, 2009, p. 287)

Another participant in its creation was the Zapotec intellectual and composer Jaime Martínez Luna. Esteva reminisced, recalling John Dewey's old pedagogical phrase, that Luna was the one who gave us this name, which we all loved, and told us: 'You all should always keep your feet on the ground and should take care of Mother Earth.' Moreover, from the moment we said: 'The way to learn here is, first, to learn by doing'.
(Martín, 2015, p. 14)

The Unitierra movement today is integrated into a network of organisations, including the foundational headquarters in Oaxaca as well as Unitierra California, Unitierra Chiapas, Unitierra Huitzo, Unitierra Manizales, Unitierra Puebla, and Unitierra Toronto (University of the Earth Oaxaca, 2022).

The promoter of Unitierra, Gustavo Esteva, is considered one of the champions of de-professionalisation, a philosophy he made into a life option. After studying industrial relations at the Universidad Iberoamericana de México, he held management positions in two companies.

> I was fired from the two places because I did not agree to do what they asked me to do. That was my 'de-professionalisation', fast, at 21 or

22. I quit that profession because I considered that I could not have a decent, worthwhile life if I stayed in it.

(Martín, 2015, p. 12)

He then tried the route of political action in the clandestine militance and the government itself. However, he found that 'if what interested me was to change, the possibility of transforming people, the State and the government were the least appropriate places to do so. They are designed to control and dominate, not for anything else' (Martín, 2015, p. 12). He, therefore, took up de-professionalisation, working for the cause of the underprivileged apart from the professional political class and guerrilla militants.

As in Illich's case, in Esteva, de-professionalisation found one of its main dimensions of work in education, or rather, in another form of education. To Esteva, education is clearly in crisis. The crisis is neither temporary nor situational but intrinsic to the very meaning of teaching:

Initially, the education system was created in Mexico to take the Indians away from the Indians. When it was proposed to imitate the gringos in treating the Indian question, legislators in Congress said that we couldn't commit genocide, but we could educate them and educate them into extinction. This was done to millions of people. It was not simply about training the workforce. There is an element that perhaps is the School's only achievement: at school, kids learn to say 'Yes, sir; yes, ma'am' and to obey wholly even the most irrational authority. Subjugation: This is what Education was conceived for.

(Martín, 2015, p. 14)

For its part, the Intercultural University project is a state undertaking. Its first headquarters opened in 2003 in the state of Mexico. By 2008, nine publicly funded campuses were operating and two privately funded ones in different states of Mexico. The initiative originated from the General Coordination of Intercultural and Bilingual Education in the Department of Public Education. As mentioned earlier, the legal umbrella for these projects is in the modification to the Constitution of Mexico to integrate the indigenous peoples' demands and in the General Lay of Linguistic Rights of the Indigenous Peoples of 2003. Despite being a publicly funded official project, it also arose mainly as a product of Mexico's political and social scene following the Zapatista uprising of 1994. Thus, from official agencies, the project joined the type of initiatives to which Sartorello (2014, p. 75) refers when he states that 'it was on account of the circumstances opened by the Zapatista uprising that the sociopolitical conditions were ripe for the action of indigenous organisations interest in designing and starting up alternative educational proposals different from the official one'.

Since the Intercultural University was created, its activities, primarily because of its dependence on public money, have been subject to considerable meddling from political powers that have not seldomly weakened the different proposals. The problem lies in that, as Schmelkes (2008, p. 332) notes, both the federal and state governments 'understand the creation of the intercultural universities as a way of stifling non-conformities among the indigenous population'. In addition, another source of criticism lies in the use of the concept of interculturality itself. Applied to a project-oriented toward students from indigenous communities, it runs the danger of interculturality being interpreted as an 'indigenous matter' and not anything that needs to concern society (Tipa, 2018, p. 68).

The idea on which this initiative is structured, as Schmelkes (2013, p. 10) has pointed out, is that 'intercultural education in conditions of multiculturality must try to turn difference into a pedagogical advantage'. This idea runs throughout the teaching and research carried out at these university centres, specifically in that 'community-based research is an important part of the learning process for students in undergraduate courses, and lecturers are strongly engaged in community work, which they draw on in their teaching and research' (Perales et al., 2021, p. 84). In consequence, one of the main goals of the Intercultural University is to create horizontal relationships between schools of higher education and local communities. By doing so, they aim to turn the tables on a relationship traditionally marked by a hierarchical interrelation based on a Western power structure in which the indigenous communities were kept out of the circles where knowledge is generated.

The disruptive conceptualisation of the learner in Zapatista decolonial pedagogy

Four dimensions can be identified on which to articulate the conceptualisation of the learner in the decolonial pedagogy carried out in Zapatista indigenous communities in Chiapas. The four dimensions are the break from the dichotomy between individual and society, the search for alternative ethics to the individualist rational model, the notion of education as a way toward emancipation, and the defence of incidental learning.

The learner does not correspond to the individual/society dichotomy

Tamayo Flores-Alatorre and María Guadalupe Olivier Téllez (2019, p. 69) have accurately placed one of the ideas comprising the backbone of Zapatista pedagogy: 'The idea of individuality makes sense in the collective group. This is a fundamental principle that forges a decolonial pedagogy for emancipation'. Language is where this idea is represented, since 'in the Zapatista language there are no objects that are individual subjects in any grammatical utterance because they consider that everything has life and heart. Rather than anthropocentrism, there is biocentrism' (Tamayo Flores-Alatorre & Olivier Téllez, 2019, p. 69). Thus, this is a dissenting educational grammar that separates itself from the dichotomy between individual and society. This dichotomy is generally placed in a preferred position in the categorisation characteristic of Western pedagogy.

In this sense, the experience told by Catherine Walsh, a professor at the University of Massachusetts, is revealing. In 2013, Subcomandante Marcos and Subcomandante Moisés invited her to visit a Zapatista school. She made her visit in December of that same year. Walsh said that visit was 'a lesson in humility, displacing and decentering what I thought I knew, how I thought I knew it, and how I thought I came to know' (Walsh, 2015, p. 10). When she saw first-hand how the indigenous people implemented their ideas about autonomy, freedom, and community, Walsh stated that the experience 'made me confront the assumptions that, despite my own declared criticalness and decolonial positioning, I had not questioned or challenged, neither in my pedagogical practice nor in my identification and authority as professor and teacher' (Walsh, 2015, p. 10).

Zapatista pedagogy faces the challenge of consolidating a disruptive grammar of freedom based on the resistance experience. In Subcomandante Marcos' words:

> When power creates a bag of oblivion in the indigenous communities, the indigenous communities turn that bag of oblivion into a bag of resistance and start to organise themselves to survive the only way they can: together, as a group. The only way these people could be sure of carrying on was by joining each other. That is why the words together, we, the word united, and the word group all mark the companions' words. It is a fundamental part – the backbone of Zapatista discourse.
>
> (Subcomandante Marcos, 1996)

Reclaiming the idea of community entails a decentralisation of identity. Under this paradigm, the point is not to look for national or local identities but to look for networks of support based on community logic. The sociologist Manuel Castells analysed what this decentralisation means in the new social movements. From his perspective, as he stated in his book *Networks of Indignation and Hope: Social Movements in the Age of the Internet*, what matters is the 'social actor's ability to become the subject, defining his action around projects constructed beyond the institutions of society, per the social actor's values and interests' (Castells, 2012, p. 220). Thus, from marginalisation and rebelliousness, the Zapatista indigenous peoples of Chiapas develop an education system that aims to overcome the classic modern dichotomy that pits the individual against the social surroundings and vice versa.

The learner escapes from individualist rational ethics

The Zapatista alternative does not see the individual as a rational, independent being. Instead, it gives priority to the contingency and need human beings have for taking care of each other and the natural environment. The starting place is that we human beings need help on both the individual and community levels. What underlies Zapatista ethics is a different stance on injustices, which is inserted into care ethics, a branch of contemporary ethics inspired in part by the works of Gilligan (1993), who questioned Lawrence Kohlberg's scale of universal moral development (Jover & Gonzálvez, 2016).

The philosopher Camps (2021, pp. 82–83) has synthesised the main postulates of care ethics in her book. It reverberates with ideas with apparent ties to decolonial pedagogy that break from the 'ethics' that have governed the field of education for so long:

> Caring, we used to say, consists of knowing how to go the extra mile to give more than what is strictly fair and necessary. Teachers care for their students if they do not look at them as mere names to be passed or failed. Civil servants care for the citizens if they can humanise their relationship with the people who go to the administration offices and know how to be more than just bureaucrats who order them to fill out a questionnaire. Employers care for their employees when they see in them something more than a 'human resource' for labour and know how to appreciate what is and what is not on their resume.

What this entails is exploring a fragmented ethic. There is no room for advocating a return to the community, and even less, in the history of emancipation, after the landmark discovery of individuality. That discovery forever shattered the closed-off spaces of community life and its often-oppressive traditions. What the Zapatistas are putting on the table is an ethic with other underpinnings. As Mignolo (1997, p. 10) observed in his study on the ethical consequences of the Zapatista revolution, it begins at 'fragmentation as a universal project [that] is appropriated and takes apart global designs'.

This ethical twist questions the metaphysics of modern subjectivity grounded in individualism. In our tradition, philosophers such as Levinas have denounced the limitations of this metaphysics. Subjectivity cannot be anchored on a social contract (which includes an economic contract), a legal framework, or a national identity. It is a deeper reality that relates to the concept of 'responsibility'. This responsibility constitutes the fundamental structure of subjectivity, which can only develop from the experience of otherness. Popke (2004, p. 311) translates these ideas to the Zapatista experience: 'If the humanness articulated by the Zapatistas is concerned to give a face to the faceless, it is also about overcoming the distance decay of our moral imperatives. We can view this as a way of conjuring a form of proximity'.

The learner is placed into a process of emancipation from oppression

The relationship between education and emancipation, or the quest for emancipation through education, has its own historical background in the past of pedagogical ideas. One of the first writers to place emancipation as the main objective of his education theory was Joseph Jacotot (1770–840) in the early 19th century. Jacques Rancière revisited his work and his ideas on education in the 1980s. The book (1987), *Le maître Ignorant* (The Ignorant Schoolmaster), results from this rapprochement. More recently, authors such as Masschelein and Simons (2013) have given continuity to Jacotot and Rancière's ideas from the academic field of pedagogy. Stamp articulates a sound synthesis of emancipation throughout these works (2013, p. 654) when he explains that 'the task for Jacotot is not to raise the ignorant by imparting knowledge. In other words, it is not to educate people experiencing poverty but to emancipate them by obliging intelligence to manifest itself'.

For his part, Paulo Freire is a critical author in the 20th century who puts the concept of emancipation in a preferential place in his theory of education. For Freire, emancipation is an aspiration that must be included in all educational practices since it involves overcoming alienation. To Freire, fighting for the emancipation of the popular classes is essential, and education is an essential tool for that purpose. In the second chapter of his book, *Pedagogy of the Oppressed*, in which he develops his criticism of bank education, Freire states (2005, p. 86):

> Problem-posing education, as a humanist and liberating praxis, posits as fundamental that the people subjected to domination must fight for their emancipation. To that end, it enables teachers and students to become Subjects of the educational process by overcoming authoritarianism and alienating intellectualism; it also enables people to overcome their false perception of reality. The world – no longer something to be described with deceptive words – becomes the object of that transforming action by men and women, which results in their humanisation.

Freire is keenly present among those who have searched for the theoretical underpinnings of Zapatista educational practices. Baronnet (2015, p. 712), for example, writes that 'the dignifying pedagogy proposed by Paulo Freire would be more relevant today than ever in Zapatista regions, showing that education does not change the world, but it does empower the people'. Along this same line, Silva Montes (2019, p. 110), following Freire's ideas, states that Zapatista education is 'constructed from the communities to emancipate themselves from capitalism and, according to Zapatism, from its four wheels: exploitation, plunder, repression, and scorn'. This capitalist spiral is the basis of the destruction generated by capitalism and the logic of exploitation, through which human and material resources are potentially an element for business and transaction. The functioning of this dynamic is what displaces other cosmovisions and epistemologies to the periphery.

The learner maintains an incidental approach to knowledge

Zapatist education includes a criticism of the modern conceptualisation of learning as the result of an intentional, organised, and sequenced process. The modern education scheme extols teaching processes subject to a contrastable formality. It undervalues the knowledge acquired in spaces not controlled by schools, subject to the political, economic, or religious powers at the time. From a decolonial perspective, the Zapatistas' educational proposal seeks to restore the balance between formal and intuitive learning.

From this perspective, decolonial pedagogy is based on a criticism of institutionalised education. This is in line with the ideas of Illich (1972, pp. 32–33), who defended that a radical alternative to a schooled society requires not only new formal mechanisms for the formal acquisition of skills and their educational use. A deschooled society implies a new approach to incidental or informal education. For Illich (1972, p. 113), 'things are basic resources for learning. The quality of the environment and a person's relationship to it will determine how much he learns incidentally.'

It must be noted that Illich's book makes no explicit mention of the indigenous people's cosmovision. Even though when he wrote the book, he was living in Cuernavaca, a town in the state of Morelos in Mexico with a considerable population of indigenous people and *campesinos*, Illich seems not to have been interested in the alternative to modern institutions that were emanating from these communities. Gustavo Esteva re-read Illich's work from the perspective of the indigenous movement, which primarily resulted from the Zapatista uprising. As Esteva (2012) repeatedly noted, the University of the Earth directly ties into Illich's proposals to the point that the headquarters in Chiapas bears his name. Unitierra thus acts as a bridge that joins Illich's defence of incidental education to criticism of modernity from the indigenous cosmology. Illich (1972) emphasised the need to build institutional alternatives far away from hegemonic models and to model a different discourse based on new epistemological referents to reconstruct the relationship between education and school. From that perspective, the *Deschooling Society* contains a decolonial epistemology that distances itself from the aspirations of industrial modernity.

Conclusion

We began this chapter noting the decolonial turn's undeniable presence in the social sciences and humanities. The recent repercussion of widespread movements such as *Black Lives Matter* and *Me Too* with clear decolonial inspiration can be analysed from the perspective of decolonial studies' impact on academics and public opinion. The case of the Zapatista movement, which made history in Mexico in 1994, features its development while also being an explicit reference in the configuration of political and social decolonial alternatives. This has led to the interest in exploring the educational proposal organised by the indigenous communities of the Zapatista Army of National

Liberation (EZLN) and delving deeper into the ideas that articulate a disruptive conceptualisation of the learner.

The challenge of Zapatista education as an alternative lies in the possibility of generating a coherent system. Its foundational postulates have made the EZLN a social movement that has opened its epistemic paradigm within the social organisations seeking to refute the social theses of globalised systemic capitalism. The movement has disrupted educational debate by its organised disobedience able to shape an alternative to the pretended universalising vision of the modern individual. Although with different approaches, this stance has inspired projects such as the University of the Earth and the Intercultural University in Mexico. Both projects are constituted as proposals in the wake of the Zapatista movement. Especially considering other worldviews and epistemologies that stand out from those of the Western industrial world, these two projects stand out for their attempt to address contemporary pedagogical challenges from a decolonial perspective.

The decolonial pedagogy of the Zapatista movement rests on four main pillars: the break from the dichotomy between individual and society, the search for alternative ethics to the rational individualist model, the notion of education as a way toward emancipation, and the defence of incidental learning. These four pillars integrate an idea of the learner that is defined in opposition to ideas incorporated in Western education, no matter how conventional-traditional or progressive they are. The pillars also highlight the weight that care ethics, the ideas of Freire, and the most radical postulates of Ivan Illich can have on the theoretical formulation of decolonial pedagogy. Due to their ability to relocate some of the central points that have sustained the pedagogical debate over the last two centuries, these four elements have a clear potential to revitalise educational discourse today. They also entail a change of perspective on educational phenomena and open the possibility of thinking about teaching and learning practices from a more plural epistemological position, a position less dependent on an economic system whose social, environmental, political, and cultural consequences are increasingly devastating.

References

Abraham, C. (2021). Toppled monuments and Black lives matter: Race, gender, and decolonization in the public space. An interview with Charmaine A. Nelson. *Atlantis: Critical Studies in Gender, Culture & Social Justice Issue*, 42(1), 1–17. https://doi.org/10.7202/1082012ar

Andrade, A., & Antonio, M. (2017). La institucionalización del proyecto zapatista: Autonomía, democracia y gobierno en el Sureste Mexicano. *Trayectorias*, 19(44), 23–42. www.redalyc.org/pdf/607/60749639002.pdf

Badiou, A. (2003, September). Conferencias en Buenos Aires. *Acontecimiento: Revista para Pensar la Política*, 13(26).

Bailón Corres, M. J. (2019). *Derechos Indígenas en México 2001–2019*. Comisión Nacional de los Derechos Humanos.

Baronnet, B. (2010). Zapatismo y educación autónoma: De la rebelión a la dignidad indígena. *Sociedade e Cultura*, *13*(12), 247–258. https://doi.org/10.5216/sec.v13i2.13428

Baronnet, B. (2015). La Educación Zapatista como Base de la Autonomía en el Sureste Mexicano. *Educação & Realidade*, *40*(3), 705–723. https://seer.ufrgs.br/index.php/educacaoerealidade/article/view/45794

Cammaerts, B. (2022). The normalisation of social justice: The "anti-woke culture war" discourse in the UK. *Discourse & Society*, 1–14. https://doi.org/10.1177/09579265221095407

Camps, V. (2021). *Tiempo de cuidados: Otra forma de estar en el mundo*. Arpa.

Carlin, M. (2014). Amputating the state: Autonomy and La Universidad de la Tierra. In M. Carlin & J. Wallin (Eds.), *Deleuze & Guattari: Politics and education: For a people-yet-to-come* (pp. 165–183). Bloomsbury Academic.

Castells, M. (2012). *Redes de indignación y esperanza: Los movimientos sociales en la era de Internet*. Alianza.

Cumes, A., & Íñigo, M. (2017). Conversación sobre epistemología Maya, teoría poscolonial y procesos de lucha identitaria con Aura Cumes. *Re-Visiones*, *7*, 1–20.

De Lissovoy, N. (2010). Decolonial pedagogy and the ethics of the global. *Discourse: Studies in the Cultural Politics of Education*, *31*(3), 279–293. https://doi.org/10.1080/01596301003786886

de Sousa Santos, B. (2014). *Epistemologies of the South: Justice against epistemicide*. Routledge.

de Sousa Santos, B. (2020). The alternative to Utopia is Myopia. *Politics & Society*, *48*(4), 567–584. https://doi.org/10.177/00323920962644

de Vos, J (2001). *Kibeltik: Nuestra Raíz*. CIESAS.

Dussel, E. (1974). *Historia de la iglesia en América Latina: Coloniaje y liberación 1492/1973*. Nova Terra.

Esteva, G. (1994). *Crónica del fin de una era*. Posada.

Esteva, G. (2008). Crónica de un movimiento anunciado. In G. Esteva, R. Valencia, & D. Venegas (Eds.), *Cuando las piedras se levantan* (pp. 21–89). Antropofagia.

Esteva, G. (2012). Regenerar el tejido social de la esperanza. *Revista de la Universidad Bolivariana*, *11*(33), 175–194. http://dx.doi.org/10.32735/S0718-6568/2012-N33-896

EZLN. (1994). *Primera Declaración de la Selva Lacandona*. https://enlacezapatista.ezln.org.mx/1994/01/01/primera-declaracion-de-la-selva-lacandona/

Forbis, M. M. (2016). After autonomy: The Zapatistas, insurgent indigeneity, and decolonisation. *Settler Colonial Studies*, *6*(4), 365–384. https://doi.org/10.1080/2201473X.2015.1090531

Freire, P. (2005). *Pedagogy of the oppressed*. Continuum.

Fukuyama, F. (1992). *The end of history and the last man*. Free Press.

Giarracca, N. (2008). Presentación. In G. Esteva, R. Valencia, & D. Venegas (Eds.), *Cuando las piedras se levantan* (pp. 11–20). Antropofagia.

Gilligan, C. (1993). *In a different voice: Psychological theory and women's development*. Harvard University Press.

González Gómez, A. E. (2019). La insurrección en curso: El pensamiento filosófico-político de Gustavo Esteva. *Revista Ciencias y Humanidades*, *9*(9), 119–138.10.21017/Pen.Repub.2016.n4.a6

Grünner, E. (1998). El retorno de la teoría crítica de la cultura: Una introducción alegórica a Jameson y Žižek. In F. Jameson & S. Žižek (Eds.), *Estudios culturales: Reflexiones sobre el multiculturalismo* (pp. 11–64). Paidós.

Gutiérrez Narváez, R. (2006). Impactos del zapatismo en la escuela: Análisis de la dinámica educativa indígena en Chiapas (1994–2004). *Liminar: Estudios Sociales y Humanísticos*, *4*(1), 92–111. www.redalyc.org/pdf/745/74540108.pdf

Holloway, J. (2002). *Change the world without taking the power.* Pluto Press.

Igelmo Zaldívar, J. (2009). La Universidad de la Tierra en México: Una propuesta de aprendizaje convivencial. In J. L. Hernández Huerta, L. Sánchez Blanco, & I. Pérez Miranda (Eds.), *Temas y perspectiva sobre educación: La infancia ayer y hoy* (pp. 285–298). Globalia.

Illich, I. (1972). *Deschooling society.* Harper & Row.

Inclán, D. (2016). Contra la ventriloquia: Notas sobre los usos y abusos de la traducción de los saberes subalternos en Latinoamérica. *Cultura-Hombre-Sociedad*, *26*(1), 61–80. https://doi.org/10.7770/CUHSO-V26N1-ART1019

Inclán, M. (2021). *El movimiento zapatista y la transición democrática en México: Oportunidades para la movilización, el éxito y la supervivencia.* CIDE.

Jover, G., & Gozálvez, V. (2016). Articulación de la justicia y el cuidado en la educación moral: Del universalismo sustitutivo a una ética situada de los derechos humanos. *Educacion XX1*, *19*(1), 311–330. https://doi.org/10.5944/educxx1.15588

Martín, R. (2015). Entrevista con Gustavo Esteva, fundador de Unitierra. *Magis*, *448*, 10–17.

Masschelein, J., & Simons, M. (2013). *In defense of the school: A public issue.* Education, Culture & Society Publishers.

Mignolo, W. (1997). La revolución teórica del Zapatismo: Sus consecuencias históricas, éticas y políticas. *Orbis Tertius*, *2*(5), 1–12.

Mignolo, W. (2009). Epistemic disobedience, independent thought and decolonial freedom. *Theory, Culture and Society*, *26*(7–8), 159–181. https://doi.org/10.1177/0263276409349275

Perales Franco, C., & McCowan, T. (2021). Rewiring higher education for the sustainable development goals: The intercultural university, Mexico case. *Higher Education*, *81*, 69–88. https://doi.org/10.1007/s10734-020-00525-2

Popke, J. (2004). The face of the other: Zapatismo, responsibility and the ethics of deconstruction. *Social & Cultural Geography*, *5*(2), 301–317. https://doi.org/10.1080/1464936041000169027

Rancière, J. (1987). *Le maître ignorant: Cinq leçons sur l'émancipation intellectuelle.* Fayard.

Rodríguez Reyes, A. (2016). El giro decolonial en el siglo XXI. *Revista Ensayos Pedagógicos*, *11*(2), 133–158.

Sandoval Forero, E. A., & Capera Figueroa, J. J. (2017). El giro decolonial en el estudio de las vibraciones políticas del movimiento indígena en América Latina. *Revista FAIA – Filosofía Afro-Indo-Abiayalense*, *7*(28–29), 1–27.

Sartorello, S. C. (2014). La co-teorización intercultural de un modelo curricular en Chiapas, México. *Revista Mexicana de Investigación Educativa*, *19*(60), 73–101.

Schmelkes, S. (2008). Creación y desarrollo inicial de las Universidades Interculturales en México: Problemas, oportunidades y retos. In D. Mato (Ed.), *Diversidad cultural e interculturalidad en educación superior: Experiencias en América latina* (pp. 329–338). IESALC.

Schmelkes, S. (2013). Educación para un México intercultural. *Sinéctica*, *40*, 1–12.

Silva Montes, S. (2019). La escuela zapatista: Educar para autonomía y la emancipación. *Alteridad*, *14*(1), 109–121.

Stahler-Sholk, R. (2007). Resisting neoliberal homogenization: The Zapatista autonomy movement. *Latin American Perspectives*, *34*(2), 48–63. https://doi.org/10.1177/0094582X06298747

Stamp, R. (2013). Of slumdogs and schoolmasters: Jacotot, Rancière and Mitra on self-organised learning. *Educational Philosophy and Theory*, *45*(6), 647–662. https://doi.org/10.1080/00131857.2012.723888

Subcomandante Marcos. (1996). *Intervención en el I Encuentro Intercontinental por la Humaniadad y contra el Neoliberalismo*. https://enlacezapatista.ezln.org.mx/1996/07/30/subcomandante-marcos-intervencion-en-el-i-encuentro-intercontinental-por-la-humanidad-y-contra-el-neoliberalismo/

Subcomandante Marcos. (2003). *El mundo: Siete pensamientos*. https://enlacezapatista.ezln.org.mx/2003/05/02/el-mundo-siete-pensamientos-en-mayo-de-2003-mayo-del-2003/

Subcomandante Marcos. (2004). *Leer un video. Sexta Parte: Seis Avances*. https://enlacezapatista.ezln.org.mx/2004/08/25/leer-un-video-sexta-parte-seis-avances/

Subcomandante Marcos. (2006). *¿Qué tan grande es el mundo?* https://enlacezapatista.ezln.org.mx/2006/02/17/en-la-ibero-puebla-17-de-febrero/

Tamayo Flores-Alatorre, S., & Olivier Téllez, M. G. (2019). La lucha por una educación autónoma en México. *Revista Mexicana de Estudios de los Movimientos Sociales*, *3*(2), 57–74.

Tipa, J. (2018). ¿De qué me sirve la interculturalidad? Evaluación de la Universidad Intercultural de Chiapas por sus estudiantes. *Altered: Revista de Educación*, *13*(1), 56–71.

Universidad de la Tierra Oaxaca. (2022). *Nuestras redes*. Retrieved June 6, 2022, from https://unitierraoax.org/nuestras-redes

Veltemeyer, H. (2000). The dynamics of social change and Mexico's EZLN. *Latin American Perspectives*, *27*(5), 88–110. https://doi.org/10.1177/0094582X0002700506

Walsh, C. (2015). Notas pedagógicas desde las grietas decoloniales. *Clivajes, Revista de Ciencias Sociales*, *4*, 1–11. http://hdl.handle.net/10644/3908

10 Southern theories

Implications for epistemic justice and sustainable development

Tendayi Marovah

Introduction

The scholarly landscape across myriad disciplines has predominantly been dominated by academics hailing from the Global North, thereby perpetuating a legacy of knowledge production steeped in Western epistemologies. Consequently, finding most research inquiries entrenched in theories and paradigms from the Global North is partially unexpected. Despite the burgeoning expansion of scholarship emanating from Southern African, Asian, and Latin American nations, there persists a substantive reliance on conceptual, theoretical, and philosophical frameworks anchored in the contexts of the Global North. This dichotomy presents dual challenges of significant magnitude. To begin with, the scholarly perspectives originating from the Global South remain relegated to the periphery in the global education discourse, often undervalued and marginalised.

Moreover, in the infrequent instances when these perspectives from the Global South manage to perforate the dominant narrative, there remains a tangible risk of distortion, misrepresentation, or oversimplification of their realities due to entrenched philosophical and conceptual biases associated with the Western discourses. As detailed in the subsequent sections of this chapter, such a dynamic engenders a state of epistemic injustice. Epistemic injustice refers to the scenario where the Global South's knowledge systems, theories, and philosophies are systematically undermined, neglected, or disregarded. If left unchallenged, this situation could have severe implications, culminating in the stagnation and potential decline of scholarly activities and knowledge generation in the Global South. This phenomenon, called epistemicide (Hall & Tandon, 2017), illustrates the detrimental ramifications of entrenched bias in the global scholarly discourse.

This chapter highlights the great potential of Southern theories or theories from the Global South to confront epistemic injustices by expanding epistemic capabilities (Boni & Velasco, 2019). Since knowledge, scholarship, and research are not neutral but are shaped by those who hold political and social power, there is a need to recognise the potential of Southern theories in addressing epistemic injustices (Boni & Velasco, 2019; Walker, 2019).

DOI: 10.4324/9781003358879-10

As Walker (2019) argued, respect, recognition, and equal moral worth are imperative conditions required for all scholars to participate as equal and valued academic citizens. Therefore, it is vital to cultivate and support epistemic virtues for research and academic discourses to be genuinely inclusive. Two broad distinct but complementary forms of epistemic injustice, testimonial and hermeneutic injustice, are advanced by Fricker (2007) and applied in academic arrangements by several scholars (Ndofirepi & Gwavaranda, 2018; Boni & Velasco, 2019; Walker, 2019). Testimonial injustice occurs when a speaker's credibility is unfairly diminished due to prejudice from the listener. This results in a complete disregard for the speakers' voices and their claims to be acknowledged as subjects of knowledge, ultimately harming their self-development. Boni and Velasco (2019) noted that testimonial injustice occurs in the process of communicative activity. This harm to epistemic confidence and self-development affects scholars when discourses are non-inclusive. In this instance, Southern theories are systems of knowledge that are broad in scope and aim to explain robust phenomena. They offer coherent and valuable conceptual frameworks to integrate existing knowledge. They target research and help distil the right kinds of theoretical and empirical questions. It becomes clear that marginalising Southern theories as evaluative or explanatory tools lead to an incoherent conceptual framing that will not provide better explanations about the phenomena under investigation than competing theories.

Hermeneutical injustice results from belonging to a group that lacks equal access to participate in creating social meanings. This means that the knowledge claims of speakers from these groups are not recognised due to a lack of available conceptual resources (Fricker, 2007). In this case, scholars from colonised, formerly colonised, marginalised, or oppressed groups are prevented from exercising a distinctive voice and deriving and sharing meaning from their theories, philosophies, or experiences. Their capacity to understand and interpret their experiences diminishes their ability to contribute to the discourse. Academic or research narratives favouring dominant groups and the ruling elite while labelling other groups as substandard do not provide a solid foundation for promoting epistemic justice. This often leads to a decline in self-esteem by mindlessly following dominant narratives without fully appreciating the epistemological justifications inherent in knowledge economy debates (Ndofirepi & Gwavaranda, 2018). The far-reaching impact of narratives that do not give equal weight to scholars and researchers from minority or marginalised groups, such as those from the Global South, compared to those from dominant circles in the Global North, can result in hermeneutical injustice. While this is not the only cause, it is significant (Marovah & Mkwananzi, 2020). Interrogating forms of epistemic injustice is critical in knowledge economies, where knowledge generation is highly valued, but knowledge systems and those who possess knowledge are often marginalised (Ndofirepi & Gwavaranda, 2018). The importance of epistemic justice in knowledge economies to promote democratic societies and socially equitable communities cannot be overstated. As Walker (2019) argued regarding the significant connection between epistemic justice and capability formation, this chapter asserts that the capabilities of researchers should be both the means and ends of the knowledge economy.

Southern theories are essential for promoting authentic scholarship, particularly in the Global South. This is because it addresses power imbalances and other inherent challenges in the knowledge economy. Drawing on the scholarship of decolonisation in Africa and other postcolonial states, research on decolonisation, and those who have applied Southern theories in their work, this book contributes to the ongoing debates on decolonising knowledge. It clearly demonstrates the potential to make meaningful contributions to the knowledge economy.

Global challenges and how they affect the Global South

As emphasised in the opening chapter, this book responds to the myriad global challenges in the Global South context. These challenges include natural disaster response, climate change adaptation, communication strategies, resilience building, gender equity, education, and disability inclusion. It is a fact that both the Global North and Global South are confronted by various socio-economic and political challenges, which have been categorised and presented in various forms. Historically, global challenges have yet to be experienced and dealt with similarly. These have been characterised by significant gaps in the way they have been experienced as well as in the way they have been dealt with. For example, differences in access to resources required for crucial developmental outcomes have only sometimes been homogenous. This could be explained in terms of divergences in levels of industrialisation and economic advancement skewed in favour of the Global North. The Global South nations, most of whom were former colonies, have remained underdeveloped due to their perceived failure to keep up with the speed and levels of industrialisation. The recent outbreak of the COVID-19 pandemic has demonstrated differences in how both spheres experienced and were affected by the phenomenon.

This chapter acknowledges that several factors speak to the current interconnected complex challenges faced by the Global South. For example, the Global South is currently perceived as experiencing extreme poverty due to three key inextricably connected factors. Most of the estimated one million people suffering from hunger and two billion who do not have access to clean water belong to the Global South. The strong positive correlation between lack of clean water, hunger, and poverty cannot be denied. It is a fact that when people do not have access to nutritious food, they lack the energy needed to work for themselves out of poverty. Additionally, lack of access to clean water and nutritious food increases vulnerability to various illnesses.

Other factors often downplayed are connected to a lack of coordinated and regulated industrial activity by capitalists funded by Global North capital monopolies whose values do not speak to the realities of the Global South. For example, to accommodate competing capitalist interests, policy ignoring local values are promulgated, resulting in the forced migration of indigenous populations, often leading to conflicts among and between various competing stakeholders. To this end, productive land, the mainstay of these indigenous communities, is unilaterally expropriated, affecting their livelihoods. Unsurprisingly, inequalities across multiple categories such as class, race, ethnicity, and gender characterise societies in the Global South. For this reason, wealth in the Global South is often confined to a few individuals connected to power whilst the rest wallow in poverty.

All chapters in this book clearly illustrate the potential epistemic power of indigenous philosophies from the Global South in evaluating and informing intervention programs dealing with power differentials providing a fertile ground for multiple forms of inequalities noted earlier. These theories can naturally inform policy across various sectors, such as community development, gender, education and disability. This book makes a significant epistemic contribution to national and international policy-making by emphasising the need to incorporate diverse perspectives from the Global South in discussions aimed at addressing global challenges in specific contexts, whether from the past, present, or future. The chapters are strategically connected and complement each other in demonstrating the usefulness of Southern theories in addressing global challenges.

I will now explain why this book is significant in advancing discussions on epistemic justice through the lens of Southern theories. In the following section, I will link Southern theories to discussions on epistemology.

Connecting with epistemic debates

The call to challenge the dominant knowledge systems and prevent the erasure of non-Western philosophies and theories, known as epistemicide, has been ongoing for a considerable period. These have taken many forms and have been named differently in various contexts, yet their common goal has been to advance epistemic justice. The proponent of the concept of epistemic justice, Miranda Fricker, did not specifically focus on the Global South but instead centred her argument on the injustices perpetuated within the knowledge economy. Fricker (2007) identifies two main types of epistemic injustice: testimonial and hermeneutic injustice. These forms of injustice can occur in academic settings, intentionally or unintentionally, and contribute to perpetuating inequalities. The two forms of injustice are distinct but also complementary to each other. Whilst with testimonial injustice, 'speakers are, variously, thwarted in their claims to acknowledgement as subjects of knowledge, and thereby harmed in their self-development, in hermeneutical injustice, 'speakers' knowledge claims fall into a blank gap in the available conceptual resources' (Fricker, 2007, p. 2). Testimonial injustice can have a detrimental impact on the knowledge and forms of knowing of scholars from the Global South, as it undermines their epistemic confidence and hinders their self-development.

In the same way, Marovah and Mkwananzi (2020) build upon Walker's (2019) work to illustrate how hermeneutical injustice obstructs the ability of oppressed or marginalised individuals to comprehend and interpret their own experiences. The importance of epistemic justice in addressing the needs of marginalised, oppressed, colonised, or formerly colonised individuals is emphasised by Walker (2019). She argues that it is crucial to prioritise the 'epistemic practices of knowledge, knowing, and being a knower' to fully comprehend the conditions necessary for achieving epistemic justice (Walker, 2019, p. 1).

A paradigm shift in the undertaking of knowledge, power, and democracy

In *Southern Theory*, Raewyn Connell (2007) argues for a radical rethinking of social science and its relationship to knowledge, power, and democracy on a global scale. Here, I bring together empirically grounded cases from around the world to explore the practical applications of Southern theories in addressing contemporary and future challenges. I depart from the mainstream social sciences that portray the world as understood only by the educated and affluent in Europe and North America, who dominate the imagination of social sciences and dictate reading lists for students worldwide. Instead, I advocate for a more comprehensive and inclusive scholarship. Based on the content and arguments presented in this book, it is evident that the Global South contributes significantly to producing knowledge and understanding of society. Through vivid accounts from various scholars across the globe in multiple disciplines, Mutanga and Marovah demonstrate the power and relevance of social theory from the world periphery in understanding our changing world. The book *Southern Theories* presents examples of empirical and philosophical paradigm shifts in epistemic justice discourse. These examples demonstrate the significance of epistemic discourses, particularly in contexts where knowledge generation is highly valued.

The implications of marginalising knowledge systems and knowers are far-reaching and have significant consequences. Traditional research methodologies, often informed by Global North thinking through their philosophies and theories, can harm participants in their self-development by undermining their claims to acknowledgement as co-producers of knowledge. This results in what Ndofirepi and Gwavaranda (2018) refer to as the harmful effects of excessive confidence in one's knowledge and personal growth. As noted by Marovah and Mutanga (2023) and Marovah and Mkwananzi (2020), this unethical practice destroys one's identity by unthinkingly following the identities of others. In the following section, I provide cases where Southern theories can inform policy and practice to deal with global issues.

Implications for Sustainable Development Goals

This book challenges the dominant powers that seek to constrain our society's self-knowledge. In an era characterised by epistemic hegemony, the book emphasises Southern theories' significant role in advancing democracy. The book argues that a lack of inclusivity in the social sciences is, at best undemocratic. The discourse within this work contests the prevalent genres, including philosophies and theories, which frequently present a worldview limited to the perspectives of men, capitalists, and the privileged classes. It proposes an alternative approach to knowledge acquisition, aiming to broaden our understanding of the world. Critically, it contests the dominant perspective that views the world through the lens of the affluent, capital-exporting nations of Europe and North America, often referred to as the global metropole.

Although it is challenging to base our understanding of society on various experiences, this book proves that global knowledge generation is feasible. This knowledge can aid societies undergoing forced transitions to understand themselves better. As such, the book recommends the incorporation of Southern theories and their principles into the core of international reconstruction and development policies. The emphasis here is on aligning Southern theories with the requirements of political power and democracy. While many national policies in the Global South prioritise human development, Southern theories often must be recognised as the bedrock, process, and objective of economic growth and social development. As the book demonstrates, though the values of the Global South differ from conventional development concepts, they can still inspire future 'development' plans.

Theories originating from the Global South, such as *Buen Vivir*, Neozapatism, *Qi* vitality, and *Ubuntu*, have garnered more focus in recent years. These theories advocate a collective economic culture that prioritises social justice, equality, equity, communal sharing, and collective rights, contrasting with the capitalist values of growth, competition, and profit. These theories guide new economic principles and systems that foster a more balanced and humane society. They facilitate initiatives to eradicate poverty, improve food security, promote sustainable energy, develop industry and infrastructure, and advance equality. These theories emphasise relationships and underscore the importance of collaborative, community-oriented, self-organised, and autonomous local production, ensuring an equitable distribution of benefits.

Community is a crucial component of most Southern theories. These theories can reframe our perspectives and methods concerning global issues and their resolution. van Norren (2022) argues that the absence of the term 'community' from the Sustainable Development Goals (SDGs) suggests overlooking Southern theories in shaping these goals. If we aspire to build trust and credibility globally, employing Southern theories that underscore community centrality would be advantageous to guide our policies and practices to achieve well-being.

Another significant principle of Southern theories pertains to the community's spiritual, emotional, and physical wellness. Chapters 5, 6, and 7 illustrate the spiritual and emotional connotations that Southern theories associate with illness. They stress the importance of unity in supporting those facing mental, physical, or emotional challenges within the community. The contrasting approach during global pandemics, such as COVID-19 pandemic, where the sick were isolated and viewed as outsiders, clearly demonstrates the lack of inclusivity in the knowledge and science that inform global health decisions.

Another critical global issue that Southern theories can innovatively address is SDG 4. These theories emphasise the importance of moral education for developing a sense of personhood, which includes citizenship education (as outlined in SDG 4.7). This approach prioritises character development over focusing on cognitive education for production processes. Drawing on Southern theories, education implies cultivating moral maturity that promotes justice, courage, and truthfulness. This means being able to deliberate and engage in dialogue that allows diverse perspectives and the freedom to express dissenting opinions. Developing listening skills, respecting diversity, and articulating logical arguments are all crucial aspects to consider when it comes to effective communication. This promotes epistemic justice by reinforcing the significance of diversity in education, as outlined in SDG 4.7. Framing education policy and practice using theories from the Global South adds value to the advancement of Global Citizenship Education.

Southern theories are valuable in challenging the idea of nature being distinct from human communities. They provide a distinctive viewpoint on environmental conservation that recognises nature and humans as interconnected components of a communal concept of life. SDGs can be achieved through this level of awareness. These include SDG 6 – Clean Water and Sanitation; SDG 12 – Responsible Consumption and Production; SDG 13 – Climate Action; SDG 14 – Life Below Water; and SDG 15 – Life on Land.

Conclusion

Global South theories play a crucial role in shaping our comprehension of present and forthcoming challenges.

These theories offer nuanced and context-specific perspectives on the complex and interconnected challenges faced by countries in the Global South. They provide valuable insights into the root causes of these challenges and potential solutions. Southern theories are grounded in the cultural and spiritual beliefs of the local communities, providing a more holistic comprehension of the cultural and societal dynamics of the regions they aim to explore. By utilising the perspectives and methodologies of Southern theories, we can strive towards establishing a more comprehensive and fairer world that acknowledges and tackles the requirements and viewpoints of all individuals, irrespective of their geographical location. Despite the increasing recognition of the significance of theories from the Global South, they still need to be more recognised in mainstream discourse and often receive inadequate attention in academic and policy circles. Overcoming these barriers requires a collective effort to promote the broader acceptance of theories from the Global South and to ensure that Southern perspectives are fully integrated into the dominant discourse. This requires a commitment to actively listen to and engage with the voices and perspectives of Global South individuals and ensure that their needs and viewpoints are comprehensively understood and considered. Additionally, it requires recognising the value and importance of Southern theories and committing to promoting their wider adoption and integration into mainstream discourse.

Lastly, Southern theories provide a valuable resource for shaping our comprehension of current and future challenges and promoting a more inclusive and equitable world. By utilising these resources, we can strive towards building a fair, impartial, and sustainable world for everyone.

References

Boni, A., & Velasco, D. (2019). Epistemic capabilities and epistemic injustice: What is the role of higher education in fostering epistemic contributions of marginalised knowledge producers? *Global Justice: Theory Practice Rhetoric*, 12(1), 1–27. https://doi.org/10.21248/gjn.12.01.228

Connell, R. (2007). *Southern theory: The global dynamics in social science*. Routledge.

Fricker, M. (2007). *Epistemic injustice: Power and the ethics of knowing*. Oxford University Press.

Hall, B. L., & Tandon, R. (2017). Decolonisation of knowledge, epistemicide, participatory research and higher education. *Research for All*, 1(1), 6–19. https://doi.org/10.18546/RFA.01.1.02

Marovah, T., & Mkwananzi, F. (2020). Graffiti as a participatory method fostering epistemic justice and collective capabilities among rural youth: A case study in Zimbabwe. In M. Walker & A. Boni (Eds.), *Participatory research, capabilities and epistemic justice: A transformative agenda for higher education* (pp. 215–241). Palgrave Macmillan.

Marovah, T., & Mutanga, O. (2023). Decolonising participatory research: Can Ubuntu philosophy contribute something? *International Journal of Social Research Methodology*. https://doi.org/10.1080/13645579.2023.2214022

Ndofirepi, A. P., & Gwavaranda, E. T. (2018). Epistemic (in)justice in African universities: A perspective of the politics of knowledge. *Educational Review*. https://doi.org/10.1080/00131911.2018.1459477

van Norren, D. E. (2022) African ubuntu and sustainable development goals: Seeking human mutual relations and service in development. *Third World Quarterly*, 43(12), 2791–2810. https://doi.org/10.1080/01436597.2022.2109458

Walker, M. (2019). Defending the need for a foundational epistemic capability in education. *Journal of Human Development and Capabilities*, 20(2), 218–232. https://doi.org/10.1080/19452829.2018.1536695

Index

Note: Page numbers in *italics* indicate figures and page numbers in **bold** indicate tables.

Aboriginal societies 12, 56
Adichie, C. N. 7, 123–125, 129
Africa: climate justice activism in 111; communality in 128–129; decolonial activism and 104, 112; decolonising knowledge production 11, 154; diverse ways of knowing 11, 63; environmental activism in 6, 111; gender inequality in 3; misrepresentations of 3, 11; patriarchy in 106, 121, 127; rational choice in 7, 125; Sub-Saharan 5, 61; *Ubuntu* and 105–109, 112–113, 125; *see also* South Africa
African feminism: Adichie on 123–125, 129; community and 123, 125, 128; critical reflection by men and women in 123–124, 128–129; critique of mono- and dual-sex systems 119, 127–128; empowerment needs 121, 123, 127–128; Gandhian feminist approach 7, 128; gender inequality and 121, 123–124; indigenously-defined 122–123; intersectionality and 121–122; neo-colonialism and 121; Nigerian influence 122–123; personal identity and 126–127; racism and 121; resistance to colonialism 121; restorative justice and 7, 128–129; subcultures/forms of 122, **122**, 128; *Ubuntu* and 7, 117, 125–129; unique discrimination and 121–122; Western feminism antagonism with 123
African womanism **122**
agency: Chinese philosophy and 19–22; Confucianism and 21–22; marginalised groups and 82; persons and 20–22; women and 3, 121
Alli Káusai 59–60
Analects of Confucius 22–23, 25
Animism: belief system in 72–73; bonds with nature in 76–77; community resilience and 76–79, 80; daily moral code 73; human-animal relationships 73; hybridisation of 5, 78–79, **80**, 81; Karen people and 72–74, 76–80, **80**; as resilience factor 74, 76; Southern theories and 2
anthropological theory 8–9
anti-apartheid movement 109–110
artificial intelligence (AI) 2
Asia 61–63, 89, 152; *see also* Southeast Asia
authenticity 29–30

Beiji Qianjin Yaofang (Sun Simao) 45
Ben Cao Gang Mu 45
Berghs, M. 5–6, 104
Bhutan: borrowed policies and 98–99; Buddhism in 6, 87, 89; characteristics of 87; conceptualisation of disability in 88–89, 93, 97–98, 100;

freedom of religion in 87; gender parity in education 91; GNH and 6, 87, 89–92, 94, 99–100; happiness in 90–91, 100; inclusive education and 6, 87–89, 93–99; modernisation of school system in 87–88, 91; monastic education in 88, 91; National Policy for Persons with Disabilities 95; parental involvement in education 88, 97–98; Special Education Needs schools 94, 96; Standards for Inclusive Education 94–96; students with disabilities 6, 87–88, 93–96; universal access to education in 91–92, 94

Bhutan Certificate of Secondary Education (BCSE) 91

Bhutan Education Blueprint 2014–2024 98

Bhutanese Buddhism: compassion (*karuṇā*) in 89, 99; conceptualisation of disability 6, 87, 89, 93, 99; inclusive education and 6, 93, 99; karma in 88–89, 97, 99; *Mahāyāna* 87, 89; practice of *dharma* 89, 99

Black Lives Matter movement 133, 147

body: Buddhism and 99; Daoism and 42; homeostasis and 41; interconnectedness and 41; Karen people and 73, 79; mind-body dualism 17–18; one-world theory and 19; *Qi* vitality theory and 33, 36–37, 41–42, 46; spiritual healing 44; tranquility and 41–42; virtues and 40; yin-yang balance of 44

Bolivia 60–61

Buddha 35

Buddhism: Chinese philosophy and 31; compassion (*karuṇā*) in 89, 99; conceptualisation of disability 87, 89, 99–100; cultivation of true nature 43; *Drukpa Kagyu* (*Mahāyāna*) 87, 89; harmony and 79; hybridisation of animism and 78–79, 81; interconnectedness and 6, 99; Karen people and 79; karma and 88–89, 97, 99; Southern theories and 2; Tantric 89; Theravada 78; Zen 35; *see also* Bhutanese Buddhism

Buddhist Karens 79

Buen Vivir (Good Living): decolonisation of knowledge and 60; development paradigm critique 11, 59, 63; eco-social justice and 5, 60, 63; harmonious living and 9, 59–60; interconnectedness and 48; Latin American social movements and 60–61; social justice and 157; Southern theories and 2, 61–62; *Ubuntu* and 61

capitalism: anti-colonial activism and 104; exploitation and 146; globalisation and 59; Global North monopolies 154–155; individualism and 48, 60; marginalisation and 53; neoliberalism and 111; non-sustainability in nature 48; pursuit of GDP 47; racialised 104; refutation of systemic 137, 146, 148

care ethics 140, 145

Caribbean 56

Centre for Bhutan Studies 90–91

challenges: decolonial 54; Global South and 1–3, 8, 154–155, 158; inclusive education implementation 98–99; political 8, 154; socio-economic 8, 154; Southern theories and 9–10, 159; sustainability 82

ChatGPT 2

Chiapas, Mexico: autonomous local authorities 136; indigenous communities in 135–136, 144; Zapatista communications in 59; Zapatista decolonial pedagogy in 7, 134, 138, 140–141, 143–147; Zapatista movement in 134–138, 142, 147–148

Child-Friendly School Initiative (Bhutan) 96

China: Confucianism in 27; Daoism in 27–29; healing practices in 41, 46; Karen people and 71, 76; *Qi* cultivation in 42; resurgence of Confucianism in 11; traditional values and 11

162 Index

Chinese medicine: body shaking practices 37; cultivation of *Qi* and 42; interconnectedness and 34, 41; meditation practice 45–46; *Qi* vitality theory and 43–46; spiritual body and 44; treatment of *Qi* 44–45
Chinese philosophy: agency/autonomy in 19–22; conflicting contingencies and 21; Confucian thought in 31; cultivating *Dao* in 46; cultivation in 16, 22–24; emotions and 22–23; gender relations and 18–19; genuine pretending in 16, 30; global challenges and 4; harmony in 16, 24–27; holistic view of 17; homoverse and 4; interconnectedness and 18; justice in 25–27; living embodiment of wisdom 35; morality and 20–21; nondualism in 16–19; person in 16, 19–21; *Qi* vitality theory 4–5, 38, 41, 43; recontextualisation of 17; virtues and 42; yin and yang 18; *see also* Confucianism; Daoism
Chinese Text Project 32n1
Christianity 17, 19, 78–79, 81
climate change 4–5, 58, 154
climate justice 104, 111
cognitive justice 10, 134
Colombia 61
colonialism: anthropological theory and 9; categories of exclusion 60; defining 118; epistemic dominance and 119, 134, 152; GDP growth and 47; gender inequality and 3, 119; social injustice and 6; Western hegemony and 2
coloniality 55–56, 118–119, 153; *see also* decoloniality
communication: decolonial turn in 53–55, 62; dependency theories and 54–55, 62; development paradigm and 55; de-Westernising 53, 63; ecology of knowledge in 53–54, 63; exclusions in 53; Good Living principles in 62; indigenous approaches to 5, 56–59, 63; interculturality and 54; testimonial injustice and 153, 155; Western hegemony and 5; Zapatistas and 59
communicative justice 58, 63
community: African societies and 128; *Buen Vivir* and 62; education and 24; happiness and 27, 99; harmonious living and 9, 24, 27, 31, 59; personhood through 106; Southern theories and 157–158; *Ubuntu* and 10, 105–106, 125; well-being and 7, 90, 93, 123, 125, 128–129, 158; Zapatista pedagogy and 140, 143–145
community resilience: animism and 76–79, **80**; ecological approach 5, 70–71; ethnic minority groups and 5–6, 69–70, 81, 92; external threats and 71; factors for 71; flexibility and 5, 78–79, **80**; indigenous religions and 5, 68–69, 74, 76, 78–80; Karen people and 71, 76, 78–81; persistence and 5, 78, **80**
Confucianism: agency in 21–22; as counter to Western cultural hegemony 11; critical reflection and 21; cultivation in 16, 22–24; Daoism and 27, 29–30; embodying love in 43; importance of education and learning 23–24; resurgence in China 11
Confucius 24, 28, 35
Confucius Institutes 11
Convention on the Rights of People with Disabilities (CRPD) 94
cosmology 18, 36, 38, 147
critical theories 11, 53
Culham, T. 4, 33–34, 37, 49–50
cultivation: Chinese philosophy and 16, 22–24; collaboration and 31; Confucianism and 22–24; Daoism and 28–29, 35; of *Qi* 33–36, 42–43, 45
cultural relativism 117, 119–120, 126, 128–129
cultural resilience 5, 81
cultural studies 53, 133

Dao: as creative force 38, 40; cultivation of *Qi* and 39, 43, 46; living embodiment of wisdom 35; virtue 26, 42

Daodejing 30
Dao De Jing (Laozi) 38–40
Daoism: balanced worldview and 5; body and 42; Confucianism and 27, 29–30; cultivation of *Qi* in 35–36, 38, 42–43; cultivation of self 28–29; first-person research 34–36; genuine pretending in 16, 30; harmony in 25; interconnectedness and 5; nature and 47; personal experience 35; *qigong* 34; Southern theories and 2; virtue and 39–40, 42; wandering in 27–28; yin-yang 39–40
decoloniality: critique of power dynamics 9; development perspectives and 118; identification of epistemicide 134, 152; of knowledge 118; social diversity and 118; *Ubuntu* and 6, 106–114; Zapatista pedagogy and 7, 134, 138, 140–141, 143–147
decolonial pedagogy: amplification of student experiences 140; care ethics and 145; challenges to knowledge production 140; emancipatory perspectives 56, 139, 143, 145; epistemic disobedience in 140; Global North and 107; indigenous communities and 134, 137–143; interconnectedness and 7; social justice and 107; *Ubuntu* and 110; *see also* Zapatista pedagogy
decolonial studies 133–135
decolonial turn: gender studies and 133; in Latin America 54–56, 62–63, 133–134; social sciences and 54–55, 147; subaltern sectors and 133, 135
decolonisation: activism priorities 104; *Buen Vivir* and 60; defining 13n2; developmentalism and 60; of development studies 117–118; of education 49, 107–108; of gender and development 119; historicist approaches 133–135; of knowledge production 6, 10–12, 13n2, 53–54, 154; post-development theories 118; power in communication strategies 55; Southern theories and 2
Decolonizing Methodologies (Smith) 12
dependency theories 54–57, 62–63
de-professionalisation 141–142
Descartes, R. 17–18, 54
Deschooling Society (Illich) 147
de Sousa Santos, B. 53, 56, 106, 134, 137
developed nations 54–55
developing countries 54–55, 118
development: *Buen Vivir* and 60; capabilities approach 118; communication for 55, 57; defining 117; education and 47; gender-based disparities 118; indigenous cultures and 59–60; Latin American questioning of 59; neo-colonialism in 47; as service 62; Southern theories and 9–10, 157; as tool of domination 60; women and 118–119, 129; world hierarchies in 47
developmentalism 59–60
Development Alternatives with Women for a New Era (DAWN) Network 118
development studies: decolonisation of 117–118; Gandhian model 9–10; gender and 117–118; Global North and 54–55; marginalisation of Southern theories 10–11; modernisation theory and 8, 54, 118; neoliberalism and 8; postcolonial perspectives 118; post-modernist perspectives 118; reflexivity and 129; Western narratives in 10–11
Dewey, J. 141
disability: activism and 110; Buddhism and 87, 89, 93, 99–100; as continuum of ability 99; decolonial activism and 104, 109–111; GNH and 92–93, 99–100; interdependent collective 110; marginalisation and 97–98; socio-cultural construction of 89; *Ubuntu* and 110–111; Western inclusiveness goals 6, 87–88; *see also* inclusive education; students with disabilities

Dorji, R. 93, 95–96
Drukpa Kagyu (Mahāyāna) Buddhism 87, 89
Dukpa, D. 88, 93
Dussel, E. 55–56, 134

eco-centrism 77
eco-cosmic citizenship 4, 33, 36, 48, 50–51
ecology: GNH and 90–91; Karen people and 77–78, **80**; as a right 111; *Ubuntu* and 104, 110, 114; *Ukama* and spiritually diverse 110
ecology of knowledge 53–54, 63, 133
eco-social justice 5, 60, 63
Ecuador 59–61
education: care ethics in 145; community and 24; Confucianism and 23–24; cultivation of *Qi* in 34; culturally-rooted 11; decolonial activism and 49, 104, 107–108; de-professionalisation and 142; development and 47; emancipation through 143, 146; happiness and 91–92; incidental learning and 7, 143, 147; institutionalized 147; intercultural policies 10, 143; nature and 47–48; neoliberal values of 107; *Qi* vitality theory and 34, 48–50; self-cultivation and 48; situated learning processes in 139; *Ubuntu* and 107–108, 110–111; Western hegemony and 2, 7, 9, 11; *see also* inclusive education; Zapatista pedagogy
emancipation 7, 54, 56, 139, 143, 145
emotions 22–24
End of History and the Last Man, The (Fukuyama) 136
environmental activism 6, 111
environmental conservation 12, 87, 90, 158
environmental degradation 4, 6, 111
environmental justice 6, 158
epistemicide 134, 152, 155
epistemic justice/injustice: African epistemologies and 11; authentic scholarship 154; Global North narratives 153; hermeneutic injustice 153, 155–156; knowledge economies and 153–155; philosophical paradigm shifts in 156; Southern theories and 7, 152–153, 155–156; testimonial injustice 153, 155–156
equality 33, 47, 157; *see also* gender inequality
Escobar, A. 10–11, 55, 57
Esteva, G. 137, 141–142, 147
ethnic minority groups: adaptiveness of 69; community resilience and 5–6, 69–70, 81, 92; Karen people and 71–72; resilience factors of 68–69
Eurocentrism 112, 118, 134
EZLN *see* Zapatista Army of National Liberation (EZLN)

#Feesmustfall movement 107
Femalism **122**
feminism: cultural relativism and 126; exclusionary practices 121–122, 127; gender equality and 119, 121, 126–129; individualism and 119, 125, 127; intersectional 126; marginalised epistemologies 117; mono-sex systems 119, 127; patriarchy and 120, 127–129; Southern theories and 119; three waves of 120–121; Western theories 7, 9, 117, 119–123; *see also* African feminism
first-person research 34–36
Foucault, M. 55
Freire, P. 56, 139, 146
Fricker, M. 153, 155
Fukuyama, F. 136

Gandhi, M. 10
Gandhian model 7, 9–10, 128
gender: Chinese philosophy and 18–19; decolonisation of 117, 133; development studies and 117–118; intersectionality of 9, 60; parity in education 91; relational identity formation 126–127; Western binary 3–4, 18; Yoruba society and 3–4
gender inequality: African feminism and 121, 123–124; Bhutanese

schools and 98; coloniality and 3, 60, 119; decolonising knowledge and 6; dual-sex systems 119, 127; engagement of men and women in 123–124, 128–129; misrepresentations of 3; mono-sex systems 119, 127; patriarchy and 120, 127–129; Western feminism and 120–121
gender relations 18–19, 118–119
gender theories 9, 117, 119
genuine pretending 16, 30–31
Global Citizenship Education 158
globalisation 57, 59, 91, 96
Global North: capital monopolies 154–155; decolonisation discourse 119; decolonising curriculum in 107; development communication 55; development paradigm and 54–55, 118; dominant narratives in 153; environmental destruction and 111; epistemologies and ontologies from 10, 152; gender theories and 117; global hierarchies and 8, 47, 112; intersectionality theory and 60; *see also* West
Global South: authentic scholarship in 154; *Buen Vivir* and 60–61; critical communication theories 53; decolonial turn in 54–56, 62–63, 133–134; dependency theories 54–55; development studies and 8, 54–56; diverse philosophical concepts 13n1; ecology of knowledge in 53, 63; environmental activism in 111; environmental changes and 8; epistemic injustice and 152–156; epistemologies and ontologies from 104, 106–107, 114, 119–120, 152, 155; extreme poverty in 154; global challenges and 154–155, 158–159; holistic philosophies in 47, 59–61; industrialisation in 154; knowledge production and 10, 152–153, 156–157; learning from nature in 47; misrepresentations of 3; right-brain consciousness in 47; self-determination and 1;

self-worth and 1; storytelling in 4; Western-informed interventions 8–9; *see also* Southern theories
GNH *see* Gross National Happiness (GNH)
Good Living/*Buen Vivir* see *Buen Vivir* (Good Living)
Green Belt Movement (GBM) 111
Gross National Happiness (GNH): in Bhutan 6, 87, 89–92, 94, 99–100; cultural preservation 87, 90; economic growth and 91; educational policy and 91–92; environmental preservation 87, 90; GNH Index and 90; good governance 87, 90; harmony and 62; impact of 90; inclusive education and 6, 93–94, 99; persons with disabilities and 92–93, 99–100; sustainable development and 87, 90–91; well-being and 6, 90

happiness: community and 27, 99; cultivation of *Qi* and 35; GDP in assessment of 91; harmony and 27, 73, 93; as human development goal 90; interconnectedness and 99; justice theories and 25; *see also* Gross National Happiness (GNH)
harmony: Buddhism and 79; *Buen Vivir* and 11; calmness and 74; Chinese philosophy and 16, 24–27, 29, 31; community and 27, 59; emotions and 27; happiness and 27, 73, 93; humans and non-humans 73; interconnectedness and 5; Karen people and 73–74; with nature 11; *Qi* vitality theory and 4, 33, 35, 40, 46, 48; *Ubuntu* and 6; well-being and 58
Hayami, Y. 73–74, 78
hermeneutic injustice 153, 155–156
Historia de la iglesia en América Latina (Dussel) 134
HIV (human immunodeficiency virus) 109
holistic philosophies: *Buen Vivir* and 5, 11, 59–61; Chinese philosophy

and 17, 41, 47; Confucianism and 22; education and 11; GNH and 6, 90, 92–93; inclusive education and 88; learning and 11; Southern theories and 47, 158; well-being and 6, 11
homoverse 4, 16
Huang Di Nei Jing (the Inner Sutra of the Yellow Emperor) 42, 43

Igelmo Zaldívar, J. 7, 133
Ikeda, K. 72, 78
Illich, I. 141–142, 146–147
inclusive education: Bhutanese Buddhism and 6, 93, 99; GNH and 6, 93–94, 99; implementation in Bhutan 93–99; parental involvement in 88, 97–98; public acceptance of 88; students with disabilities and 87–89, 93–98; teacher attitudes and preparation 96–97; *Ubuntu* and 110–111
India 11
Indigenous Australians 12
Indigenous Center for Integral Training – University of the Earth: Ivan Illich (CIDESI) 141
indigenous communities: animism and 72–73; assimilation policies and 12; in Chiapas, Mexico 135; colonial hegemony and 135; communication and 5, 56–59, 63; community life plans in 62; cosmovision 147; cultural resilience and 81; decentralisation of identity 144; decolonial activism and 111, 136–138; decolonial pedagogy and 134, 137–143; development solutions in 59–60; Good Living principles in 61–62; harmonious living and 59–60; interculturality and 10, 143; knowledge systems 1, 9–10, 12, 56, 58; political participation 59
indigenous philosophies 105–106, 155; *see also* Animism; *Buen Vivir* (Good Living); *Qi*; *Ubuntu*
indigenous religions: community resilience and 5, 68–69, 74, 76, 78–80; hybridisation of 5, 78, 80; *Ubuntu* and 105–106

individualism: capitalism and 48, 60; competitiveness and 5, 58; Daoism and 29; modern subjectivity in 145; mono-sex systems 119; neoliberalism and 111; Western feminism and 7, 119, 125, 127; Western theories and 7, 29, 111, 123
interconnectedness: Buddhist philosophy and 6; *Buen Vivir* and 48; Chinese philosophy and 18; compassion (*karunā*) and 89; Daoism and 5; decolonial pedagogy and 7; happiness and 99; human-environment 4; nature and 76–77; *Qi* vitality theory and 4–5, 33, 41; reality and 18; Southern theories and 4–7, 10, 13, 47; *Ubuntu* and 10, 61; yin and yang 18
interculturality 10, 54, 143
Intercultural University *see* Universidad Intercultural (Intercultural University)
intersectionality 9, 60, 121–122, 126
Iranian cultural identity 11–12
Iranian Revolution 12
Islamic cultural identity 11–12

Jinjing Qigong 37
justice and rights: Chinese philosophy and 25–27, 31n2; collective social change 108; communal context for 32n2; communicative 58, 63; decolonial activism and 104, 109; harmony and 26–27; restorative process 108; transitional 108; *Ubuntu* and 108–109, 126, *126*, 128; well-being and 2; *see also* eco-social justice; restorative justice; social justice

Karen Environmental and Social Action Network 77
Karen Liberation Army 75
Karen National Association (KNA) 75
Karen National Union 74, 75, 77
Karen people: acceptance of Buddhism 79; animistic belief system 72–74, 76–80, 80, 81; antagonism with Burmese 74, 75, 77; belief in territorial

spirits 73; collective identity and 76–77, 79–80, 80, 81; community resilience and 71, 76, 78–80, 80, 81; conversion to Christianity 78–79; coolness and 73–74; cultural resilience and 81; daily moral code 73, 80; defense of homeland 77–78, 81; eco-centrism 77, 80; environmental activism by 77; harmony and 73–74; human-non-human relationships 73, 77; hybridisation of religion 5, 78–79, 80, 81; indigenous culture and 68; interconnectedness with nature 76–77; *Karenness* and 76; *kawthoolei* and 77, 82n1; linguistic family 72; mountainous cultivation 77; origins of 72; political oppression of 68, 74, 75; politico-religious social order 78; shared cultural identity and 71; wrist-tying ceremony 76, 79–81

karma 44, 88–89, 97, 99
kawthoolei 77, 82n1
Khoo, Y. 4, 33–34, 37, 40, 49–50
Kirina, T. K. 6–7, 117
knowledge economies 153–155
knowledge production: decolonisation of 6, 10–11, 13n2, 140, 154; epistemicide and 134, 152, 155; epistemic injustice and 152–153, 155–156; Eurocentrism and 112, 118, 134; exclusions in 53, 120; Global South and 10, 152–153, 156–157; hermeneutic injustice and 153, 155–156; postcolonialism and 53; racialisation and 135; testimonial injustice and 153, 155–156; Western epistemologies and 152, 155

Laozi 38, 40, 45
Latin America: *Buen Vivir* and 60–61, 63; community life plans in 62; decolonial turn in 54–56, 62–63, 133–134; dependency theories 54–57, 62; de-Westernising communication in 53, 63; epistemicide 134; indigenous communication in 5, 56–57; indigenous epistemologies 56, 58–59; intercultural education policies 10; knowledge production and 53–54; Modernity/Coloniality Group 55; social movements in 57, 59–61

left-brain consciousness 47
Le maître Ignorant (Rancière) 146
liberal feminism 9, 120
liberation philosophies 57, 134
Lin, J. 4, 33–34, 37, 41, 49–50

Marcos, Subcomandante 138–140, 144
materialism 11, 19, 21
Maxwell, T. W. 100
McGilchrist, I. 36, 47
meditation: Buddhist 34; Chinese medicine and 44–45; cultivation of *Qi* in 33–34, 44, 46, 50; Daoist 34, 36; movement of *Qi* in 40; Nei Dan (internal cultivation) 39; *qigong* and 37, 39; Wai Dan (external cultivation) 39; walking 40–41
Me Too movement 133, 147
Metz, T. 106, 113
Mexico: agreements between EZLN and 138; communication in Oaxaca 62; democratisation in 136; Intercultural University project 142–143; NAFTA and 135; Oaxaca commune and 137; recognition of indigenous rights 136, 142; San Andrés agreements 137–139; Unitierra movement 141; Zapatista-inspired projects in 135, 141; *see also* Chiapas, Mexico
Mignolo, W. 55, 140, 145
mind-body dualism 17–19
modernisation 8, 54, 87–88, 91, 118
Modernity/Coloniality Group 55
Mohism 31
moral education 158
morality 20–21
Motherism **122**
Myanmar: Anglo-Burmese war in **75**; Baptist missionaries in 78; Karen people in 68, 71, 74, 76–78

Nasa indigenous people 62
National Policy for Persons with Disabilities (Bhutan) 95

Native American studies 12
nature: Buddhism and 79, 89; as commodity 54; cultivation of Qi and 36–37, 40–43, 45–46, 48; disconnection from 4, 44; harmonious living and 11, 59, 79; Karen people and 72–74, 76–77; learning from 47–48; re-sacralisation of 58; Southern theories and 158
Nego-feminism **122**, 128
Nei Dan (internal cultivation) 39
neo-colonialism 6, 9, 47, 54, 121
neoliberalism 8, 107, 111
Neozapatism 7, 157; *see also* Zapatista pedagogy
Networks of Indignation and Hope (Castells) 144
New Zealand 12
Nigeria 122–123
nondualism 16–18
North American Free Trade Agreement (NAFTA) 135
Nzegwu, N. 3–4, 9, 119, 127

Orientalism (Said) 112
Other 53–56

Partido Revolucionario Institucional (Institutional Revolutionary Party) (PRI) 136
Pedagogy of the Oppressed (Freire) 146
persons/personhood: agency/autonomy in 20–22; Chinese philosophy and 16, 19–21; disability and 110; individualist views of 20; morality and 20–21, 158; social nature of 20; *Ubuntu* and 105–106, 113; Western philosophy and 19, 21, 106
Plato 19, 21, 35
pluriverse 57–58, 63
postcolonialism: decolonising knowledge production 154; development studies and 118; knowledge production and 53; modernity/coloniality paradigm 56–57; *Ubuntu* and 110; white/western theory 135
post-modernist development 118
power: colonial exclusions and 60; coloniality of 9, 55–56, 118; communication strategies and 55; decolonial theories and 9, 55–56; *Qi* and 37, 39, 51n4; social sciences and 156; Western structures 143, 155; women's agency and 3, 121

Qi: cultivation of 33–34, 41–43, 45, 48; cultivation of virtue in 39–40; existence and 18; meditation and 46, 50; nondualism in 16, 18; personal experience of 37, 40–41; Southern theories and 2; well-being and 4, 35–36, 46, 50
Qian Jin Yi Fang (Sun Simao) 45–46
qigong 34, 37, 39
Qi vitality theory: Chinese medicine and 44–46; contemplative practices in 33; cosmology of 38; cultivation of virtue in 40; Daoism and 35–36; education and 34, 48–50; harmony and 4, 33, 35, 40, 46, 48; interconnectedness and 4–5, 33, 41; social justice and 157; universal life forms and 48; virtue and 43

race 9, 25, 60, 120, 122, 155
racialisation 135
radical feminism 9, 120–121
resilience: Animism and 74, 76; climate change and 58; defining 68, 70; ecological approach 69–70, 80; engineering approach 69–70, 80; evolutionary processes 70; organisational research in 68–69, 81; theoretical approaches to 68–69; *see also* community resilience; cultural resilience
resilience mechanism 70
restorative justice: African feminism and 7, 128–129; TRC and 105–106; *Ubuntu* and 108, 126, 128–129
retributive justice 7, 126, 128–129
right-brain consciousness 47
Royal Government of Bhutan (RGoB) 91

Said, E. 112
Salamanca Statement (1994) 93
Schuelka, M. J. 6, 87, 93, 95, 97, 100
second-person research 34–35
Sen, A. 118

SERAZ-LN *see* Sistema Educativo Rebelde Autonomo Zapatista de Liberacion Nacional (SERAZ-LN)
Sgaw Karen script 79
Shen 44, 51n4
Shen Nong Original Herbal Sutra 45
Shenren 42
Shona people 105, 110–111
Sistema Educativo Rebelde Autonomo Zapatista de Liberacion Nacional (SERAZ-LN) *see* Zapatista Rebel Autonomous Educational System of National Liberation (SERAZ-LN)
Smith, L. T. 12
Snail-sense feminism **122**, 128
social class: African feminism and 122, 128; colonial exclusions and 60; inequalities and 154, 157; Karen people and 80; third-wave feminism and 120
socialist feminism 9, 120–121
social justice: anti-colonial activism 104; *Buen Vivir* and 157; conceptualisation of disability 89; decolonial activism and 133; decolonial pedagogy and 107; eco-social justice and 5, 60, 63; educational equity and 6; *Qi* vitality theory and 157; *Ubuntu* and 107, 113, 157
social movements: *Buen Vivir* and 60–61; decentralisation in 144; decolonial turn and 133; feminist 127; in Latin America 57, 59–61, 63; *see also* Zapatista movement
social sciences 54–55, 133, 147, 156–157
South Africa: anti-apartheid movement 109–110; #Feesmustfall movement in 107; HIV/AIDS in 109; transitional justice in 108; TRC and 104–106, 108, 114; Treatment Action Campaign (TAC) 108–109; *Ubuntu* and 61, 104–105, 107–108, 114
Southeast Asia 5, 76; *see also* Karen people
Southern theories: advancement of democracy 157; alternative development models 9–10, 157; alternative living and 61–62; *Buen Vivir* and 2, 61–62; community in 157–158; cultural understanding and 7; diverse approaches 13n1; environmental conservation and 158; epistemic justice and 7, 152–153; feminism and 119; global challenges and 9–10; global development and 1; global dialogue and 10; holistic view of 47, 158; informing policy and practice 156–158; integration in dominant discourse 159; interconnectedness and 4–7, 10, 13, 47; justice theories 32n2; knowledge systems 152–153; marginalisation of 2, 8–11, 153; moral education in 158; personhood in 158; social sciences and 156; sustainable development and 7, 157–158; *see also* Global South
Southern Theory (Connell) 156
Standards for Inclusive Education (Bhutan) 94–96
Stiwanism **122**
storytelling 4
students with disabilities: attitudes towards 88, 97; GNH and 92–93; inclusive education and 89, 93–98; increase in 96–97; marginalisation of 97–98; parental expectations for 98; post-school transitions 95; *Ubuntu* and 110; *see also* inclusive education
Sub-Saharan Africa 5, 61
Suffering in Silence (Heppner) 72
Sumak Kawsay 5, 11, 60
sustainable development: *Buen Vivir* and 5, 9; cultivation of *Qi* in 34; GNH and 6, 87, 90–91; happiness in 91; Southern theories and 7, 157–158
Sustainable Development Goals (SDGs) 88, 111, 157–158

Tagore, R. 11
Tantric Buddhism 89
Taoism *see* Daoism
Tendon and Channel Qigong 37
testimonial injustice 153, 155–156

170 *Index*

Thailand: Buddhism in 79, 89; Karen people in 68, 71–72, 78; minority ethnic groups in 75
Theravada Buddhism 78
tranquility: body and 41–42; cultivation of *Qi* and 37–38, 45–46, 50; *Dao* and 39; meditation and 45
TRC *see* Truth and Reconciliation Commission (TRC)
Treatment Action Campaign (TAC) 108–109
truth: Chinese philosophy and 19, 25; collective 112, *112*; decolonial turn and 55; individual 112, *112*; Plato on 19; restorative 108, 112, *112*; Southern theories and 158; types of 105; *Ubuntu* and 108, 112–113; Western philosophy and 19, 25
Truth and Reconciliation Commission (TRC) 104–106, 108, 114
Tutu, D. 105
two-world theory 19

Ubuntu: African feminism and 7, 117, 125–129; *Buen Vivir* and 61; climate justice and 111; community and 10, 105–106, 125; concept of 104–106; decolonial activism and 6, 106–114; ecological interdependence in 111, 114; education rights and 107; environmental justice and 6; as ethical practice 112, *112*, 113; humanistic perspectives in 110, 112, 125; inclusive education and 110; interconnectedness and 10, 61; interdependent collective 106, 108–110, 112–113, 125–126; justice and rights 108–109, 126, *126*, 128–129; moral feeling and 112–113; performative actions 113; personal identity and 125–126, *126*, 127, 129; personhood in 105–108; philosophical positions 125–126, *126*, 127–129; rational choice 125, *126*, 127–129; relational identity formation 125, 127; restorative justice and 108, 126, 128–129; social harmony and 6;

social justice and 107, 113, 157; South Africa and 61, 104–105, 107–108; Southern theories and 2; TRC and 106, 108, 112, 114; truth and 108, 112–113; well-being and 105, 113, 125
Ukama 110; *see also Ubuntu*
Unhu see Ubuntu
UNICEF 97
UNICEF-Bhutan Report 98
United Kingdom 107
United Nations 87, 90
United States 12, 107
Unitierra *see* Universidad de la Tierra (University of the Earth) (Unitierra)
Unitierra movement 141
universalisation 57
universal thinking 58
Universidad de la Tierra (University of the Earth) (Unitierra) 7, 134, 141, 146–147
Universidad Intercultural (Intercultural University) 7, 134, 141–143, 146
University of the Earth *see* Universidad de la Tierra (University of the Earth)

virtue: body and 40; Chinese philosophy and 41; Daoism and 39–40, 49; *Qi* and 39–40, 43–44, 46, 48, 50; *qigong* and 37
Visva-Bharati University 11
Viteri Gualinga, C. 59–60

Wai Dan (external cultivation) 39
Walker, M. 153, 156
Walsh, C. 55–56, 144
well-being: community and 7, 72–73, 90, 93, 123, 125, 128–129, 158; development paradigms 11; environmental 60; GNH and 6, 87, 90; harmony and 58; individuals and 72–73; *Qi* and 4, 35–36, 46, 50; Southern theories and 62–63, 72; *Ubuntu* and 105, 113, 125; Western theories and 25–26
We should all be feminists (Adichie) 7, 129
West: AI tools and 2; capitalist paradigms 13n1; communication inequalities and 5; decolonial theories and 9; disability theories

in 6; education theory and 2, 7; feminism and 7; gender theories 18; imperialism and 11; structural inequalities in 119

Western theories: anthropological theory 8–9; conceptual thought in 35; decolonisation of 6, 10, 13n2; development studies 8; dominance of 2, 5, 8; education systems and 2, 9; feminism and 120–122; gender theories 9; Global South and 8–9; individualism and 7, 29, 111, 123; justice in 25; left-brain consciousness in 47; marginalisation of indigenous thought 10, 12; matter-spirit dualism in 17–18, 22; mind-body dualism 99; personhood in 106; person in 19, 21; Southern perspectives and 13n1; two-world theory 19

women: agency and 3, 121; creative force 48; development and 118–119, 129; dual-sex systems 119; gender inequality and 3, 6, 98, 119; mono-sex systems 119; pre-colonial roles 3; *see also* gender

World Happiness Day 90
World Happiness Reports 90–91
World Happiness Summit (WOHASU) 90

Xianren 42
Xiu Dao 46
Xunzi 22–23

yin-yang 18, 39, *39*, 44
Yoruba society 3–4
Yuan Qi 46, 51n4

Zapatista Army of National Liberation (EZLN) 135–136, 138–139, 148
Zapatista movement 7, 134–138, 142, 147–148
Zapatista pedagogy: care ethics in 140, 145; decoloniality and 7, 134, 138, 140–141, 143–147; dichotomy between individual and society 143–144; disruptive conceptualisation of learner in 143–147; emancipatory perspectives 146; incidental learning and 7, 143, 147; indigenous communities and 138–140, 144; institutionalisation of 139–140; intercultural bilingual education in 138; refutation of systemic capitalism 146, 148; situated learning processes in 139; Southern theories and 2; *see also* Neozapatism
Zapatista Rebel Autonomous Educational System of National Liberation (SERAZ-LN) 7, 134, 138–139
Zapatistas 59
Zen Buddhism 35
Zhen Qi 44–45, 51n4
Zhenren 42
Zhuangzi 25, 27–28, 30
Zimbabwe 4, 105, 110

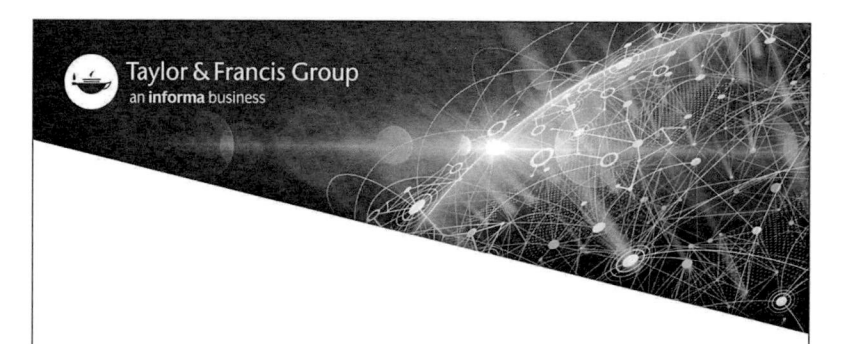